NEGRO EDUCATION
IN
AMERICA

Its Adequacy, Problems, and Needs

THE COMMISSION ON YEARBOOKS OF THE JOHN DEWEY SOCIETY
ARCHIBALD W. ANDERSON, EDITOR-IN-CHIEF

All yearbooks of the John Dewey Society
are prepared under the general coordination of the Commission on Yearbooks.

NEGRO EDUCATION IN AMERICA

Its *Adequacy, Problems, and Needs*

EDITED BY

VIRGIL A. CLIFT
ARCHIBALD W. ANDERSON
H. GORDON HULLFISH

HARPER & ROW, PUBLISHERS

New York, Evanston, and London

YEARBOOK COMMITTEE

VIRGIL A. CLIFT, Chairman
Professor of Education and Head
of the Department, Morgan State
College

ARCHIBALD W. ANDERSON
Professor of Education
University of Illinois

INA CORINNE BROWN
Professor of Anthropology,
Scarritt College

JOHN L. CHILDS
Professor Emeritus,
Teachers College
Columbia University

MAE P. CLAYTOR
Professor of Psychology,
Morgan State College

JOHN CONSTABLE
Foreign Service Reserve Officer
United States Information
Agency

JOHN W. DAVIS
President Emeritus
West Virginia State College

DAN W. DODSON
Professor of Education
New York University

KATHARINE DRESDEN
Professor of Education
Chico State College

REGINA M. GOFF
Professor of Education
Morgan State College

NELSON H. HARRIS
Head, Division of Education,
Shaw University

H. GORDON HULLFISH
Professor of Education
Ohio State University

W. A. LOW
Professor of History
Maryland State College

ROBERT E. MARTIN
Associate Professor of Government, Howard University

WILLIAM H. MARTIN
Dean of Hampton Institute

CHARLES H. THOMPSON
Dean of the Graduate School,
Howard University

GUY H. WELLS
Former President of Georgia
State College for Women, Executive Director of Georgia Council
on Human Relations

Contents

Foreword

IN RECENT years, all news media in this country have given extensive coverage to events connected with public school desegregation. Public attention has been directed not only to this specific question but also to the broader question of race relationships generally. In the light of this current public interest, the appearance of a book dealing with the education of the Negro should require no justification. What is required, however is a description of the approach followed in preparing this volume and an explanation of why this yearbook is the kind of book it is.

This yearbook has been sponsored by the John Dewey Society for the Study of Education and Culture. The full name of this organization contains the key to the approach which has been followed in this book, as well as in all of its other yearbooks. The general purpose of the Society is to study education in its cultural relationships. The Society is convinced that one of its most important functions is to explore significant and controversial public problems which have educational implications. The Society is dedicated to the belief that only through study and exploration can tenable and effective procedures be developed for dealing with unresolved issues and problems.

This does not mean that the John Dewey Society expects its yearbook committees to maintain an impossible and unrealistic "neutralism." The Society is committed to a democratic value system and dedicated to the solution of social and educational problems through democratic means. Yearbook committees are free to follow their own procedures, reach their own conclusions, and make their own recommendations. The Society expects, however, that the conclusions reached will be the outcomes of honest study, and that the recommendations made will contribute to the advancement of democracy. Uncritical partisanship, expressed in intemperate philippics, does not contribute to the objective inquiry and constructive thinking which John Dewey Society yearbooks are expected to achieve.

The members of the Committee which undertook the preparation of this yearbook have in large measure attained these goals. Many of them are intimately connected with the central problem of the book and have deeply-felt opinions about it. All of them have strong convictions about the moral issues involved. Nevertheless, they have managed to deal with the subject as students and scholars rather than as polemicists.

A second part of the reason this yearbook has taken its present form is to be found in the circumstances surrounding the original decision of the Executive Board of the John Dewey Society to appoint a Yearbook Committee to study the problem of the education of the Negro in the United States. This Committee was appointed during the period prior to the U.S. Supreme Court decision of 1954. At that time, the first of the court decisions requiring the admission of Negroes to segregated universities had been handed down, but no one could have confidently predicted that within a few years the "separate-but-equal" doctrine would be so completely repudiated.

The Executive Board, nevertheless, recognized that a problem did exist, that it had been in the process of development over a long period of years, and that it appeared in some form in every part of the country and was not confined to the relatively small group of states in which schools were legally segregated. To put it another way, the Executive Board and the Yearbook Committee were both concerned with the education of the Negro as a broad and continuing social and educational problem of tremendous public significance. The issue of segregation was to be regarded as an important part of the problem but it was not to be regarded as the whole of the problem, nor even as the central issue. Even if, by some miracle, every school in the country could be desegregated overnight, the basic problem of this book would still remain. This basic problem is that of providing equality of educational opportunity. Even more broadly stated, it is the problem of how education can help the members of a minority group become freely and fully functioning first class citizens of American democracy. The task of the Yearbook Committee was to deal with Negro education as a specific instance of this broad and basic problem.

A problem thus broadly defined requires an equally broad approach in its study. This approach the Yearbook Committee has attempted to take. And although all of the data examined in the study of a problem need not necessarily be presented in the final report, those connected with the preparation of this volume have been unanimous in feeling that this particular subject is one which requires the summary of information from many fields if the problem is to be fully understood and a constructive and intelligently informed attitude toward its solution is to be developed.

Most of the members of the Executive Board, the Yearbook Commission, and the Yearbook Committee are engaged in the education of teachers. They are acutely aware of the extent to which teachers lack the necessary background to understand fully the many dimensions of the problem with which this book deals. And if teachers lack this background, those whom teachers teach will not acquire it. One of the major responsibilities of the Yearbook Committee, therefore, has been to supply this background and to define the problem in terms of that background.

Part I is devoted to the first phase of this task. It describes how the special problems connected with the education of Negroes have developed historically and includes anthropological, sociological, and psychological data which help to explain just what is, and is not, included in questions of race and race relationships. Part II explores the many ramifications of these questions as they specifically affect education. The chapters comprising it collectively present the continuing aspects of the educational problem in their broadest dimensions.

Had the situation remained relatively stable, most of the task of the yearbook as originally conceived would have been completed by Parts I and II. Every major social problem, however, has changing elements as well as continuing elements. Sometimes changes evolve slowly. Sometimes they occur with what seems to be dramatic suddenness. The latter has been the case with some aspects of this problem. While the Yearbook Committee was in the midst of its work, the Supreme Court decisions nullifying the "separate-but-equal" doctrine and substituting a policy of "gradualism" in desegregating schools were handed down.

These decisions have not materially altered the broad outlines of the problem of using education to integrate Negroes fully into the framework of American democracy. The decisions did, however, give the question of segregated education an immediate urgency and did initiate a series of developments which had to be taken into account by the Yearbook Committee. These decisions and subsequent developments are dealt with in Part III.

Part IV considers the future task. The two chapters in this section, although originally written during the period of optimism following the Supreme Court decision recognized that these decisions would not solve the problem of Negro education but were only the opportunity for further progress. Some ways of achieving this further progress are described. Events, however, have continued to catch up with the progress of the Yearbook. Just as the final revision of the manuscript was being completed, the wave of "sit-in" lunchroom demonstrations occurred. Later, this development was followed by the efforts of the "Freedom Riders" and action by the Attorney General of the United States to secure desegregation of interstate public transportation. These events revealed a growing disillusionment with the progress in school desegregation achieved under the policy of "gradualism." They also revealed a growing dissatisfaction with the failure to extend the same principles into the areas of other civil rights. Whenever possible, within the time limits available, attempts have been made to bring the discussion up to date and to deal with these newest developments and to place them in perspective as they relate to the other aspects of the general problem which is the central concern of this Yearbook.

The John Dewey Society has a special debt of gratitude to the Yearbook Committee which prepared this volume. This Committee has worked hard over a longer period of time than any other yearbook committee in the history of the Society. In many respects, it has had the most difficult task ever assigned to such a group. The difficulties it has encountered in trying to keep pace with a rapidly changing problem have been related. In addition, it has encountered other delays and problems of a wholly unpredictable kind. Space does not permit a detailed history of the preparation of this Yearbook, interesting and sometimes amusing though those details might be.[1] A few things, however, should be mentioned.

The Yearbook Committee originally began work under the Chairmanship of John W. Davis, who was then President of West Virginia State College at Institute, West Virginia. A few years later, when President Davis was asked to become Director of the United States Operations Mission to Liberia, Virgil Clift of Morgan State College, Baltimore, Maryland, joined the Yearbook Committee as Associate Chairman. When increased governmental responsibilities caused President Davis to withdraw from the Committee, Dr. Clift assumed full responsibilities as Chairman.

Although Dr. Clift had many obligations and was out of the country for a time on an official State Department mission to Pakistan, he presented the first draft of the Yearbook manuscript on schedule. This was delivered to the Yearbook Commission just as Dr. Clift left to serve for two and one-half years on the United States Operations Mission to Libya.

In order to take care of revisions in the manuscript during Dr. Clift's absence from the country, especially because the events following the Supreme Court decisions required additions to the manuscript as well as an unusual amount of rewriting to bring other chapters up to date, a special Revision Committee was appointed. This Committee consisted of William Heard Kilpatrick, H. Gordon Hullfish, and the present writer. It was made responsible for recasting the manuscript into its present form. On Dr. Clift's return, he worked with the Revision Committee.

The John Dewey Society wishes to express its appreciation to

---

[1] One example of the totally unpredictable occurred when the Chairman of the Yearbook Committee, Virgil Clift, was in Libya. His luggage, containing the first draft of the yearbook manuscript, was following him in a government transport plane. Over the ocean, the plane had engine difficulty and the cargo had to be jettisoned. This is the only case on record of a John Dewey Society yearbook manuscript ending up in the middle of the Atlantic Ocean.

President Davis, to Dr. Clift, to the members of the Yearbook Committee, and to all others who gave so generously of their time and efforts to produce this manuscript. Special mention should be made of the debt owed to Frank Klassen for his diligent and excellent work in handling proofs and preparing the index. The Society is proud to present this Yearbook to the public and expresses the hope that it may contribute in some measure to the solution of an important educational problem.

ARCHIBALD W. ANDERSON
Editor-in-Chief, John Dewey Society
Commission on Yearbooks
University of Illinois
Champaign-Urbana, Illinois

Preface

MUCH is being written and said these days, both in the United States and abroad, about the education of the American Negro. In America, what is being written and said is often influenced by strong emotions, hot-headedness, ignorance of facts, sympathy, anger, or fear.

Recently, those of us who have spent time abroad are being frequently compelled to face many questions about this American problem. The experience of trying to explain the total situation in an intelligent and satisfactory way to friends of the American people abroad has impressed me with the fact that many of us have given too little serious and critical attention to the various aspects of segregated education. It is my hope that this Yearbook will help both to identify and to clarify some of the critical issues.

The issues concerning segregated education lie within the framework of a wider, pressing problem in American education. This problem, stated briefly, is our need to provide adequate educational opportunities for all American citizens. Only as this problem is solved will minority groups be able to contribute to the welfare of the nation. Many of the authors represented in this Yearbook, whatever their philosophical differences may be, feel that the over-arching conceptual scheme of social and educational development advocated by John Dewey has many far-reaching implications for minority groups in general and for the educational role of the Negro in particular.

The contributors to this volume are cognizant of the ways in which different types of education may be used to produce and sustain differing societies. All are devoted to democracy and to an education that reflects its values: that man must use intelligent approaches to those problems upon the solution of which both the kind of society and education depend. They have made a serious attempt to present factual material which may be useful to others who wish to think instructively about the issues.

The authors were selected because their professional activity has shown them to be aware of the need for an integration of ideals and concrete actualities. They have tried to avoid, in this writing, the presentation of generalities. Rather, they have tried to answer questions which are basic to our educational dilemma. Some of the more important of these questions are: What social and moral values may serve as a source of direction for the resolution of issues, and the solution of problems, that relate to the education of the Negro in the United States of America? What is the historical setting out of which the present situation emerged? Has the American Negro contributed any important theories or ideas that bear upon his own education? Do findings in sociology, psychology, anthropology, and other social sciences promise to help us understand better the problems which confront us? What courses of action can majority and minority groups take—what courses of action should they take —as they try to make education conform to the demands of recent legislation and litigation?

The chairman of the Yearbook Committee wishes to express appreciation to President Martin D. Jenkins of Morgan State College for the assistance he gave with the original planning of it and for his generosity in handling much of the correspondence addressed to me by contributors while I was out of the nation.

Special acknowledgment and thanks must go, also, to Professor Archibald Anderson, Chairman, Commission on Yearbooks of the John Dewey Society, and to Professor H. Gordon Hullfish—my former teacher, who has inspired many people, including me—at Ohio State University. Without the capable work of Professors Anderson and Hullfish on the final editing of this volume, its publication might never have occurred.

VIRGIL A. CLIFT
Chairman of the Yearbook Committee

*Morgan State College
Baltimore, Maryland*

Introduction

THE United States citizen has been sorely tried in recent years. He emerged victorious from man's most general and devastating war only to discover that its fruits were cold war, police action, international strife, and tension—not peace. He was precipitated into a position of world leadership and there discovered that the heritage he knew to be responsible for his wealth and his power did not cast so bright a light throughout the world that all men would quickly embrace it. He found his cities unravaged by war and, with wisdom and generosity, gave aid to allies and former enemies whose homelands were so destroyed they could not recover on their own initiative. He then discovered that the helping hand is not always viewed as a friendly one. He was comforted by the knowledge that the scientific advances and technological know-how which had hastened the end of the war had given him an edge that would deter any country wishing to start another, only to discover: first that his security could be threatened internally both by those whose loyalty was to another way of life, and by those who, in the name of advancing security, threatened it by hysterical word and ill-considered act; and, second, that scientific insights and technological know-how were not his exclusive possessions. He knew that in educational developments he had out-stripped the world but came to learn that Russia, though starting late, had, by concentration and the means available to the totalitarian government, made specific and spectacular gains in scientific fields that forced him to question both his educational purposes and practices.

Nor is this all. While World War II was in progress, in order to avoid the aftermath of World War I, he had helped create, in the United Nations, a machinery for the maintenance of peace. He discovered later, however, that when men gather around tables and in assemblies they may deepen the differences he had thought such acts would lessen. He learned that he was over-matched on the propaganda fronts of the world, despite his known skill in selling everything below the level of ideas. He was forced to realize that others could grow in economic strength, despite their indifference to economic laws or principles he was sure had cosmic sanction. He had, in the words of William James, "a more or less dumb sense of what life honestly and deeply means." Yet he found it difficult to be articulate as his anxieties increased in the face of the rapid development of earth-encircling instruments of potential total destruction, of the upthrust of a new nationalism in a sea of world unrest, and of the submergence of national cultures by a ruthless and encroaching force.

Somewhat sadly the United States citizen has been forced to conclude that the end of his trials will not occur within the predictable future. Perhaps he should have known this all along. He is, after all, a free man among free men. He had gained his freedom within conflict, and within conflict he would be forced to maintain it. Short of turning his affairs over to government or to a man on a white horse, which he has not been disposed to do he has to depend on the continuous play of idea upon idea in order to advance. But always, of course, sure of his right to believe as he does, whatever the issue, he is encouraged by the very conditions of his being to resist change, to find his security in his past habits and values. Thus, paradoxically, though he knows his culture cannot stand still, that the freedom he grants to others by insisting upon it for himself has made change a fact of his life, he nevertheless continues to encircle himself with beliefs that resist change.

At no point in his national life is this paradox more evident than when, as he strides forward on the new plateau of human decency created by the decision of the United States Supreme Court that outlawed segregation in the public schools, he stumbles over thought habits in which an accepted sense of white supremacy is grounded. He knows that he will never leave this plateau, except as he rises to ever higher ones; yet his habits often tell him to deny not only the fact of his gain but, also, its inevitability as men try to live by the democratic aspiration. Not all citizens stumble, of course; nor do all stride forward with equal spirit—some, indeed, drag their feet and, in addition, deliberately attempt to block the movement of others.

In the volume, *White and Negro Schools in the South*,[1] the authors note that the "Court decision adds a new dimension to the educational problems of the Southern region, that of mixing the two races in the public schools."[2] They are right. Those who wrote the present volume equally recognize this, as they also recognize that the Court, in all of its decisions cut down the barbed wires of segregation practices, has added a new dimension to the moral problem of the nation. The educational problem, because the immediate impact of decisions relating to the schools was upon habits that have been regionally nurtured, has seemed to many to be an exclusive problem of the South. Yet neither the educational problem nor the moral one, if indeed these may be separated, is regional. They are problems of all the people.

No one among us, whether of North or South, may assume the right to defy the Court where the education of the future citizens of the nation is involved. And what is true of individuals on this score is equally true of the individual states. The right to remain free of federal domination, a right men with our history may be expected to hold to tenaciously, does not include the right of some within a state to use official machinery to keep others within it ever on the fringes of citizenship. But if the Southerner has no inherent right to look upon his prejudices as if they were divinely sanctioned, the Northerner, in turn has an obligation to recognize that social change, North or South, is not a simple or easy matter. The habits here at issue are deeply rooted, pervading both individual and institutional lives. This indisputable fact provides no warrant for the arrogance of those who would set themselves above the law of the land. The presence of the law, on the other hand,

---

[1] Truman M. Pierce, ed., *et al*, Englewood Cliffs: N. J. Prentice-Hall, Inc., 1955.
[2] *Ibid.*, p. 305.

provides no justification for others to act as if no further problems remain. The simple fact is otherwise.

Although students of national history have recognized the ultimate inevitability of the decision, and even though previous court decisions have been powerful levers in the struggle to equalize educational opportunities that have resulted in important improvements in Negro education, the South, nevertheless, was not ready for the segregation decision. The typical Southerner finds it very difficult to substitute the more radical doctrine of placing Negroes and whites in the same school for the doctrine he only recently accepted of providing equal educational programs for the two races.[3]

The laws that govern in the United States are not struck out of the blue. They reflect, though they may not duplicate, general trends within social policy. The decision of the Supreme Court of May 17, 1954, for instance, which outlawed state-enforced segregation in the public schools, reflected the emerging conscience of those among us who recognize that this nation has an obligation, in its new status as a world leader, to do away with those discriminatory practices we have long tolerated even while knowing them to be indefensible. Further, the sensitivity of the Court to the consequences the decision would have within those states which maintained segregated schools led it to hear arguments on methods of enforcement before writing the implementing decision, handed down on May 31, 1955.

The Court, therefore, created no bludgeon. It anticipated no single pattern of compliance. It placed its faith, rather, in the commitment of all citizens, North and South, to the basic values of the democratic aspiration, expecting communities to develop plans for complying with the decision and to comply, in fact, "with all deliberate speed." While it delegated responsibility to the Federal district courts to pass judgments upon plans of action, whenever enforcement action was brought before them, it expected the processes of democratic citizenship to be the chief instruments of compliance.

Its expectations have been but partly realized, as the world well knows. If, as was suggested above, the South was not ready for the

[3] *Ibid.*, p. 305.

decision, some elements within it were more than ready to use it for political, even private, gain.

The three-year period following the Court's 1954 decision saw a phenomenal growth of groups organized for the primary purpose of maintaining segregation. Some 50 have been in existence at one time or another. Their claimed membership, running into the hundreds of thousands, far outstrip their opposition. And it ranges from prominent politicians and "solid" business and professional leaders in certain groups to what some segregationists themselves condemn as rabble-rousers, publicity seekers, and fastbuck boys who never had it so good before, what with selling five-dollar memberships and keeping their books to themselves.[4]

In consequence, many citizens, especially in the Deep South, who would have supported the decision, either because they respected law or because they honored Christian principles or because they felt the compulsion of their democratic commitment or because they thought it futile to oppose an inevitable movement, were unable to offset the fast-rising pressure of the segregationists. They soon found themselves reduced to silence because of fears of predictable and unpredictable patterns of reprisal. They were thus forced to stand aside as legislation they disliked was adopted. A chapter in *With All Deliberate Speed,* which summarizes the efforts made by the states in the Deep South to defy the decision during the three-year period after it was handed down, is forced to conclude:

In every state of the region there was a far stronger pattern of legislation aimed at preserving racial segregation than there was in 1954, although the new pattern generally avoided any outward appearance of being based on race; in no state had there been admitted a Negro student to a public school on the elementary or secondary levels; and throughout the region there was a core of resistance which surpassed that in existence in 1954.[5]

[4] Don Shoemaker (ed.), *With All Deliberate Speed—Segregation-Desegregation in Southern Schools* (New York: Harper & Brothers, 1957), p. 16. This volume, prepared by staff members and associates of the Southern Education Reporting Service, provides, in its own words, "a journalistic summation of three turbulent years" since the decision.

[5] *Ibid.,* p. 109.

Fortunately, the South exhibited the plurality characteristic of the culture generally and notable instances of compliance occurred. Public officials, including school officials, in certain border states and the District of Columbia, initiated community planning and action that led, varyingly, to immediate or gradual desegregation. In each successful instance, one fact stood forth, the firm attitude of public officials.

What were the common elements that accounted for the relative ease with which most of the border states obeyed the Court decision? One, certainly, was the impact of official attitudes. Almost immediately after the decision was handed down, governors, attorneys general and state boards of education declared for prompt compliance and pledged their best efforts to accomplish it peacefully. In these days the segregationists were off balance and the integrationists had things pretty much their own way. In some cases, the official attitude softened somewhat when citizen opposition began to lift its head. But generally the border officials from the first held the position that the law had been defined by the Court and it was up to the states to go along.[6]

No comparable attitude, to the distress of friends of freedom throughout the world, was displayed in the autumn of 1957 by Governor Orville Faubus of Arkansas. His intervention to deny the officials of Little Rock an opportunity to initiate their plan for the entrance of selected Negroes to the high school stands in sharp contrast to the supporting attitudes of the governors of those states where integration, in whole or in part, has gone forward.

It was against this background—or, perhaps more accurately, within this interplay of movement and counter-movement—that the *Sixteenth Yearbook* of the John Dewey Society was written. Its authors were not concerned to produce a tract, deeply as they believe in the rightness of the Court's action to set us straight with our historical commitment. Theirs, rather, was a quest for knowledge, to discover the ways in which the Negro has participated in American education and to assay the nature of that participation. Their careful analyses reveal that the American Negro has persisted patiently and courageously to lift himself educationally so that he

[6] *Ibid.*, p. 61.

could both enjoy the fruits of democratic citizenship and contribute to it in full measure. And they reveal, further, that however much the habits of others have restricted the Negro's educational opportunities, quantitatively and qualitatively, he has demonstrated his capacity to pull an equal share of the load of citizenship. His contribution to all aspects of the culture free men now share is beyond debate. This volume forecasts, then, without resort to preachment, an enrichment of the lives of all as we learn to live sensitively and imaginatively with the commitment that none among us shall suffer the hurtful consequences of discrimination.

H. GORDON HULLFISH

Ohio State University
Columbus, Ohio

PART I

THE BACKGROUND

I

The Education of Negroes Viewed Historically

W. A. Low, Professor of History
Maryland State College

I. Introduction

THE story of the American education of the Negro begins with the modern African slave trade. It ends with the education of the Negro as an American. From beginning to end, the story raises the fundamental question of the extent and quality of cultural integration in time—the question, in this instance, of the education and Americanization of the Negro in his transition from slave to citizen. This and related questions should be kept in mind in any consideration of the history of the American Negro. By what historic steps, for example, did an alien people become acclimated to the new land? What was the nature of the challenges that social and cultural conditions placed in the way of integration? Finally, what underlying forces impinged upon the Negro in the processes of Americanization?

It may be well to note at the outset that, almost exclusively unilateral and monolithic in origin, a concept arose and remained in being which defined the presence of the Negro in America as constituting something of a distinct, bizarre, or peculiar problem. Perhaps the definition arose out of the inherent nature of the conquest. Yet, its subsequent prevalence and existence were enforced upon the conquered and their descendants by sheer physical, political, and cultural dominance.

This definition of the situation excluded the Negro as an African and denied him the right to perpetuate an African culture and homeland; but it did not acknowledge him as an American. Rather, the implication was that the Negro lived in America by sufferance as a caste in a somewhat cultural purgatory, a timeless, nebulous, no-man's-land somewhere between Africa and America.

Thus, by an acquiescence enforced upon him, the transplanted Negro in continental America was to lose his spiritual and meaningful orientation to Africa, the meaning of old gods and languages, myths, and legends. Whatever meaningful residues of African cultures were to survive, the remnants were to live in remote patterns and problems of anthropology and sociology. They did not survive as vital, cogent forces in the stream of consciousness of Negro history.[1] *Africa became irretrievably lost; yet this loss, paradoxically, opened the way through the enforced denial of Africa, for the acceptance of America.* This fact is basic to an understanding of the history of the American Negro; it is especially pertinent in the story of both his larger and his academic education. In later years, if some Negroes turned their faces toward Africa—for example, in pre-Civil War attempts to colonize Liberia, or in verse, art, and music, or in an intellectual protest against caste, or in the ill-fated Marcus Garvey movement, or in sympathy for Africans living under the yoke of European imperialism—they did so as inhabitants of America. They acted as men who lived in the shadow or light of historical, political, or social forces, but not as true representatives of transplanted Africans seeking to return to a homeland. The student of history looks in vain for serious manifestations and expressions of any kind of African Zionism or Pan-Africanism in the history of the American Negro.

The Negro has been too busily engaged in attempts to overcome the ever present ordeal of daily living in America, often literally

---

[1] Compare with views held by some writers, such as Melville J. Herskovits, *The Myth of the Negro Past.* New York: Harper & Brothers, 1941, p. 292, and Miles Mark Fisher, *Negro Slave Songs in the United States,* Ithaca: Cornell University Press, 1953, pp. 43-61.

from hand-to-mouth, under exacting conditions of slavery or caste, to pursue seriously any movement toward alienism. Understandably, under these circumstances, the tragic beauty of Negro spirituals or the brilliant artistry of Negro jazz came to represent a spiritual and emotional flight from reality. Yet, escapism in Negro history seems to be characterized more by humanism than by romanticism or Pan-Africanism. Moreover, the pressures against the maintenance of African cultures were great. The homeland was so completely removed from the day to day meaning and logic of the American experience, that any inclination to refuse the new home carried grave dangers to survival. Therefore, the possibility of the non-acceptance of the new home was rejected, along with Africa. There was simply no other place than the new home for the Negro to turn—unless possibly to a spiritual home in heaven where he could, even as a slave or caste in a Christian society, figuratively lay his burdens down. *Herein lies the paradox of the American Negro's life: a historic devotion, allegiance, and loyalty to America in spite of the intense harshness with which he was often treated here.*

It may be seen then that conformity made an early appearance in Negro history, remaining a dominant characteristic even when non-conforming ideologies prevailed within the larger American scene. And conformity left its mark. In the first place, its inertia flavored Negro history with traces of skepticism. There was a calculated caution in the Negro's approach to new, non-conforming ideologies, lest such ideologies become reason or bait for further punishment, greater perils and ordeals. To conform to the social order was a key to more relative security in an environment already flush with insecurity and hostility. Conformity implied the probability of fewer punishments, lesser perils. By contrast, any inclination toward non-conformity was a signal of approaching danger, to be carefully avoided.

There is thus a powerful resistance to change in Negro history. The Negro has patiently preferred to maintain an outlook of wait-and-see. Consequently, some of the great movements in American history that ostensibly implied a democratic uplift in the status of the Negro, or for that matter of the common man generally, were likely to be evaluated in terms of results in the future rather than in terms of promises in the present. This fact is seen, for example, in the dispositions of the Negro toward the revolutionary doctrine of the late eighteenth century, abolitionism in the mid-nineteenth century, and Populism and Progressivism at the beginning of the twentieth century.

In the second place, anti-intellectualism became a corollary to conformity. For the Negro, either the expression or experience of non-conformity or radicalism carried the onus of being "smart"; that is, of purporting to know and to be intelligent when the social order generally demanded and expected a show of ignorance and inferiority on the part of the Negro. Anti-intellectualism became a device to crush the democratic spirit of freedom along with any shred of elemental human dignity during the period of slavery. It remained a strong force, subsequently, against the pursuit of truth and democracy after the political collapse of the slave regime. Both the larger and the academic education of the Negro have thus confronted the dilemma of conformity and anti-intellectualism, on one hand, and democratic philosophies for the Negro's right to the pursuit of knowledge and freedom on the other.

Yet, the presence of anti-intellectualism has not destroyed the Negro's respect for achievements in formal training. For achievement has been the means by which the Negro could recover or redeem his pride and dignity. This fact is revealed in the life and scholarship of Carter G. Woodson, the founder and, until his death, the guiding spirit of the *Journal of Negro History* and the Association for the Study of Negro Life and History. Often and long denied access to schooling, the Negro has not been immune to the fascination of formal training. Oddly enough, he has respected academic education and honors even when it was clear that a little learning had been inflated into sophistry or concealed behind the façade of a certificate, diploma, or degree. At the expense of substance, the symbols of learning have been honored in the education of the Negro. A "professor," for example, though often genuinely respected for his role and position, has not been necessarily prized for his erudition or insight into truth. Skeptically, many Negroes have traditionally been inclined to regard him as being only one step removed from an "educated fool," especially if his academic education kept him too far afield from the realities of Negro life.

The theory underlying anti-intellectualism indicated that the alleged superiority in intellect of the conquerors or masters was beyond question; that, conversely, the inferiority of the conquered or slave was to be taken for granted; that for the Negro to assume, assert, or demonstrate an equal or superior intellect was to deny the validity of his being in American life. Consequently, the doctrine of anti-intellectualism, identified with the Negro's alleged inferiority, was widely proclaimed, nurtured, enforced, and easily associated with the rationale of white supremacy.

Fear was generated in the atmosphere of anti-intellectualism. Its potential runs like a fine thread throughout Negro history. In addition to having some of its roots in American violence, fear also found sources in the psychology of Negro life. The Negro was inclined to doubt the alleged superiority of the conquerors and masters. He never accepted completely the inferiority that was thrust upon him. This rejection was demonstrated by numerous insurrections during the slave period[2] and by the literature of protest written since his emergence into citizenship. This inclination to rebel against what he regarded as the injustice of his position and the dilemma of his existence was a basis for fear. Furthermore, the Negro had reason to fear the consequences of his political and economic weakness in the face of the power of the conquerors and their descendants.

The nature of the conquest and its aftermath indicated, as the Negro himself was to experience, that life in America would not be easy, that it would be an ordeal. Yet with this realization by the Negro there grew the resolved determination to endure Americanization. And, strangely, the bonds of slavery and caste seem to have brought in their wake a moral vigor in counterbalance to the Negro's political and economic weakness, a result that strengthened the Negro's will to endure.

In spite of the ordeal the Negro faced, then, the process of inte-

[2] For studies on slave revolts, see Herbert Aptheker, *American Negro Slave Revolts*, New York: Columbia University Press, 1943; and Joseph Cephas Carroll, "Slave Insurrections in the United States, 1800-1865," unpublished dissertation, The Ohio State University, 1936. For an interesting treatment on inferiority, see Charles H. Wesley, "The Concept of the Inferiority of the Negro in American Thought," *Journal of Negro History*, Vol. 25 (October, 1940), p. 20.

gration actually occurred. Aware of the tremendous forces imping-
ing upon his daily existence, he was not inclined to resort to
theoretical or far-reaching explanations of his lot. Without losing a
sense of humor, he adopted patterns of behavior that were hardheaded and down to earth. Experience was thus the great and lasting teacher in the education of the Negro.

II. The Ordeal of Slavery

There are estimates that upward of ten or more million slaves,
brought in filth-ridden ships from Africa, were actually landed in
the New World in the three centuries following the Protestant Reformation. This estimate is not an accurate indication of the full
demographic and, far more, cultural decimation of a people, however. Millions more died in the African conquest, committed suicide,
or perished in the agonies of the Middle Passage. Perhaps as many
as a fourth of the captives died enroute to America. Most of the
slaves in the English colonies on the mainland arrived during the
eighteenth century, notably between the time of the Spanish Asiento
and the end of the American Revolution. Either by importation or
natural increase the number had reached 700,000 in 1790, when
the first census was taken in the United States, having tripled in the
thirty-five years since 1755.[3] This was an important demographic
factor in early American life.

There were also economic factors. Slave labor was basic to the
tobacco economy of colonial Virginia and Maryland. To a lesser
extent it was also a factor in the production of rice in South Carolina. Moreover, being vitally related to the production of tobacco
and the scheme of English-American mercantilism, it was a factor
in the development of the British imperial system during the seventeenth and eighteenth centuries, when tobacco, rum, sugar, and slaves
were important commodities in the circuit of trade between Europe,

[3] For an estimate of the number of slaves brought from Africa to continental
America, see W.E.B. DuBois, *The Suppression of the African Slave Trade to the
United States of America, 1638-1870*, New York: Longmans, Green and Company,
1896, p. 5. For estimates of the number of slaves in colonial America, see Franklin
Dexter, "Estimates of Population in the American Colonies," *Proceedings*, Amer-
ican Antiquarian Society, N.S., Vol. 5, 1894, pp. 22-50.

Africa, America and the West Indies. As the decline of the tobacco kingdoms of Virginia and Maryland gave way to the rise of the cotton kingdom of the Lower South, slave labor once again became a principal factor in the economy of America. In the cotton South, as in the heyday of the tobacco lords, labor on the plantations was hard; punishments were often severe. On the plantations, however, the Negro was exposed to the first great educating influences of the American environment.

There were, of course, cultural factors, with the greatest spiritual influence coming through Christianity. At the beginning of the eighteenth century a great question to appear was this: Should slaves be Christianized and, if so, would their status then be changed? This question posed one of the first great moral dilemmas in American life, projecting significant overtones into the course of American history. Christian theory, of course, held that all men were equal in the sight of God and brothers under His fatherhood. This ideal did not sanction slavery. But, on the other hand, hardheaded merchants, who desired to continue their lucrative profits from the slave trade, and slave owners were reluctant to give up their property. So most religious groups in America sanctioned slavery, while at the same time endorsing policies of Christianization. Such policies were likewise endorsed by the Crown, which ruled that the conversion of slaves would not change their status. In fact, Royal governors to the American colonies were instructed to aid in the conversion of slaves. Many slave owners opposed this effort, believing that Christianity would eventually mean freedom of slaves.[4] But this opposition seems to have diminished in time as slaves became further and further removed from the African background. This fact is well shown in the schism of the Methodist Episcopal Church in 1844, when Southern Negroes followed their masters on the issue of slavery: the question was no longer one of Christianization but of abolition of slavery. On the eve of the Civil War in 1860, for example, there were more than 200,000 Negro members alone in the Methodist Episcopal Church, South. Attrition was rapid, however, immediately after freedom

[4] Marcus W. Jernegan, *Laboring and Dependant Classes in Colonial America, 1607-1783*, Chicago: University of Chicago Press, 1931, pp. 39-40. The author says that attitudes antagonistic to conversion were often successful.

when the questions of Christianization and abolition no longer existed.

Arguments of justification, or rationalization, undergirded the religious sanction of slavery. One of the earliest to appear was that slavery made the fruits of civilization available to the "heathen" African. Other arguments held that the Bible sanctioned slavery; that slavery was a good thing for both the Negro and the country. Some of these arguments could still be heard as late as the eve of the Civil War, and, indeed, traces of them are yet to be found. Nevertheless, despite doubts, opposition, and the severe conditions of the colonial experience, the Christianization of the Negro proceeded as the first great step in his larger American education.

There is, for example, evidence that the Puritans favored conversion. In a tract published in London in 1673, Richard Baxter favored Christian instruction of slaves. John Eliot and Cotton Mather of New England favored instruction, also. And Samuel Sewall, a judge in Massachusetts, not only favored instruction but was quite outspoken against slavery, believing it to be a curse against God and humanity.

The Church of England, moreover, made efforts at conversion through its Society for the Propagation of the Gospel in Foreign Parts, organized in London in 1701. For example, an early catechizing school was founded in New York City at Trinity Church in 1704.[5] Instruction was given by Elia Neau regularly until 1712, when blame for a local slave uprising was attributed by some masters to Neau's work. High officials disagreed, but enrollment was temporarily curtailed. Neau died in 1722, but instruction continued under others until about mid-century. Reverend Thomas Bray in Maryland was another who encouraged instruction and conversion. His followers, known as Bray's Associates, continued his work, notably in Philadelphia and North Carolina, until the 1760's. These specific attempts by the Church of England are singularly noteworthy, though of greater importance to the movement was the prestige of the Church and of influential clergymen.

[5] A general and reliable reference to the early academic education of the Negro is Carter G. Woodson, *The Education of the Negro Prior to 1861*, New York: G. P. Putnam's Sons, 1919. A general reference for later years is Horace Mann Bond, *Education of the Negro in the American Social Order*, New York: Prentice-Hall, Inc., 1934.

Early efforts to teach the Negro were made by Catholics in New Orleans. The Ursuline Nuns attempted to teach Negroes and Indians in 1727 and, a few years later (1734), a school for Negroes was established and conducted on Chartres Street.

The most conscientious efforts, however, were made by Quakers. From the earliest days, slavery in colonial America troubled the consciences of Quakers. In face of opposition, Quakers permitted slaves to attend their meetings, even before they had decided to stop buying or to free them.[6] Indeed, Paul Cuffe, a prosperous Negro, set up a school in Massachusetts in the eighteenth century. John Woolman's influence, it should be said, was especially noteworthy.

Significant, also, was the influence of Anthony Benezet. He began an evening school in his home in Philadelphia in 1750 and conducted instruction there for twenty years. He was far more enlightened than many of his contemporaries at a time when enlightenment flourished. He spoke out against the idea of inferiority:

I can with truth and sincerity declare that I have found amongst the negroes as great a variety of talents as amongst a like number of whites; and I am bold to assert, that the notion entertained by some, that the blacks are inferior in their capacities, is a vulgar prejudice, founded on the pride or ignorance of their lordly masters, who have kept their slaves at such a distance, as to be unable to form a right judgment of them.[7]

Benezet exerted his influences at home and abroad in having a free school erected in 1770, with Moses Patterson as the first teacher. Upon his death in 1784, he bequeathed his fortune for the continuation of this school. Known as Benezet House, located on Locust Street in Philadelphia, the school was a fitting monument to a man who proudly devoted much of his long life to the academic education of the Negro.

Like Benezet, many Quakers clearly saw the need not only to give Christian instruction to the Negro but to abolish slavery as well. While Benezet was still alive, Philadelphia Quakers decided in 1776 to put an end to slaveholding. It is no mere coincidence that the de-

[6] Thomas E. Drake, *Quakers and Slavery in America*, New Haven: Yale University Press, 1950, pp. 1-33, 71.
[7] George S. Brooks, *Friend Anthony Benezet*, Philadelphia: University of Pennsylvania Press, 1937, p. 46.

cision came during the same year of Jefferson's Declaration of Independence. Quaker ideals triumphed over economic self-interest. The Quakers went further, moreover, and formed the Pennsylvania Abolition Society, one of the most influential of its day, having a roster of members eminent in England, France, and the United States, including Benjamin Franklin, William Pitt, Noah Webster, and Thomas Paine. The aims of the Society were to promote the gradual and moderate abolition of slavery; to give aid to the free Negro; and to establish schools for Negroes whenever possible.

Although Quakers were in the vanguard in pressing for education and freedom of Negroes, they were not alone. A great number of slaveholders gave instructions and granted manumissions in the liberal atmosphere of the Revolutionary period. Thus the free Negro population increased; by 1850, for example, half of the Negroes in the state of Maryland were already free—that is, were not legal chattels. The free Negro, always present in colonial America, therefore emerged as a definite factor of influence. He took the lead, for example, in establishing separate churches as a protest against inequalities. Such was the early story of African Methodism in Philadelphia and Baltimore.[8]

Efforts toward the education and freedom of the Negro were curtailed, of course, by the rapid rise of the slave power in the cotton South. Nothing illustrates this fact more clearly than the South's frantic disturbance over a slave insurrection in 1831 led by a Virginia Negro, Nat Turner. After the insurrection, "black" codes were devised, curtailing the movements of Negroes, forbidding the teaching of Negroes. The codes were not always strictly enforced, however, because Negroes continued to learn somewhat clandestinely. Some schools for Negroes were in operation in Danville and Richmond in Virginia as late as a decade before the Civil War and Berea College in Kentucky pioneered during the period in admitting Negro students, even though repercussions from John Brown's raid were to close its doors to Negroes. The Ursulines in New Orleans, furthermore, were still conducting a school for free *gens de couleur* in 1838. It may be said that legacies from the earlier work of religious

[8] See Charles H. Wesley, *Richard Allen, Apostle of Freedom*, Washington: The Associated Publishers, Inc., 1935.

and civic groups, mainly in the North and Upper South, provided sporadic incentives for the academic education of the Negro during the generation prior to the Civil War.

The chief spiritual force in the larger and academic education of the Negro lay without doubt in the bonds and unity of Christendom. Though the dominant power in the South was remarkably successful between 1830 and 1860 in deterring the ethical principles which pointed to the larger education of the Negro, the abolitionist crusade against slavery made it increasingly clear that this "peculiar" institution was morally wrong. Whatever causes may be assigned to the Civil War—and these are certainly many—it is surely true that the moral issue of slavery was a disrupting influence in the minds and actions of most Americans.

III. THE ORDEAL OF CITIZENSHIP

The victory of the North in the Civil War left deep scars in Southern life. There was not only the demographic factor of the Negro; there was also the vacuum left by the collapse of the slave power. Most of the Negroes in the nation at the end of the War were concentrated overwhelmingly in the Old South. Moreover, the political and economic domination of the old planter aristocracy ended as the "peculiar" property upon which much of this power rested became "contraband" of war and was later freed by the Emancipation Proclamation and the Thirteenth Amendment. Perhaps not without malice and revenge, the reconstruction that came in the wake of the military defeat of this power left even more marks upon national life. In an atmosphere that was not without controversy, tension, and violence, freedom of the Negro made its appearance under the political sponsorship of Congressional Republicanism.

Regardless of the pros and cons of Reconstruction, echoed even today in sound historical scholarship, the period opened a way for the greater Americanization of the Negro. This is shown in the introduction and support of organized education for Negroes in the generation following Lee's surrender at Appomattox. The older antebellum idea that *any* Negro education was questionable gave way to the newer idea that the Negro might be educated, even at nominal public expense, if his education remained under control of persons who would not permit the system to endanger white supremacy or allow the Negro to forget his "place." *The newer idea, then, arising in the post-bellum period, while it gave sanction to the acceptance of Negro education, left a margin of doubt as to the extent and quality of the program.* The Reconstruction philosophy of freedom for Negroes, however, buttressed by the American heritage of freedom, was enclosed within this margin. Thus, a moral question was posed in the new citizenship of Negroes, even as a similar question underwrote conversion to Christianity.

It must be borne in mind, however, that strong opposition arose to Negro education. This carried the familiar ring of earlier days—namely, that the education or integration of the Negro would be a dangerous threat to the vital interests of whites. Some Southerners, indeed, were not disposed to accept the idea of public education at all. One Virginian, writing under the name of "Civis" in 1877, first denounced any public education whatsoever, and then turned bitterly against the "hideous doctrine of negro equality," which he identified with Negro education.

I oppose it [public education] because its policy is cruelty in the extreme to the negro himself. It instills in his mind that he is competent to share in the higher walks of life, prompts him to despise those menial pursuits to which his race has been doomed, and invites him to enter into competition with the white man for those tempting prizes that can be won only by a quicker and profounder sagacity, by a greater energy and self-denial, and a higher order of administrative talent than the negro has ever developed.[9]

The idea of equality, of course, plagued the minds of the many Southerners whose dogma and credo held that the Negro's right to vote or to go to school would be tantamount to the "mongrelization" of the white race. Discrimination and resentment against the Negro, his church, school, home, or business, were likely to occur in proportion to the depth of this belief. Resentment sometimes flamed

[9] Bennet Puryear, *The Public School and its Relation to the Negro*, Richmond, Virginia, 1877, p. 17. By Civis. Republished by request, from the *Southern Planter and Farmer*, Clemmitt and Jones, printers.

into violence, fanned by the harsh arrogance of those convinced of the sanctity of white supremacy. Negro schools were frequently the targets of such resentment. Opposition found "full and free expression" in the interior of many Southern states.[10] In some communities Negroes were forcibly prevented from attending schools; teachers were not permitted to teach. Churches that often housed schools were sometimes burned. Some of the teachers, many of whom had lived along the fugitive Underground Railroad, suffered intimidation, insult, scorn and ostracism; a few were killed.[11] The Negro's right to an academic education during Reconstruction was circumscribed by the shadows cast by his former status.

It must be remembered, nevertheless, that violent opposition abated as years passed. Though barriers of caste were to be raised in the New South (1877-1913) as Southern white rule was restored, the idea of support for the academic education of the Negro began to receive sympathetic acceptance. By the turn of the century, some communities of the South were giving limited financial support to a segregated Negro education that was controlled by whites, unequally supported, and devoted almost exclusively to elementary or industrial education.

Whatever were the conditions surrounding the post-Civil War education of the Negro, the period did witness the first great program of organized education for the Negro. There was, for instance, the program of the federal government as conducted by the War Department. As refugees and "contraband," Negroes were early cared for and given some instruction under the military commands of General Rufus Saxton in the Sea Islands and vicinity, under Colonel John Eaton in Mississippi, and under General N. P. Banks in Louisiana. Later, acting as an agency of the War Department, the Freedmen's Bureau (1865-1872) enlarged upon these military beginnings under the leadership of Edwin Stanton, Secretary of War; General Oliver O. Howard, commissioner; and John W. Alvord, the Bureau's superintendent of instruction. The Bureau undoubtedly

[10] Paul S. Pierce, *The Freedmen's Bureau*, Iowa City: University of Iowa Press, 1904, p. 80, cites House Ex. Doc., 39th Congress, no. 70, p. 179.
[11] *Seventh Annual Report*, Freedmen's Aid Society, Methodist Episcopal Church, 1874, p. 15.

aided in the establishment of a system of schools for Negroes, giving "central organization, encouragement, protection, and financial support to the efforts of philanthropists, freedmen, and states."[12]

Civic and religious groups cooperated with the Freedmen's Bureau and, in addition, developed programs of their own. One of the first civic groups was the Boston Educational Commission, later known as the New England Freedmen's Aid Society. In the same year (1862), the National Freedmen's Relief Commission of Philadelphia and New York was founded. Later these groups temporarily formed the United States Commission for Relief of National Freedmen with headquarters in Washington, D.C. By 1865 this consolidated body was replaced by the American Freedmen's Aid Union which, after two more changes in name, went out of existence in 1869. Other organizations formed to aid freedmen were the African Civilization Society, the Baltimore Association for the Moral and Educational Improvement of Negroes, and a similar organization in Delaware.

Churches also made valuable and comprehensive efforts in the institutional history of Negro education. The American Missionary Association set up schools for Negroes in Newport News, Portsmouth, Suffolk, and Yorktown in Virginia, Washington, D.C., and Columbus, Ohio, as early as 1863. Furthermore, the Friends Association for Aid to Freedmen, the Board of Freedmen's Missions of the United Presbyterian Church, and the Freedmen's Aid Society of the Methodist Episcopal Church gave important aid to freedmen. Significant work was performed, also, by the American Baptist Home Mission Society, the American Church Institute of the Episcopal Church, and the conferences of the African Methodist Episcopal Church.

Some of the leaders in these civic and religious organizations had been prominent in the abolitionist movement; among them were Levi Coffin, Salmon P. Chase, Henry Ward Beecher, John M. Walden, and Richard S. Rust. Some were prominent business or civic leaders, such as Mathias W. Baldwin, locomotive industrialist; Edward Atkinson, textile manufacturer; and William Claflin, Governor

---

[12] Pierce, *op. cit.*, p. 83. There are several more recent studies of the role of the Bureau in the individual states.

of Massachusetts. No doubt many persons in the movement carried over their former religious and humanitarian zeal against slavery. Certainly, many Northern teachers who went South did so out of religious and humanitarian motives.[13]

Philanthropy was another great source of support. Financed mainly by wealthy Northerners whose fortunes came from the nation's industrialization, large educational foundations were organized within thirty years after the War. Recognized and regarded as a civic and moral duty, philanthropy aided Negro education materially in such categories as building construction, endowment, scholarships, teacher training, and industrial education.[14] Two major funds, the Daniel Hand and Anna T. Jeanes, were set aside exclusively for Negroes.

It can hardly be said, however, that philanthropy imparted a democratic philosophy to the academic function of Negro education. Despite its intent to do good, it considered the temper of the South realistically and circumvented the basic question of the application of democratic ideals to Southern Negro education. It was careful not to aggravate the controversial issue of race adjustment and Negro equality; and, further, Southern whites were usually selected to administer the funds. Thus, Northern philanthropy inadvertently perpetuated an old tradition of paternalism as a philosophy in solving the Negro "problem."*

The Peabody Education Fund, whose donations eventually amounted to about $3,500,000, began in 1867. Barnas Sears, a minister from the North, became its first general agent. He was succeeded upon his death in 1880 by Jabez Lamar Monroe Curry, a native of

[13] Henry L. Swint, The Northern Teacher in the South, 1862-1870, Nashville: Vanderbilt University Press, 1941, pp. 35, 46.
[14] Two general studies on philanthropy are: Ullin W. Leavell, Philanthropy in Negro Education, Nashville: George Peabody College Press, 1930; and Jesse B. Sears, Philanthropy in the History of American Education, Washington: Government Printing Office, 1922.
* A parallel example of a postwar policy which tended to revive and sustain the old power structure may be found in the white population. The Amnesty and re-enfranchisement granted former rebels enabled them, in many places, to institute a campaign of discrimination against Southerners who had been loyal to the United States throughout the war.—Editor

Georgia and former Confederate colonel.* In addition to grants to schools, the Fund also supported the establishment of museums at Yale, Harvard, and the City of Baltimore. Another fund was established by John F. Slater in 1882. A million dollars began the fund, but later donations doubled this amount by 1920. Atticus G. Haywood, a Georgian president of Emory College, was the first agent; he was succeeded by Curry, Wallace Buttrick, and James H. Dillard. Within a year after its inception twelve grants were made to Negro schools located chiefly in Virginia, North Carolina, South Carolina, Georgia, and Alabama.[15] Shaw, Hampton, and Tuskegee shared its earliest and principal benefits to Negro schools. Prior to World War I, the trustees began a program to establish "county training," or industrial, schools which gave impetus to the beginning and development of some of the first high schools in Southern communities.[16]

Other large funds came into being with the turn of the century. Andrew Carnegie gave $10,000,000 in 1902, establishing libraries on the campuses of many Negro schools and colleges. The General Education Board was enriched by John D. Rockefeller with an amount that began with $1,000,000 in 1902. There were also the Rosenwald Fund and the Anna T. Jeanes Fund. The latter was endowed by a kind, reticent Quaker with more than a $1,000,000 in 1907, for the purpose of assisting in the establishment of rural schools "for the great class of Negroes to whom the small rural and community schools are alone available."[17]

Lastly, there were the programs of education sponsored by individual Southern states. The inception of such programs was high-

* Although a Northerner, Sears was widely acclaimed, at the time of his death, for his understanding of southern education problems. Curry, although a "gentlemen of the Old South," was "a great admirer of Horace Mann and his educational work in Massachusetts." Curry was a staunch supporter of public education and, in the main, followed along the general lines laid down by Sears. cf. William E. Drake, *The American School in Transition.*—Editor

[15] Leavell, *op. cit.*, p. 64.

[16] See Edward E. Redclay, *County Training Schools and Public Secondary Education for Negroes in the South,* Washington: The John F. Slater Fund, 1935.

[17] For the story of the Jeanes Fund, see Arthur D. Wright, *The Negro Rural School Fund,* Washington: The Negro Rural School Fund, Inc., 1933, and Benjamin G. Brawley, *Doctor Dillard of the Jeanes Fund,* New York: Fleming R. Revell Co., 1930.

lighted by the issues of Reconstruction; continuance was influenced by the politics of the New South. Already revamping their state constitutions to comply legally with Congressional demands for Negro freedom and citizenship, Southerners began to make some of their first provisions for public education. Maryland, for example, made its first provisions for organized public education in 1864 and 1867. The Assembly set up a uniform system of free public schools, creating school districts and a state board of education. States farther south likewise made legal provisions: Arkansas and Louisiana in 1864; Florida in 1865; North Carolina in 1868 and 1876; Virginia in 1869 and 1870; South Carolina in 1877.

In the atmosphere of Reconstruction and the New South, however, public education for Negroes, and for many white Southerners, existed primarily on the law books. As late as 1900, one careful student condemned the public system of education in the South as a "misnomer" and "totally and radically inadequate."[18]

Maryland in the Upper South was far from the worst state in developing a program. Yet its support was dismally inadequate in comparison with many Northern states. For example, in the year following the close of the Civil War, Maryland appropriated no funds whatever for the education of Negroes. The first annual report (1866) of the superintendent of schools recommended that the State should provide separate schools for Negroes but admitted later that "nothing has been done for this class in the State."[19] An examination of expenditures in later years is revealing: for example, the amount paid to "colored schools," excluding Baltimore, was $4,580.31 in 1870; about twenty dollars was added to this amount the following year.[20]

The lack of public support for Negro education was general throughout the South. In many communities only about half of the children of school age attended any school at all, and only about half of those enrolled attended with a fair degree of regularity. The length of the school term was only a few months and classes were

[18] Edgar W. Knight, Public Education in the South, Boston: Ginn and Company, 1922, p. 422.
[19] Annual Report, Maryland State Board of Education, 1866, p. 64.
[20] Ibid., for years cited.

conducted often in a crowded, one-room shack or church-house by a teacher who would have been earning a high salary of $200 for any entire year before 1900. The Southern states were spending an average of $4.92 per year on a white child in 1900 and $2.71 on a Negro child.

The vast majority of Negro schools, public or private, gave instruction mainly in the rudiments of education immediately after the Civil War. As the century wore on, some groups began to improve the quality of their programs, to provide better buildings, and to extend the period of schooling upward. The basis was thus laid during Reconstruction for the development of Negro higher education. Some groups began to emphasize the necessity of more adequately trained ministers, teachers, or tradesmen at scores of schools that were variously styled as "normal," "institute," "academy," "seminary," "college," or "university." Some of these appellations were surely misleading, in the light of then existing American standards. Some critics maintained that Negro higher education institutions were unrealistically adapting their programs to the needs of the Negro peasant. Others held that, despite the conditions of his life, the Negro was capable and should be exposed to the highest and best qualities of the educative process.

Many of these earliest Negro schools survived, of course. Some changed their names or purposes. Some were absorbed by the states. And some lived as landmarks, public or private, in the institutional history of Negro education. A few illustrations will suffice. In Alabama the American Missionary Association sponsored and supported the establishment of a school at Talladega in 1867; theological training was given in 1872, but later this privately supported seminary became Talladega College. Fisk University (1866) in Nashville, Tennessee, and Tougaloo University (1869) in Mississippi were also set up by the American Missionary Association. A school in Pine Bluff, Arkansas, originally known as the "Branch Normal," became the Arkansas Agricultural, Mechanical, and Normal College by legislative act in 1872. In Augusta, Georgia, a school was organized in 1867 as the Augusta Institute; later this school became Morehouse College in Atlanta. It was supported by the American Baptist Home Mission Society, which also aided in the founding and support of

Virginia Union University (1865), Shaw University (of North Carolina, 1865), and Benedict College (1871). In the State of Mississippi the legislature set up Alcorn College in 1871; the name and source of support (excluding federal aid) remained unchanged. In Holly Springs, Mississippi, the Methodist Episcopal Church in 1867 founded a school known later as both Shaw University and Rust College. Moreover, in North Carolina in 1867 the Presbyterian Church founded Scotia Seminary which was later named Barber-Scotia College. In the same year and state at Charlotte, Biddle University was founded; it later became Johnson C. Smith. Lincoln Institute in Missouri, founded by Negro war veterans of the 62nd and 65th Infantries in 1866, became Lincoln University by law in 1921. In Maryland the Baltimore Conference of the Methodist Episcopal Church founded the Centenary Biblical Institute at Baltimore in 1866. Subsequently known as Morgan College and Morgan State College, this school eventually maintained branches in Princess Anne, Maryland, and Lynchburg, Virginia. It may be seen, then, that the period of Reconstruction witnessed the essential origin of Negro institutions of higher learning, opening the way for each to develop along its own unique lines.[21]

Federal aid was a factor in this development, mainly under the Morrill Acts of 1862 and 1890. Some Negro schools received federal

[21] A general story of the origin of the Negro college is told in D. O. W. Holmes, *The Evolution of the Negro College*, New York: Columbia University Press, 1934. The question of the oldest Negro college in the United States is debatable. Lincoln University in Pennsylvania, formerly Ashmun Institute, claimed the honor at a centennial observance in 1954. However, at least two other colleges could claim the distinction, Wilberforce and Cheyney. A number of histories of individual colleges has been written, including the following: Myron W. Adams, *A History of Atlanta University*, Atlanta: The Atlanta University Press, 1930; Samuel C. Armstrong, *Twenty Years Work of Hampton Institute*, Hampton: Hampton, Virginia Normal School Press, 1893; Walton C. John, *Hampton Normal and Agricultural Institute*, Washington: Government Printing Office, 1923; W. M. Davis, *Pushing Forward: A History of Alcorn A. and M. College*, Okolona: The Okolona Industrial School, 1938; Walter Dyson, *Howard University, the Capstone of Negro Education*, Washington: The Graduate School, Howard University, 1941; Cecil D. Halliburton, *History of St. Augustine's College*, Raleigh: St. Augustine's College, 1937; Thomas E. Jones, *Progress at Fisk University*, Nashville: Fisk University, 1930; F. A. McGinnis, "A History of Wilberforce University," Doctor's Dissertation, University of Cincinnati, 1940; W. Sherman Savage, *History of Lincoln University*, Jefferson City, Mo., 1940.

land grant funds under the first act. But not all Southern states complied with this act. Mississippi was the first Southern state to comply; the first land grant college for Negroes was established at Alcorn. Virginia followed the next year (1872), naming Hampton Institute as the recipient after some legislative controversy. South Carolina also designated Claflin during the same year.

Other Southern states designated federal land grant funds for Negro education only after the passage of the Morrill Act of 1890. This act was designed to prevent the expenditure of land grant funds in any state where "a distinction of race or color is made." Even in states that maintained separate institutions, the act required programs to be of "like character," and funds were to be distributed on a "just and equitable" basis. The act was a step in the direction of assuring financial equality in Negro education, therefore, despite the existence of dual schools. It gave strength, also, to the "separate but equal" doctrine. Consequently, some states hastily designated existing Negro schools to receive land grant funds for the first time or set up new Negro schools outright. In the latter category were the Georgia State Industrial College, the Agricultural and Technical College of North Carolina, and West Virginia State College. In the former, funds were designated by 1900 for schools already in existence in Alabama, Arkansas, Florida, Kentucky, Louisiana, Maryland, Missouri, Tennessee, and Texas; and funds were shifted in Virginia and South Carolina—from Claflin to Orangeburg, from Hampton to Petersburg.

The federal government, through what was then its Bureau of Education, insisted that land grant funds should be used in accordance with provisions of the Morrill Acts, but this insistence was more advisory than mandatory. Occasionally, an opinion of the Attorney General was obtained; but, inasmuch as the Bureau was not a law-enforcing body, its efforts to correct infractions were confined largely to persuasion or a threat to investigate or to discontinue funds. The Bureau's outstanding work was largely in the collection and dissemination of data.

The decade after the turn of the century is illustrative. The commissioner of education, Elmer E. Brown, was of the opinion that the way in which land-grant institutions were complying with provisions of the Morrill Acts should be established through a factual study. Obtaining an opinion from the Attorney General, he was assured that, under the Secretary of Interior, he was empowered to "ascertain and certify as to whether each institution is entitled to receive its share" of Morrill funds.[22] Accordingly, Brown officially authorized one of the earliest general surveys of land-grant institutions to determine the extent of compliance with the law. The findings were not too encouraging.

Kendrick C. Babcock and Arthur C. Monohan, specialists in the Bureau, were given the assignment. With the exception of one institution, they visited all land-grant institutions east of the Mississippi River. Their report, submitted on June 17, 1911, revealed that land grant institutions repeatedly gave "false items." The authors found that Negro institutions were devoted primarily to academic and teacher training and did not regard agriculture and mechanic arts as the "leading object" as required by the Morrill Act of 1862.[23] They reported further that Negro colleges not infrequently gave instruction on a "grade as low as the 4th or 5th of the public schools."

Other surveys were made by the Bureau, significantly in 1916 and 1928.[24] Findings and recommendations were both extensive and intensive. The recommendations for Negro institutions were generally acknowledged and accepted, however, within the framework of a dual system of education. Higher standards for the Negro were urged in the face of uncomplimentary conditions.

IV. THE EFFECT OF THE ATLANTA COMPROMISE

The period of Reconstruction had established the significant principle, however it may have been circumvented, that Negroes were entitled to be educated as free men. But the principle was surren-

[22] Records of the Department of Interior, National Archives, MS letter dated February 23, 1911. The opinion is not abstracted in pamphlets on rulings relating to the Morrill Acts.

[23] *Ibid.*, MS report dated June 17, 1911.

[24] Thomas Jesse Jones, *Negro Education. A Study of the Private and Higher Schools for Colored People in the United States*, Washington: U.S. Office of Education, Bulletin No. 38-39, 1916, and Arthur J. Klein, *Survey of Negro Colleges and Universities*, Washington: U.S. Government Printing Office, Bulletin No. 7, 1928.

dered during the period of the New South, when many influential Southern leaders were determined to keep the Negro "in his place." What this added up to was to keep him politically inarticulate and disenfranchised as in ante-bellum days, while offering a modicum of education as a compromise. The surrender may well be called the "Atlanta Compromise,"[25] since it was at the Atlanta Cotton States and International Exposition in 1895 that Booker T. Washington, in a memorable speech, gave persuasive sanction to the course of Southern sectionalism in the New South and the role assigned therein to the Negro.

Pragmatic and realistic, like many of his slave predecessors, Washington skilfully gauged the temper of his times and concluded that a program of cooperation (and possibly conformity) was likely to bring the Negro the highest utilitarian success and the greatest personal security and safety. His plea was that the Negro, a loyal Southerner, deserved a place of recognition in the rising progress of the South. Looking upon questions of social equality as the "extremist folly," he advised Southern Negroes to "Cast down your buckets where you are," educating the "head, hand, and heart"[26] through "the shop, the field, the skilled hand, habits of thrift, and economy, by way of the industrial school and college."[27]

Washington was influenced strongly by Hampton Institute. Like many of his classmates, he fell under the spell of Samuel C. Armstrong, a founder of Hampton, a former Union general, and a student of Mark Hopkins while at Williams College. Armstrong's emphases were that Hampton students should have a high regard for the dignity of labor; that they should train Negro youths to "go out and teach and lead their people, first by example, by getting land and homes; to give them not a dollar they could earn for themselves; to teach respect for labor; to replace stupid drudgery with skilled

[25] An excellent chapter by this title is found in C. Vann Woodard, *Origins of the New South, 1877-1913*, Baton Rouge: Louisiana State University Press, 1951, pp. 350-368.
[26] From the Atlanta address as quoted in Booker T. Washington, *Up From Slavery*, Garden City: The Sun Dial Press, 1900, pp. 218-225.
[27] From an address before the Harvard Alumni in 1896 after receiving an honorary Master of Arts as cited in Lewis Copeland, ed., *The World's Great Speeches*, Garden City: Garden City Publishing Company, 1942, p. 332.

hands; and to these ends to build up an industrial system, for the sake not only of self support and intelligent labor, but also for the sake of character."[28] He built his program at Hampton on the foundation blocks of skilled labor and moral character.

Armstrong's influence upon the academic course of Negro education was significant. Graduates of Hampton carried his teachings throughout the South. Writing his autobiography at Tuskegee, then famous for its program, Washington had only high praise for his old and ailing teacher. "It would be difficult," he wrote, "to describe the hold he [Armstrong] held upon the students of Hampton, or the faith they had in him . . . he was worshipped by his students."[29] One of Washington's schoolmates, Harold J. Trigg, likewise remembered Armstrong's influence, paying high tribute to his former teacher, then deceased, in an address before Hampton's graduating class of 1903:

I take pleasure in referring to General Armstrong as my teacher. His Sunday night lectures on moral philosophy will never be forgotten by those hearing him. No man who sat before him in those days could forget his teachings and efface from the tablets of his memory the impressions of that living, burning soul of truth and righteousness. The influence of those lectures has been multiplied many times in the lives of the youth of this Commonwealth through Hampton graduates. The most difficult principles of moral science were beyond the comprehension of the boys, but they believed them nevertheless, because they believed in their teacher and were willing to practice his teachings by faith. He knew how to say "Be wise as serpents and as harmless as doves," and I venture the assertion that there is not a boy of us who lives today that cannot hear that voice in those words ringing in his soul.[30]

The Southern whites could and did applaud the Compromise as a "platform upon which blacks and whites can stand with full justice to each other."[31] Humanitarian educators like J.L.M. Curry, Charles Dabney, and Charles D. McIvar endorsed the Compromise. Men

---

[28] Armstrong as quoted by Walton C. John, *op. cit.*, p. 5.
[29] Washington, *op. cit.*, p. 56.
[30] From a MS in the records of Hampton Institute; loaned through the courtesy of Major Walter R. Brown.
[31] The editor of the *Atlanta Constitution* as cited in Washington, *op. cit.*, p. 226.

like Governor Charles B. Aycock of North Carolina could build and endorse the support of Negro schools as defined by the Compromise, while at the same time conducting a relentless program of white supremacy against the Negro's right to vote, against the fiction of "Negro domination."

Northern philanthropists applauded the implication that the Compromise held for the business community: economy, industrial production, monopoly, anti-labor action, and profitable Southern markets. Gaining fame and influence, Washington moved easily in circles of the powerful and rich. And though not advocating political power or "social equality" for the Negro, he himself came to wield an influence greater than that of any Negro, and of many Southern whites for that matter. He dispensed the patronage of influential philanthropists and frequently served as a spokesman for the Negro people.

Many Negroes likewise applauded the Compromise. At last they had found a national hero and spokesman who could replace Frederick Douglass, the old abolitionist who died early in 1895. Through Washington's prestige they experienced a measure of recognition and pride. Besides, since Reconstruction days the great majority of Negroes openly and realistically accepted segregation in fact, if not in principle. It was unsafe for the Negro to do otherwise, as widespread lynchings, riots, and a thousand degrading indignities in the New South demonstrated. Thus, it was not at all difficult for the Negro to go along with a Compromise which promised to abate rather than engender racial conflict.

Negroes, of course, found a measurable sense of success and pride in their segregated schools, churches, homes, and businesses. It is true that the system of segregation kept some doors closed that had never been opened, but it also provided some limited opportunities. A movement to replace white teachers in Negro schools was well under way, for example, in Baltimore in 1895, the year of Washington's Atlanta speech. The Baltimore *Afro-American*, a Negro newspaper first published in 1892, devoted a long editorial to protest the employment of white teachers in Negro schools of the city. This was almost exactly one month after Washington's Atlanta address. Another editorial a few weeks later urged Negroes to vote for the candidate for mayor who promised to discontinue "mixed schools" of Negro and white teachers.[32] Washington himself went to Tuskegee only after Armstrong insisted that he should be employed instead of a white teacher. Here was a facet of the Negro's interest in Negro education.

Endorsement of the Compromise was also written into law. In the year after Washington's Atlanta speech, the Supreme Court, in the case of *Plessy* v. *Ferguson,* gave sanction to both the theory and practice of segregation if accomodations were equal.

Despite the sanction by law, however, some Negro leaders openly opposed the Compromise as a retreat from the principle that Negroes should be educated as free men. It was challenged strongly by a New England Negro, W.E.B. DuBois, who barely missed taking a teaching job at Tuskegee. Instead, DuBois went to Atlanta University in 1896, having there a brilliant and distinguished career in scholarship and letters. He favored a program of education that would teach the Negro to think and recognized the need of higher learning in the Americanization of the Negro. DuBois moved boldly during 1905-06 in his attack upon the Compromise. He insisted that as free men Negroes were entitled to every right and privilege of any other American. He led the "Niagara Movement," the spiritual ancestor of the National Association for the Advancement of Colored People, making known his stand in a set of publicly announced resolutions in Atlanta, August, 1906:

We want full manhood suffrage, and we want it now, henceforth and forever. Second: We want discrimination in public accomodations to cease. . . .
Third: We claim the right of free men to walk, talk, and be with them that wish to be with us. . . .
Fourth: We want the laws enforced against rich as well as poor; against Capitalist as well as Laborer; against white as well as black. . . .
Fifth: We want our children educated. . . . And we call for education meaning real education. We believe in work. We ourselves are workers,

[32] *Afro-American,* Baltimore, Maryland, November 2, 1895.

but work is not necessarily education. Education is the development of power and ideal. . . .[33]

The controversy between Washington and DuBois continued until Washington's death in 1915. During these years there can be little if any doubt of the winner in terms of power, prestige, and popularity. Even DuBois himself admitted shortly after Washington's death that Washington was the greatest leader since Frederick Douglass.[34] This admission, however, did not end DuBois' fight against the principles of the Compromise.

Washington seems to have lived for and in keeping with his times, a superb diplomat, realist, and materialist, though a biographer states that, despite his Compromise, Washington really favored the ultimate equality of the Negro.[35] On the other hand, far less the materialist and far greater an intellectual and scholar, DuBois stood openly and unequivocally, but at times bitterly, upon the timeless belief of Americans in freedom. Time may yet in its perspective accord him a greater stature, without bitterness, for not compromising the moral challenge which he plainly recognized as underwriting the so-called problem of the Negro in American life.

V. THE CHANGING EDUCATIONAL PATTERN

A great migration of Negroes from the farm to Southern and Northern cities came after Washington's death. In an important sense the movement was a flight from poverty, oppression, and the boll weevil. The unprecedented urbanization and industrialization of the Negro was thus under way. Needless to say, the heralded industrial education of the Compromise—an education far removed from the realities of labor unionism, the factory system, mass

[33] Ridgely Torrence, *The Story of John Hope*, New York: Macmillan Company, 1948, pp. 150-151. John Hope, newly appointed president of Atlanta University, endorsed the Niagara Movement. DuBois tells the story of his fight against the "Tuskegee Machine" in his autobiographical *Dusk of Dawn*, New York: Harcourt Brace and Company, 1940, pp. 72-96.

[34] Basil Mathews, *Booker T. Washington*, Harvard University Press, 1948, p. 302.

[35] *Ibid.*, p. 299.

production, and corporate enterprise—had not even remotely prepared the migrant peasants to live in the machine age of the twentieth century.*

Profound changes took place in both the academic and the larger education of the Negro between World War I and World War II. In brief, these were:

1. A significant establishment of Negro public high schools, a development that was pronounced in large urban areas, both North and South. Sometimes the establishment was made from schools already in existence at the elementary level.

2. Enormous increases in both the relative and actual sizes of the enrollment, supply of teachers, number of graduates, and capital outlay. There were programs of consolidation, new curricula, and many changes suggested by general American patterns and trends in elementary and secondary education.

3. Similar changes at the college level. Many Negro colleges dropped their high school programs; some added graduate instruction. Many degree-conscious Negroes graduated in ever-increasing numbers from Negro and Northern colleges. Regional accrediting agencies added more and more Negro colleges to their lists.

4. State supported and land grant institutions surpassed the private Negro colleges in enrollment and financial support. The need thus arose for the United Negro College Fund.

5. Negro education was subjected to the scrutiny of the scholar. Following the lead of study in Negro history, studies in Negro education appeared regularly in the *Journal of Negro Education,* first published in 1932. Moreover, many federal, state, and local surveys were conducted and a great deal of independent research by individuals was initiated.

6. Some studies pointed out conditions in academic education in comparison with existing American standards and objectives. Others

* This statement is equally true, of course, of almost all American education, North and South, in the late nineteenth and early twentieth centuries. One of the most obdurate problems confronting professional students of education during the past 75 years has been this "educational lag" between the demands of an urbanized and industrialized society and a schooling persistently characterized by attitudes retained from an earlier agrarian economy.—Editor

noted the appalling gap between education for Negroes and whites, the predominance of teacher training in Negro colleges, the lack of democracy in the administration of Negro colleges and schools. One serious student, for example, listed exactly 364 problems that confronted the Negro college, the most outstanding being the need of the Negro college to shift its "general administrative policy and practices from the autocratic and authoritarian (however benevolent) to something nearly approximating democracy."[36]

7. The most profound change was the quest for equality. In great part this quest was conducted quietly and diplomatically, though forcefully, by Negro teachers and their former students, even within a segregated system controlled mainly by whites.

The quest for equality, in large measure, represents a reassertion by the Negro of the legal rights granted during Reconstruction. A "new" Negro,[37] far less docile than the post-Reconstruction generation, while aware of his status in contemporary life, sought adjustment through the courts, remembering that he, too, lived within the organic framework of the American democratic heritage. Perhaps in no area of Negro life was the quest more dramatic and significant than in the field of public education, particularly higher education. This fact is well illustrated in the Murray and Gaines cases.

Donald Gaines Murray, a Negro graduate of Amherst College in 1934, applied for entrance to the School of Law of the University of Maryland, located in Baltimore, on January 24, 1935. Refused admission, he filed his complaint in the local courts. The courts of Baltimore ordered his admission, but the University took the decision to the Court of Appeals of Maryland in October of 1935. It permitted Murray to enroll in September, pending action of the higher courts. The Court of Appeals upheld the decision of the lower courts and Murray continued his studies, being graduated in 1938.

The arguments in the Murray case reflected contrasting ap-

---

[36] John W. Davis, "Problems in Collegiate Education of Negroes," *West Virginia State College Bulletin*, June, 1937, p. 12.

[37] Alain Locke, ed., *The New Negro*, New York: A and C Boni, 1925; see also his "The Negro: 'New' or 'Newer'?" in *Opportunity*, Vol. 17 (January, 1939), p. 14.

proaches to the theory of "separate but equal," a legal heritage of *Plessy* v. *Ferguson*. The University argued that it was not technically a state agency (having once been under private control), and that out-of-state scholarships provided for the higher education of Negroes. Murray's counsel disagreed, pointing out that the University was in reality a publicly financed institution; that the Morrill Act of 1890 entitled the Negro to equitable instruction; that instruction at the University's Negro branch in Princess Anne (renamed Maryland State College in 1947) was far from equitable and equal; and that out-of-state scholarships for Negroes would not suffice. Failure to admit Murray, his counsel argued, was an abridgment of his rights as a citizen.

Murray's counsel was led by Charles Hamilton Houston, the first Negro editor of the *Harvard Law Review*. Houston was assisted by Thurgood Marshall, a graduate of Lincoln University (Pennsylvania) and Howard University. Houston devoted a great deal of his professional life to the attainment of the Negro's equality within the ideals of the American democratic heritage. He lived to see some of the fruits of his victory, but warned Negroes not to "shout too soon" in an issue of the *Crisis*, a publication initiated by DuBois to fight the Atlanta Compromise. The victory in the Murray case became a precedent and several months after its close, a similar suit was filed by the attorneys of Lloyd Lionel Gaines, a graduate of Vashon High School in St. Louis and Lincoln University (Missouri). His chief counsel was Sidney R. Redmond, also of St. Louis, who was assisted by Houston and Leon A. Ransome.

Gaines' case is more celebrated than the Murray decision because it was eventually argued before the Supreme Court. The decision was handed down on December 12, 1938, declaring that the State was bound to furnish "within its borders facilities for legal education substantially equal to those . . . afforded for persons of the white race, whether or not other Negroes sought the same privileges." Chief Justice Charles Evans Hughes, in arriving at this conclusion, based much of his decision—in direct quotes—upon findings in the Murray case.

Other legal suits followed the Murray and Gaines cases, employing essentially the same basic pleas. Heman Sweatt filed against the University of Texas and Ada Sipuel filed against the University of Oklahoma. In August of 1949 a half dozen suits were filed by Negroes to enter the various professional schools of the University of Maryland.[38] Indeed, resort to legal action was not an unusual practice by 1950. As a result, some Negroes entered Southern universities where formerly admission had been denied. A week before Houston's death, the high court of Maryland ordered the University to admit a Negro student, Esther McCready, to its School of Nursing. From his hospital bed in Washington, D.C., a segregated hospital for Negroes (Freedmen's), Houston may have recalled as he read of this that fourteen years had passed since his victory in the Murray case. He may have remembered what he said about "shouting too soon," knowing as he did, that the mills of the gods sometimes grind slowly.

There can be little doubt that the acceleration of legal attacks upon the system of caste in organized education was helpful in securing increased appropriations and some equalization of teacher salaries, as well as encouraging experiments at regional education and limited legal integration or "mixing" in some public schools, notably in the state of Indiana. The impact of World War II, with the subsequent integration of the armed forces was an important factor, also. Finally, the unanimous decision of the Supreme Court on May 17, 1954, gave legal force and sanction to the educational theory of integration, as opposed to the old doctrine of "separate but equal," reaffirming the living ideas of the American Dream. This decision was the capstone of the Negro's legal attack. Here was another milestone in the larger and the academic education of the Negro in his transition from slave to citizen.

VI. REALIZING THE AMERICAN DREAM

It may be too soon to measure the stature of Charles Hamilton Houston in this transition. Although Houston showed the moral and ethical strength that were characteristic of Frederick Douglass, there is a sense in which he represents a forward step. Whereas

[38] *Norfolk Journal and Guide,* Norfolk, Virginia, August 6, 1949.

Douglass relied chiefly upon persuasive oratory, Houston relied upon his skill and clarity in the delineation of legal suasion and succeeded in fashioning a weapon specifically designed to secure and maintain the rights of Negroes. He moved carefully in his legal attack upon the theory of "separate but equal" to bring into force fundamentals beyond existing statutes. The *Washington Post* of his home town praised him upon his death, as a "crusader for a principle that lies at the heart of American democracy."

Within the professional lifetime of Charles H. Houston, a profound and significant change took place in the emancipation of American Negroes. He was one of the principal architects of this change. His great gifts as a lawyer were devoted from the beginning of his career to an unremitting battle to win for Negroes genuine equality before the law. Formidable statutory barriers of discrimination on grounds of race crumbled under the skill and stubbornness of his onslaught. It is a tragedy that he could not have lived to see the final victory of the cause he championed and did so much to win.[39]

This editorial would have been appropriate and timely on May 17, 1954, four years after Houston's death, when the Supreme Court made known its stand against segregation. Though Houston was dead, the Court seemed cognizant of the fact that the American Dream was still very much alive. For behind the dream lay preponderant values in the Western heritage: the classical and Christian concepts of the worth of the individual; the Reformation concepts emphasizing the equality of all men in the sight of God; the Enlightenment concept that by the application of intelligence man can make progress toward the betterment of himself and society.

Behind the Dream also lay the real experience of the Negro in the American environment, his larger education and integration into the stream of American life. This experience is itself a study of the scope and quality of the Americanization of the Negro. The historic steps in the process, applicable to the Negro's academic education as well, may be summarized as follows:

1. The early decision to give Christian instruction to slaves; the decision was acted upon despite opposition.

[39] *Washington Post*, Washington, D.C., April 25, 1950.

2. The instruction of Negroes through religious, civic, and benevolent groups, both before and after manumission.

3. The restraints placed upon the Negro and his education by the slave power of the cotton South, notably after Nat Turner's insurrection.

4. The right of Negroes to be educated as free men, established after the military and political collapse of the slave power in the South.

5. The religious and Northern influence in the establishment and support of Negro institutions during and following the period of Reconstruction.

6. The program of industrial education as symbolized and popularized by Booker T. Washington in the Atlanta Compromise.

7. The advent of public support, premised somewhat upon the principles of the Compromise, wherein segregated institutions and systems eventually flourished and expanded, notably by the time of World War II, under the legal fiction of "separate but equal."

8. The legal protest of the "new" Negro, determined either to make the legal fiction of "separate but equal" more nearly a reality or to replace the fiction altogether with integrated schools. The result, of course, was the May 17, 1954, decision of the Supreme Court against segregation.

It is well to keep in mind that these historic steps in the experience of the Negro took place within the moral order peculiar to the Western heritage, especially colored by the concepts of American democracy. *It may be seen that in each step there was, on one hand, the question of the existence of American ideals; while, on the other hand, there was the question of the existence of specific situations in which the ideals were in some part, if not fully, denied. Herein lies the historic moral dilemma surrounding the existence of the Negro in American life.* If there is to be a "solution" to the so-called Negro "problem" in America, this dilemma has to be resolved; the gap between ideals and practices has to be closed.

The problem is an American one and history has revealed a trend toward its solution, despite the resistance of anti-democratic forces. For example, the question in 1700 of the Christianization

of slaves no longer existed in 1800. Again, the question of the abolition of slavery, already on the horizon in 1800, had disappeared by
1900. Further, the question of the education of the Negro as a free
man, an anti-climax in 1900, was hardly a grave one for the nation
at the time of the decision against segregation in May of 1954.

Thus, inasmuch as the crux of the problem is moral in nature,
solutions are to be sought within the moral confines of American
democracy, of conduct in American life which results in bringing
undemocratic practices into harmony with democratic ideals. This
hope has been the essence of the Negro's thinking, feeling, and being,
even the very gospel of his religion.[40] The Negro, along with other
Americans, has held the faith and hope that democracy would become progressively a more living and meaningful reality for all. This
has been his continuing dream, despite the necessary compromises
dictated by adverse political, economic, and social conditions.
The devotion of the Negro to this aspiration constitutes a tribute
to his moral stamina.

[40] See Benjamin Mays, *The Negro's God,* Boston: Chapman and Grimes, Inc.,
1938, p. 225.

II

Unique Contributions of
Negro Educators

William H. Martin, Dean of Faculty
Hampton Institute

I. The Need for Assessment

In the Preface of Horace Mann Bond's illuminating volume, *The Education of the Negro in the American Social Order*, E. George Payne said:[1]

Too little importance has been attached to the status and contribution of the minority cultural groups to American life and civilization. Particularly is this neglect evident in the case of the Negro, in spite of the fact that perhaps the most outstanding achievement in educational progress of any single group in the United States, or elsewhere, has been the advancement of Negro education since the Civil War.

The statement was sound when it was written; it is sound today. Indeed, the need to examine the Negro's contribution is more urgent now. Recent political, cultural, economical, and social developments call for changing perspectives and for a reassessment of the social role the Negro may play now and in the years that lie ahead. These developments have brought into sharp focus several fundamental questions relating to education: What contribution

[1] Horace Mann Bond, *The Education of the Negro in the American Social Order*, New York: Prentice-Hall, Inc., 1934, p. vii.

60

has been made by Negroes to American education? What specific contributions have been made by schools and colleges? What experiences can be identified to provide some clue to the Negro's potentialities in the larger educational picture?

Since emancipation the Negro has contributed significantly to American life and civilization. His ascent, reflecting his growing sense of responsibility as he became an integral part of American democracy, illustrates the soundness of the American doctrine which emphasizes the improvability of man. He has made genuine and specific contributions, of increasing quality and quantity, to American education within recent years.

Whether the accomplishments discussed have been unique will rest, of course, upon an interpretation of the term. To say that ideas and practices contributed by Negro educators are unique, in the sense of being discrete, would be a gross error. For, as the history of education reveals, practices in any given period are necessarily adaptations or reconstructions of earlier ones. This is no less true of ideas and practices which have contributed to the development of an indigenous American educational system. The point pressed here, however, is that ideas and practices may be called unique when the situations to which they are applied are unique. Thus, the ideas and practices to be discussed are unique when viewed against the backdrop of the problems with which Negro educators have had to deal. Among these problems have been: the low economic status of the race; differential per capita expenditures in public schools; correspondingly inferior and often inadequate facilities; and indifference among some white administrators.

What has been achieved by the Negro has not been accomplished *in vacuo,* of course. Such an inference would tend to minimize the magnificent stimulus provided through the years by organized philanthropy, the growing spirit of liberalism which caught hold in the South in the late 1930's, the cooperative efforts of non-Negro organizations concerned in making democracy a reality, and the aid provided by non-educational Negro organizations that have worked relentlessly for the cause of Negro development and progress.

A fact of the situation, an anomaly in a democratic culture, has been, of course, the existence of separate schools. These schools, staffed in the main by race educators, have initiated experimentation in important areas of school practice. In addition, it should be noted, Negro contributions to American education have not been confined to Negro institutions, nor have any contributions failed to interact with the broad sweep of American life and culture. In recent years, Negroes associated with interracial and intercultural educational enterprises have achieved distinction in research, teaching, administration, and other areas of educational service.

II. EARLY IDEAS AND THEIR IMPLEMENTATION

From the status of producer of raw material in an agrarian economy, the Negro, after emancipation, was ushered into a nineteenth century social milieu that was becoming increasingly more complex. He found himself part and parcel of the greatest experiment in social living yet devised by man, one that was, initially, far too advanced for the newly-emancipated citizens. Although at the time of emancipation, as Bond noted, they were "devoid even of any experiences in the difficult art of independent living, the Negro slaves, once emancipated, brought to their new official status an immense urge for progress."[2] They revealed a passion for learning and a desire to guide their lives by America's historic faith in education.

Since the beginning of American education, leading thinkers have attempted to structure educational programs in terms of purposes that flow from the culture. In seventeenth century American education, with life steeped in religious fervor, educational enterprise reflected certain religious ideals. Indeed, throughout the broad sweep of its development, the American educational system shows the continuing attempt to gear educational thinking and practice to important values of the times. This fact influenced Negro educators. They believed, also, that an educational program should be in harmony with the prevailing temper of the time.

Before the end of the nineteenth century, and extending into

[2] *Ibid.*, p. 21.

the first decade of the twentieth, Negro leaders developed a quality of educational statesmanship that has persisted to the present time. Some of their efforts antedate the founding of public schools and colleges for Negroes. These individuals were characterized by courage, foresight, determination, and devotion to the cause of Negro advancement and progress. The founding of Haines Institute in Georgia by Lucy C. Laney and the development by Mary McLeod Bethune of Bethune-Cookman College at Daytona Beach, Florida, illustrate these qualities. The vision of Charlotte Hawkins-Brown in the development of Palmer Memorial Institute in North Carolina, which now is the only Negro finishing school, reinforces the view that some of the early leaders were deeply concerned to meet the existing educational needs of the Negro.

Perhaps Booker T. Washington accomplished more than any one else to propagate the doctrine of social regeneration by means of industrial training.* He not only developed a school based upon an articulated philosophy, but provided leadership that awakened an apathetic South to appreciate and accept his program. No other Negro educator has presented an educational philosophy in such clear-cut terms and then pursued its implications so faithfully. His life and works form one of the most dramatic chapters in American educational history.

Imbued with the ideas that labor can be dignified and that happiness comes to those who serve others, Washington's professional career was devoted to the effort to translate into the educational operations the philosophy he had started to form while studying at Hampton Institute with General Samuel Chapman Armstrong. The principle that an educational program should be projected against the life of the people was basic to his educational thinking. Accordingly, he sought at Tuskegee Institute to demonstrate the intimate interplay of ideas and practice. As he entered upon his work, visits were made to nearby towns and farm areas. These preliminary investigations eventuated in his amassing data about the needs of the people, to the end that Tuskegee's potential service might be enhanced. He firmly believed that an educational

* Stuart G. Noble, *A History of American Education:* New York: Farrar and Rinehart, Inc., 1938, p. 305.

program should be undergirded by a functional philosophy of education. "Institutions, like individuals," wrote Washington, "are properly judged by their ideals, their methods, and their achievement in the production of men and women who are to do the world's work."[3] In expanding this philosophy he said:[4]

One school is better than another in proportion as its system touches the more pressing needs of the people it aims to serve, and provides the more speedily and satisfactorily the elements that bring them honorable and enduring success in the struggle of life.

The program of industrial education that developed at Tuskegee was not a narrow one. It recognized the necessity of providing a well-rounded program for the development of Negro youth. In Washington's terms, "Mere hand training, without thorough moral, religious, and mental education counts for very little."[5] A well-rounded education in his view, consisted of the training of the hands, the head, and the heart.

Bond[6] has summarized the objectives that evolved at Tuskegee as follows: (1) the development of attitudes and habits of industry and honesty in, and the disciplining of raw, country youth through institutionalized activities; (2) the development of specific skills in definite crafts and occupations; and (3) the preparation of teachers for the public and private schools of the South who might, through spreading the gospel of thrift, industry, and racial conciliation, aid in constructing a firm economic foundation upon which the future aspiration of the race might stand.

The experiences offered to implement these objectives were of a practical kind. Consequently, students at Tuskegee were taught by the so-called activity method. They were provided opportunity "to study actual things instead of books alone."[7] Stating this differently, Roscoe Conkling Bruce, Director of the Academic De-

[3] Booker T. Washington, *Tuskegee and Its People: Their Ideals and Achievements,* New York: D. Appleton Company, 1910, p. 1.
[4] *Loc. cit.*
[5] Booker T. Washington, *Working With the Hand,* New York: Doubleday, Page and Company, 1904, p. 5.
[6] Horace Mann Bond, *op. cit.,* p. 119.
[7] Booker T. Washington, *Up from Slavery,* New York: A. L. Burt Company, 1901, p. 126.

partment, said: "They (the students) ascend to general principles through the analysis of concrete cases."[8] In a word, the student started with the known and proceeded through related knowledge and experiences to the unknown.

Washington's main purpose was to send men and women into the communities of the South who would make constructive contributions to community living. In consonance with the philosophy of Pestalozzi, he saw in education the possibility of "the social regeneration of humanity," based upon the principle of pupil activity. Accordingly, effort was made to provide a type of education which would equip his student with knowledge and skill to show the people how to put new energy and new ideas into farming as well as into their intellectual, moral, and religious life.[9]

As the program at Tuskegee flourished, it eased the feelings of many white Southerners who were apprehensive about the consequences in the development of the Negro in the classical education to which he was being introduced by the New England humanitarians. In his address delivered at the Atlanta Exposition in 1895, Washington stated, to the satisfaction of the Southern whites, "In all things that are purely social we can be as separate as the five fingers, yet one of the hand in all things essential to mutual progress." He admonished the Negro to ". . . cast down your bucket where you are—cast it down in making friends in every manly way of the people of all races by whom we are surrounded. Cast it down in agriculture, mechanics, in commerce, in domestic service, and in the professions." This address was received with mixed emotions. The white South hailed it as a platform upon which all could agree. Some Negro church groups issued resolutions condemning the Tuskegee program, and advised Negroes against sending their children to the institution.[10]

In spite of this opposition, the "Tuskegee Idea," as it is sometimes called, became the basis for a number of schools subsequently organized. In fact, the "industrial" high schools found in

[8] Booker T. Washington, *Tuskegee and Its People*, p. 65.
[9] Booker T. Washington, *Up From Slavery*, p. 127.
[10] For a more detailed treatment, and a different interpretation, of the controversy, see Chapter I, Section IV.

many southern cities today were so named out of deference to the Washington philosophy. Many of these schools carry his name. Furthermore, several private schools based on the Tuskegee pattern were established. Some were organized by graduates of Tuskegee; others were developed by educators who gave allegiance to the philosophy. Fargo Institute in Arkansas, Utica Institute and Prentiss Institute in Mississippi, and Snow Hill Industrial School in Alabama are specific examples of the effort to apply and extend the Tuskegee point of view.

III. Organization, Administration, and Supervision

As public schools for Negroes became more numerous, leaders of the race were conspicuous by their absence as members of policy-making bodies. The control of Negro schools was rarely vested in the hands of Negro administrators.[11] Yet as opportunities have been afforded them, Negroes have revealed creative imagination and sound educational insight at all administrative levels—federal, state, and local.

Although education in this country is a state function, the Federal Government over the years has exhibited a genuine interest in the development of education through the United States Office of Education. Established in 1867 as the Department of Education, the office has assumed as one of its major roles that of collecting and disseminating information about education. Ambrose Caliver, who had served as Dean of Fisk University, was appointed to the office in 1930 as the first government specialist in Negro education. In 1952 he was appointed Assistant to the Commissioner of Education.

In line with one of the major functions of the U.S. Office of Education, Caliver has published materials bearing on many phases of Negro education. Moreover, he has directed and participated in conferences and workshops involving professional and lay leaders. During the years in which the Negro has worked for equal educational opportunities, his advice and counsel have been sought by school officials throughout the South. It was largely through his

11 Horace Mann Bond, *op. cit.,* pp. 391-396.

survey of the situation that Oklahoma saw the futility of attempting a graduate program at its Negro state college.

Analysis of his published books and bulletins reveals that he has consistently placed the spotlight on critical problems related to the education of the Negro. These problems have included student personnel, rural education, secondary education, the education of teachers, vocational education and guidance, supervision of Negro education, higher education, inter-group education, and the education of Negro leaders. In addition, he has made available regularly up-to-date statistics on the education of the Negro, as well as relevant bibliographic material.

In recent years, Caliver has devoted much of his time and energy toward upgrading the literacy of Negroes and bringing into the open the problem of school segregation. His most important contributions to American education may be summarized as follows:

1. Conceived and directed the National Conference on Fundamental Problems in Education of Negroes, 1934.

2. Helped promote the education of Negroes through a series of annual radio programs, beginning in 1930 and culminating in a series of dramatized programs in 1941-42, on the participation of Negroes in American life; and through the annual meetings of the National Advisory Committee on the Education of Negroes during the Conventions of the American Association of School Administrators.

3. Contributed to the promotion of literacy education, beginning with the WPA in 1934 and culminating in the Literacy Education Project (toward which the Carnegie Corporation contributed $50,000); the introduction of literacy education bills in the Congress; and the establishment of the Literacy and Fundamental Education Committee of the U.S.A.

4. Participated significantly in planning and directing the National Survey of Higher Education of Negroes through which great impetus was given to the ideas of regional cooperation and, it is claimed by some, stimulated the development of the United Negro College Fund.

5. Contributed to the promotion of inter-group education, beginning in 1940 with the study of education of teachers for Minority-

Majority Relationships and culminating with development of a kit and packet of materials on inter-group education of teachers and leaders of adult community groups respectively (in cooperation with the NEA-ATA Joint Committee); and the preparation of an extensive memorandum for the U.S. Attorney General in connection with the preparation of his brief on school segregation on cases argued before the U.S. Supreme Court in 1953.

Other Negroes who have been, or are now, connected with the U.S. Office of Education have performed specific functions for varying periods of time.

With respect to state school administration and supervision, it is interesting to note that five states had Negro state superintendents of education during the years immediately following the Civil War.[12] One of these chief state school officers was Jonathan Gibbs, the first state superintendent of instruction in Florida. A graduate of Dartmouth College, "he established the system and brought it to success, dying in office in 1874."[13] In general, however, with the exception of some activity during the reconstruction period, Negro participation in education at the state level remained virtually nonexistent until recent years. In fact, little consideration was given to the organization and administration of Negro schools until, under the stimulation of the General Education Board established in 1902, financial support was provided for state supervisors of Negro schools. These supervisors were, in the main, white. It should be noted, however, that in recent years several Negroes have served as members of state boards of education. Among these were James Rowland in West Virginia and Dwight O. W. Holmes in Maryland. The selection of Negroes for service on state boards, however, has not kept pace with the liberal tendency shown in the appointment of Negroes to supervisory positions at the state level. A study this writer conducted in 1954 revealed that eighty-four Negroes in supervisory and consultative positions were employed in fourteen Southern states, ranging from one appointment in Okla-

[12] Ambrose Caliver and others, "Education of Negroes: Progress and Present Status in the Segregated Pattern," *School Life*, XXXVI (March, 1954), p. 87.
[13] W. E. B. DuBois, *The Negro*, New York: Henry Holt and Company, 1915, p. 220.

homa to twenty-one in North Carolina. These supervisors and consultants have devoted their energies generally to improving instruction in Negro schools, a function they have shared with some of the state colleges and universities.

A noteworthy program designed to improve Negro public schools is now operating in the State of Tennessee. H. A. Bowen, former Dean of the School of Education, Tennessee Agricultural and Industrial State University, has described the program thus:*

Tennessee's way of providing state-level educational services to Negro public school staffs is somewhat unusual. These services are spearheaded by a three-person consultative team whose members function in the State's Department of Education and also hold professorial rank on the Tennessee A. and I. University faculty. This unusual arrangement was developed cooperatively by W. S. Davis, President of the University, and W. E. Turner, Director of the State's Division of Negro Education. They conceived of it as a way of providing liaison persons to channel the State Department's and the University's personnel and services to the local areas and of keeping these two agencies sensitive to the actual needs in the local areas.

This three-man team considers its primary responsibility to local groups as one of helping them to identify educational needs and to plan, implement, and evaluate programs based on these needs. Therefore, many of the team's operations at the state level, such as assisting in the development and exchange of promising ideas and practices, serving as consultants to groups, directing conferences, etc., are directed toward this goal.

Inasmuch as a fundamental belief in Tennessee is that the use of pooled intelligence to solve mutual problems is our most promising approach to improvement, much of the in-service education work is done through groups which largely plan and implement their own improvement efforts. All members of the team work with all of these groups and continuously seek to see the state-wide program as a whole. Nevertheless, to facilitate work, some allocation of duties has been agreed upon.

At the local level Negro membership on boards of control has remained negligible, policy-making for Negro schools remaining, by and large, within the province of all-white school boards. The all-Negro communities found in several states are, of course, exceptions to this rule.

* Letter, July 15, 1954.

Within the last decade, however, some progress has been noted at the local level. G. J. Sutton, local mortician, served from 1948 to 1954 as a member of the Board of the San Antonio (Texas) Junior College District. At Los Angeles, Rayfield Lundy, a local attorney, served as board member of the Willowbrook School District from 1950 to 1953, becoming the President of the Board for the fiscal year 1952-53. In appraising Lundy's work, C. C. Carpenter, Assistant Superintendent of Schools in Los Angeles County wrote:[14]

He was most energetic and conscientious as a school board member and during his term of office, the school board made considerable progress in the area of curriculum and in providing much needed school building and in improving the quality of food service in the cafeteria.

In the District of Columbia, Margaret Just-Butcher, West Hamilton, and Wesley S. Williams have served as members of the District's Board of Education. In her capacity as board member Mrs. Butcher, before the decision was handed down by the Supreme Court, pressed for an end to school segregation in the nation's capital. At Newport News, Virginia, C. Waldo Scott, local physician and surgeon, was appointed as board member in 1952 for a period of three years and was re-elected in 1955 for another three years. Rufus E. Clement, president of Atlanta University, was chosen by the people of Atlanta in 1953 as a member of the Board of Education. Negroes also have served on the public school boards in Augusta and Gainsville, Georgia.

One of the most fruitful contributions made to school organization is reflected in the work of the so-called Jeanes Supervisors. This type of supervisory program grew out of efforts to improve rural schools in Henrico County, Virginia, while Jackson Davis was serving as superintendent. Greatly concerned about the South and its problems, he had become deeply conscious of the appalling conditions under which the great masses of the people lived, particularly the Negroes. His imagination was stimulated when, on one of his official visits, he viewed the superior job Virginia Randolph was doing at the Mountain Road School, a one-room school, which she had transformed into both a place where children learned by

[14] Letter, August 10, 1954.

active experience and a center of community activity. Jackson Davis encouraged her and secured from the officials of the newly-created Jeanes Fund a grant to expand this important work. With the title of Jeanes Supervising Industrial Teacher, Virginia Randolph visited other schools and aided teachers in improving the caliber of their work. The report of her first year's work stimulated systems throughout the southern states to ask for a "Jeanes teacher."

The Jeanes teachers through the years have assisted county superintendents in matters relating to Negro schools. Though it was intended that their work was to be supervisory in nature and concerned with the improvement of instruction, much of the work has been administrative. For example, the following statement makes explicit the duties performed by early Jeanes teachers:[15]

The Jeanes teacher teaches in the various rural schools simple industrial work, helps the regular teacher with her work, raises money for the extension of school terms, the erection of new buildings, the improvement of buildings and grounds, the supplementing of teachers' salaries and the purchase of school materials, helps the women of the community to can and sew, holds teachers' meetings, distributes supplies, and in general does anything to promote the welfare of the Negro people and especially of the Negro schools of the county in which she works.

From these meager beginnings, which grew out of the vision of Jackson Davis and the leadership of Virginia Randolph, the work of the Jeanes teacher spread throughout the South. According to a report by Alethea Washington, in 1908 there were sixty-five Jeanes teachers in as many counties in ten states. In 1931, there were 329 Jeanes teachers in nearly as many counties in fifteen states.[16]

In recent years, the program of Jeanes teachers has been administered through funds provided by the Southern Education Foundation, Inc. The work of these supervisors has gone forward since 1947 under the leadership provided by Kara Vaughn-Jackson,

<hr/>

[15] Arthur D. Wright, *The Negro Rural School Fund, Inc.*, Washington, D.C.: The Negro Rural School Fund, Inc., 1933, p. 19.
[16] Alethea H. Washington, "The Supervision of Instruction," *The Journal of Negro Education*, II (July, 1932), p. 235.

who holds the position of Special Jeanes Teacher for the Southern Education Foundation and serves as Executive Secretary for the National Association of Jeanes Supervisors. Aside from the work with the national organization, she has concerned herself with the problem of in-service improvement of teachers through directing workshops throughout the South.

In the field of city school supervision, Helen A. Whiting, between the years 1928 and 1931, provided stimulation in Charlotte, North Carolina, at the elementary level that eventuated in the development of a progressive program that drew national and international recognition through the Harmon Foundation of New York; through Teachers College, Columbia University; and through a permanent exhibition of specimens of work in Germany. Subscribing to the concept that the curriculum should be life-related, this system made no attempt to restrict the program to a formal course of study. Rather, emphasis was placed upon orienting the program to student interests and needs. Viewing the child as a totality, the schools sought to protect and improve the physical, mental, and emotional health of the child.[17] In general, school people have been slow to assume obligation for the development of children beyond the usual school term or school day. The program developed by Helen A. Whiting, however, provided healthful and creative activities for children during the vacation period.

Since 1930 a great many American educators have become increasingly conscious of the need for improving instruction in the public school. Prior to this time selected cities had engaged in curriculum reorganization programs on a system-wide basis. As a part of this movement for school improvement, the South was greatly influenced by the work of Hollis L. Caswell and Doak S. Campbell. They popularized a concept for defining the scope of the curriculum known as the "social functions procedure." The procedure was described thus:

This concept of organization of the instructional program suggests that the school program should provide in so far as possible for children to

[17] For a detailed description of specific activities see Walter G. Daniel, "The Curriculum," *The Journal of Negro Education*, II (July, 1932), pp. 277-303.

gain an increasing understanding of the issues and problems encountered outside the school, should aid them in developing desirable controls of conduct that operate in meeting such issues and problems, and should give them opportunity to participate extensively in such real situations.[18]

One of the most successful efforts of Negro leadership to implement this point of view was made at Huntington High School, Newport News, Virginia. Under the leadership of the school's principal, Lutrelle F. Palmer, a core program was developed, based upon an adaptation of the Virginia course of study. Palmer's faith in democracy as an organizing principle in school administration encouraged imagination and experimentation among his teachers. In an unpublished manuscript, prepared by William H. Robinson, then a member of the faculty at Huntington High School, a vivid account is given of the development of the program which basically was an English-social science fusion. Palmer, who brought to his position a rich background, stimulated his teachers to experiment with this promising curriculum practice. In general, however, teachers who attempted to work in the core program soon discovered that their pre-service experience did not provide them with competencies for working in an experience-centered program. To overcome this problem, Palmer inaugurated an in-service program which aided the teachers in developing techniques and skills for projecting the program of the school.

In addition to state-wide efforts there has been considerable curriculum activity centered in individual schools. In this connection it is appropriate to mention that Jennie D. Porter, of the Harriet Beecher Stowe School, Cincinnati, projected a program that contributed to curriculum theory and practice. Based upon widely accepted principles of education, emphasis was placed in this school upon grouping students where they could develop optimally. In order to make maximum use of the plant, the platoon plan of work-study-play was instituted. All experiences were an integral part of the curriculum and were broad in nature.

A unique experiment in functional education was developed at Fessenden Academy, Martin, Florida, under its director John A.

[18] Hollis L. Caswell and Doak S. Campbell, *Curriculum Development*, New York: American Book Company, 1935, p. 173.

Buggs.[19] This is an American Missionary School, embracing grades seven through twelve; the program was organized (1) to continue and enlarge the school's activities in the field of experimental education; (2) to develop individual initiative in pupils; (3) to foster group action on community problems; (4) to provide teachers and pupils with a curriculum elastic enough to permit creative self-expression; (5) to equip students with the necessary mental, moral, and physical tools which will permit them to function in the community; (6) to provide an outlet for the self-expression of individuals and groups in the community; (7) to continue and increase work in behalf of community betterment; and (8) to help pupils to seek, obtain, and discharge faithfully their full privileges and responsibilities as citizens in a democracy.

Breaking with grade differentiation as found in the conventional school, students were grouped into four general divisions; (1) Preparatory, (2) Survey, (3) Specialized, and (4) Vocational. Grouping was based on standardized test data. The purpose was to achieve situations that would permit students to function optimally. Three aspects of the program in the Survey Division suggest the forward-looking nature of this program.

1. The program was based upon projects carried out by each group, designed to provide concrete experience and training in cooperative living and exercising individuals' initiative.

2. Audio-visual aids assumed a great deal of importance to the extent that the largest educational expenditure was for the purchase or rental of visual-aids equipment and materials.

3. The time schedule was organized so as to provide substantial blocks of time with a single teacher.

Basic textbooks are not used at Fessenden because, according to Buggs, "there are none adequate for our programs." It should be noted that the curriculum is open to continued evaluation and re-direction.

The program at Dunbar High School, Little Rock, Arkansas, has

[19] John A. Buggs, "The Fessenden Plan of Functional Education," *The Clearing House*, XX (September, 1945), pp. 12-16.

been reorganized to provide for fused courses in English and social studies, and in science and mathematics; for a horizontal grade organization rather than the conventional vertically arranged subject organization; and for improvement of reading among students through remedial and developmental emphasis.

S. E. Duncan, former State Supervisor of Negro Schools in North Carolina, who worked effectively in moving Negro schools forward in his state, reported periodically on outstanding programs that were judged to be educationally sound.[20] As examples of such programs we may note Stevens-Lee High School, Asheville, which has experimented with a core program for over a decade, and Carver High School, Mt. Olive, which has developed a program involving cooperation between the school and community designed to improve instruction. In addition, this latter school has developed a core program concentrated at the 12th grade level.

IV. HIGHER EDUCATION

Since Thomas Jesse Jones[21] made his early study dealing with Negro higher institutions, facilities in Negro colleges have been improved and expanded, and the educational attainment of the faculties has been upgraded, with the result that the caliber of the work done in these colleges has improved. In addition, several institutions have developed sizeable endowments. In the wake of these developments there emerged a disposition to experiment with aspects of the curriculum, to contribute to curriculum theory, and to experiment with various kinds of administrative arrangements.

Administratively, educators have long recognized the feasibility of cooperation and consolidation in educational institutions. Dwight O. W. Holmes, among others, made a study of the problem.[22] As

[20] See S. E. Duncan, *From Here and There,* Raleigh Division of Negro Education, State Department of Public Instruction, for a description of outstanding programs in North Carolina.

[21] Thomas Jesse Jones, *Negro Education—A Study of the Private and Higher Schools for Colored People in the United States,* U.S. Bureau of Education Bulletin No. 38, 1916.

[22] Dwight O. W. Holmes, *The Evolution of the Negro College,* New York: Bureau of Publications, Teachers College, Columbia University, 1934.

a consequence, Atlanta University, Morehouse College, and Spellman College agreed, on April 1, 1929, to affiliate in a university plan according to which graduate and professional work was carried on by Atlanta University, and the college and pre-professional work by Morehouse College and Spellman College. With increasing cooperation, since 1933, the summer school has been conducted by Atlanta University, with Morehouse College, Spellman College, Clark College, Morris Brown College, and Gammon Theological Seminary affiliating.

In 1930, with the active encouragement of certain philanthropic foundations, New Orleans University and Straight University effected a merger, creating Dillard University. The new institution was named in honor of James Hardy Dillard, whose service to the cause of Negro education in the South will be long remembered. The most recent effort at consolidation resulted in merging Samuel Huston College and Tillotson College, both in Austin, Texas The institution now is designated by the name Huston-Tillotson College.

The fact that Negro institutions have not been bound by tradition has permitted unfettered opportunity to experiment.* The widespread effort to develop programs of general education attests this. On the theory that there are certain areas of knowledge with which each citizen should have experience, Negro colleges have attempted to organize their programs in line with this belief. In analyzing these programs, it is possible to identify at least four types of general education programs: (1) those that have concentrated the general education program in the first two years of a four-year program; (2) those that have organized the general education program to parallel the specialized phase of the curriculum; (3) those that provide a common freshman year of general education, with courses in the area running in diminishing proportion through the entire four years; and (4) those with a two-year program of general education which permits exploration in a specialized field during the period of lower division study.

* There is a suggestion in Section I of Chapter I that an anti-intellectual quality, as a reaction against impeding cultural conditions, has characterized Negro institutions of higher learning.—Editor

To detail the nature of some of the programs in general education and exclude others would do an injustice to many colleges that have experimented in this area. It is appropriate to point out, however, that the late Dean Irving A. Derbigney, of Tuskegee Institute, after a study of programs in twenty Negro colleges, reached the conclusion:[23]

The Negro college has, with limited resources, made much progress in organizing and carrying out programs of general education. The colleges all wish to meet the needs of their students in this important area. A small number of these colleges have made some effort to ascertain these needs specifically. Likewise, most of the colleges included in this study are interested in preparing their students for active participation in the life of the communities in which they will live and of the nation at large.

The disposition to experiment with ways of improving the organization and administration of the curriculum is reflected also in the way some institutions have dealt with the problem of articulation. In an effort to improve coordination as students move up the educational ladder, some authorities have sought to bridge the gap by utilizing the junior college as a kind of isthmus; some colleges have sponsored the so-called "senior day"; others encourage consideration of beginning college problems in senior high school home-room groups.

One of the most promising experiments with the problem of articulation was conceived by Alonzo G. Moron, former President of Hampton Institute. Designated as the "Pre-College Summer Session for High School Graduates," the program takes cognizance of the high percentage of failures found among college freshmen, especially in English and mathematics, and of the difficulties experienced by this group in making a successful transition from high school to college life. Hailed by educators and by the press as a unique idea, this program, inaugurated in 1953, seeks specifically, "to help a selected group of high school graduates to gain a better command of the basic tool subjects and also to make a more satisfactory

[23] Irving A. Derbigney, *General Education in the Negro College*, Stanford, California: Stanford University Press, 1947, p. 235.

personal adjustment in whatever college they may enroll. . . ."
It is too early to engage in a large-scale evaluation of this project.
The project has striking possibilities, however, of pointing the way
to the elimination of many of the problems encountered by the
high school graduate upon entering college.

Morehouse College and Fisk University are participating in a
program, known as the Program of Early Admission to College,
which they hope will provide a better articulation for students of
superior ability. The students who participate in the program have
completed the tenth or eleventh grade of high school and have
demonstrated ability to move faster academically than their peers.
The following statement from Fisk University suggests that the
program is moving along successfully.

We have seen enough already of the progress and achievement of superior
students to justify our conviction that many students can accomplish
far more in the environment of the Basic College than they could accomplish in their high schools. There is already evidence to confirm our
belief that a fair number can accelerate, saving time and also doing a
higher quality of work than they would do without the opportunities
and the competitive stimulus of the Basic College.[24]

It was to be expected that the Negro college would contribute
significantly to the area of teacher education, one of the major
purposes of most of these colleges being the preparation of teachers.
And, in fact, an important contribution to curriculum theory and
practice has been reflected in the development of teacher education
programs oriented to community needs. Breaking with the notion
that a college can operate in juxtaposition to community life,
a number of colleges have endeavored to integrate community
life within the curriculum. Some of the colleges have focused
student experiences on the "practical problems of community life
and living faced by the students." Several colleges have tried to
translate educational theories into practice through the utilization
of off-campus schools and communities as laboratories. In connection with this tendency, Fisk University, between 1944 and 1947,

[24] *Bridging the Gap Between School and College:* A Report on Four Related
Projects Supported by the Fund for the Advancement of Education, June 1953.
pp. 102-103.

developed a rural life program known as the Fisk-Allen White Rural Community project. It provided the setting for an internship plan that enabled students to try to implement theoretical knowledge as they planned experiences in concrete community situations and to test their understanding of the meaning and implication of the specific situations they confronted outside of college.[25]

Grambling College in Louisiana has developed a program designed to prepare its students for community living and for the profession of teaching by providing an experience curriculum based on the needs, ambitions, and opportunities of the students for whom it assumes responsibility. The broad outlines of this program, first developed at Grambling College and later at Jackson College in Mississippi, emerged under the leadership of Jane E. McAllister, who has distinguished herself as a leader in the field of teacher education. Reorganized in 1936 as a program of rural teacher education, the program reaches beyond the limits of the campus to a large number of parishes in the state.

At Jackson College a functional program of teacher education, based upon the "needs of the people," has developed. It undertakes to prepare teachers who will be able to contribute to the improvement of community living. In consequence, the general education program deals with such practical problems as homemaking, diet, shelter, and health. To provide a typical community experience, all prospective teachers are required to do their student teaching in a community school and share in the experiences offered by the community.

Aside from the tendency to organize programs for the education of teachers that provide certain kinds of community experience, some educators have experimented with matters relating to curriculum scope and sequence. In this connection, Eva C. Mitchell of Hampton Institute has developed a program based upon integrating student teaching and related courses in the education of elementary teachers. Accordingly, she has brought theory and practice together and, in the process, has provided the pre-service teacher with continuous experiences in working with children

---

[25] *The Fisk Rural Life Program: A Plan for the Development of Negro Leaders for the Rural South,* Nashville: Fisk University, 1945, p. 9.

throughout the entire pre-service period.

Negro colleges have given much attention to the development of programs to promote the in-service improvement of teachers, with the workshop used as a promising means. Almost simultaneously with the beginning of the workshop movement in 1936, George N. Redd, now Dean of Higher Studies at Fisk University, introduced into the summer school of Texas College a program which, though not called a workshop, released a selected group of experienced teachers from regularly scheduled courses to deal with problems which were intimately associated with their work. So successful was this initial experience, that Redd later inaugurated at Fisk University a plan of summer workshops and seminars that pushed the workshop idea far beyond what was being done in a number of colleges. Specifically, he visited prospective participants of his summer program in the states of Arkansas, Tennessee, and Mississippi during the regular session in order to see these teachers first-hand and to aid them in locating and defining problems upon which they would work during the summer.

A statewide program to promote the in-service improvement of teachers has operated in Oklahoma for over a decade. In cooperation with the State Department of Education, Langston University, and selected school systems, so-called regional workshops have been held at strategic points throughout the state. Between 1951 and 1953 these short workshops were conducted under the joint directorship of Clifford Powell, State Department of Education, Kara Vaughn-Jackson, Southern Education Foundation, and the writer, then of Langston University. The emphasis during the first three years centered around problems of instructional improvements, shifting in 1954 to a consideration of guidance in the Oklahoma separate schools.

With increasing concern over the status of Negro principals, planning in Southern States culminated in holding at Tuskegee Institute the first Regional Principals' Workshop, June 8–August 14, 1953. Centered around the improvement of professional competencies, fifty principals representing fourteen states participated. Alonzo J. Davis, former Dean of the Tuskegee Institute School of Education, served as director. This program, sponsored jointly by State Agents for Negro schools, the Southern States Cooperative Program in Educational Administration, and the Southern Educational Foundation, was expanded in 1954 to include workshops at Tuskegee Institute, Virginia State College, Atlanta University, and Prairie View State College, Texas.

An experiment that has striking possibilities for re-directing the education of teachers is being directed in the Virgin Islands by Hampton Institute. With a grant from the Ford Foundation, Hampton initiated two programs in the fall of 1953 that were addressed to the professional improvement of teachers in the Islands. One provides all-expense scholarships to promising high school graduates who wish to prepare for teaching in the Virgin Islands. The other is a program of in-service education for teachers that enables them to continue their professional training while working in their respective schools. During the first year, courses in professional education were offered by Hampton faculty members. During the 1954 summer session an experimental college was operated at St. Thomas, with emphasis upon courses designed for the broad cultural and intellectual development of the in-service teachers. The experimental college was continued in St. Croix, Virgin Islands, during the summer of 1955, and has since alternated each summer between the two islands. This program is significant in that it explores ways of extending college services and occurs in a setting in which genuine experimentation may be carried forward in meeting specific needs of students, without the hampering influence of tradition, certification requirements, and so on.

Negro colleges were developed, of course, to provide opportunities that had been denied the Negro by custom or law. They have been to a striking degree, democratic institutions, reflecting some of America's most cherished ideals in their practices. Especially noteworthy have been their efforts to advance intergroup understanding. The private colleges, armed as they were with charters that made no mention of race, have contributed significantly to those efforts.

Since 1944, Fisk University, with the cooperation of the Race Relations Department of the American Missionary Association, Congregational Christian Churches, has sponsored a Race Relations Institute each year. This Institute has drawn into its program some of the most outstanding scholars in this country. Social workers, teachers, and community leaders of both races have gone to Nashville annually to deepen their understanding of the problems of race relations, and to gain insights into ways of effecting better relationships in their respective communities.

From the point of view of planning, resources, and basic information, the Race Relations Institute at Fisk is unique. The participants live and work together, thereby getting an experience that many have been denied. The Institute has provided an opportunity for many people to develop an understanding of the complex factors of race relations.

Another way in which Negro colleges and universities have sought to promote inter-group understanding is through programs of student exchange. As one example, Hampton Institute introduced a program in 1946 which involved exchanging Hampton students with those from other colleges for the purpose of advancing inter-racial and inter-cultural relationships. The initial exchange was with Antioch College, then with Grinnell College. In 1947-1948 Oberlin College and Willimantic State Teachers College (Connecticut) were added; Denison University entered the program in 1950; in 1951, Bucknell, in 1952, Hiram College, and in 1953, Heidelberg College (Ohio) joined the increasing number of participating colleges.

Howard University, the largest Negro higher institution, has since its founding made a distinct contribution to racially-integrated education. This institution, like Hampton, Fisk, and Talladega, was not chartered as a Negro institution. In fact, the record shows that its first students were not Negroes. Howard has been hailed as the most cosmopolitan of the Negro institutions and a recent report shows that, in addition to Negro students, the student body includes students from twenty-four foreign countries. Other activities in Negro colleges that are designed to foster inter-group understanding include the establishment of international relations clubs and of Student Christian Associations, the admission of students without regard to race, the employment of intercultural faculties, and sharing library facilities with students of other racial groups.

Earlier it was pointed out that some Negro higher institutions have amassed sizeable endowments. With the rising costs of operating expenses, however, the private colleges have experienced considerable difficulty. An exhaustive study of Negro colleges made in 1930 revealed that increased financial support had to be found or many institutions that had made outstanding contributions to higher education would be forced to cease operation or seriously curtail their programs. As the situation worsened, F. D. Patterson, then President of Tuskegee Institute, invited twenty-seven privately endowed colleges in 1944 to form a cooperative fund-raising organization. From this beginning the United Negro College Fund emerged. It enjoys the distinction of having been the first cooperative fund-raising venture in the history of higher education.

The fund now has thirty-two member colleges which benefit from an annual nationwide campaign. The funds it secures are used for current operating expenses including scholarship aid to deserving students, teaching and science laboratory equipment, faculty salaries, and the improvement of library service. Its influence has been significant during the years of its existence. Some twenty-seven similarly organized groups of privately endowed colleges have followed the pattern it set and now sponsor campaigns seeking financial aid.

V. Measurement and Evaluation

The contribution of Negro educators to measurement and evaluation, as an examination of bibliographies and periodical literature will reveal, has been directed more toward research and interpretation than toward the production of instruments. Some of the problems dealt with in these writings are the identification of children of high intelligence, achievement of school children, delinquent children, race differences, and test behavior of Negro children. A number of the studies were based upon instruments developed in connection with them. Few have been standardized, however.

Time-honored tests reputed to measure intelligence have been under attack by Negro educators for a number of years. Price,[26] one of those who questioned these tests, supported and defended the

[26] J. St. Clair Price, "Negro-White Difference in General Intelligence," *Journal of Negro Education*, III (July, 1934), pp. 424-452.

thesis that up to the present time there have been no adequate comprehensive measurements of the intelligence of Negroes. And results from group tests in recent years have tended to show that there are differentials in tests scores as between socio-economic groups. In fact, the evidence tends to point up the cultural biases of the individuals who have constructed the instruments that have claimed to measure intelligence. Allison Davis[27] of the University of Chicago points out that culturally oriented tests, administered experimentally, are needed to provide a fair measure of the real intelligence of the children tested.

The instrument Davis used was developed in collaboration with Kenneth Eells and is called, the *Davis-Eells Test of General Intelligence or Problem-Solving Ability*.[28] Viewing intelligence in terms of problem-solving ability, the test deals with certain problem areas that are interesting and child-orientated. It measures the basic resources of reasoning, insight, problem-organization, and the like. In the administration of the test, the effort is made to create a permissive situation in which a "game" rather than a "test" atmosphere is established. The *Primary Test* is designed for grades 1 and 2, while the *Elementary Test* is to be used with children in grades 3 through 6. The scores on the test may be converted into an index of problem-solving ability or an intelligence quotient.

For over a decade, William J. L. Wallace, now President of West Virginia State College, actively participated in the construction of a number of objective tests in general and physical chemistry with members of the various subcommittees of the Committee on Examinations and Tests of the Division of Chemical Education, American Chemical Society. For a time, he was chairman of the sub-committee on publications. The instruments he helped to construct are:

1. Editorial Assistance with others, Cooperative Chemistry Test in Qualitative Analysis—Form T. 1943.
2. Collaborator, American Chemical Society Cooperative General Test for College Students—Form 1946.

[27] Allison Davis, "Socio-Economic Influences on Learning," *Phi Delta Kappan*, XXXII (January, 1951), pp. 253-256.
[28] Published by the World Book Company

3. Co-author, American Chemical Society Cooperative Physical Chemistry Test—Form W. 1946.
4. Co-author, American Chemical Society Cooperative General Chemistry Test for College Students—Form 1948.
5. Co-author, A. C. S. Cooperative General Chemistry Test for College Students—Form Z.

Mae Belle Pullins Claytor, Professor of Psychology at Morgan State College, developed an instrument, *General Knowledge Test of the Negro,* which was published by the California Test Bureau in 1945 and revised in 1951. A diagnostic instrument, it attempts to measure specific knowledge of the accomplishments of Negroes within six areas—namely, political and military events, social and economic events, education, fine arts, literature, and athletics. The test seeks to afford a more adequate means of evaluating contemporary information about the Negro than did existing standardized tests in American history. Dr. Claytor also constructed a General Knowledge Test of Local, State, and National Government for High Schools and Colleges, published in 1952 by C.A. Gregory Company; a Comprehensive Examination in Psychology, published in 1949 by C.A. Gregory Company; and a Home Adjustment Questionnaire, published in 1951 by C. H. Stoelting Company.

William E. Anderson, Director of Research and Evaluation at Alabama State College, has published since 1945 a series of tests under the general title, "Standard Achievement Tests." These instruments, designed in the main for high school students, cover the field of reading, American literature, Negro history, and American history. These tests have been used widely in statewide meets, research projects, and high school evaluation programs. They are all accompanied by percentile norms and the standardization groups range from 1320 high school students and 290 college sophomores, for the English literature test, to 8,000 high school and 2,000 college students, for the reading survey test. In addition Anderson developed a personality instrument which represents, in an abbreviated form, adaptations from instruments in use in personality measurement. It has been used rather extensively by graduate students in studying problems of personality of adolescents and adults.

In recent years considerable research has been conducted in the area of human relations. William H. Brown, Director, Bureau of Educational Research, North Carolina College, published in 1952 the experimental edition of an instrument designed to study viscidity within small groups. There are two forms, "Looking at Groups" and "Another Look at Groups." A detailed discussion of Brown's instrument has appeared in the literature.[29] Both forms of the test contain the same items and are designed to obtain from individuals an expression of their feeling about the group to which they belong. The feeling of members of a particular group gives an indication of the kind of human relations that characterize the group. Its present form is experimental, and according to Brown:[30]

Further research is needed to demonstrate the validity of the inventory as a measure of viscidity in groups, and further studies of viscidity should include the use of some measures of permissiveness. However, the findings up to this point are significant in teacher-training and leadership training, since cooperative endeavors are likely to be more productive when individuals hold attitudes toward their associates which make for high viscidity.

Another aspect of the measurement and evaluation movement concerns evaluation of the curriculum. Resulting from the Cooperative Study of Secondary School Standards, involving six regional accrediting associations, there has been a shift from the use of inflexible standards to the utilization of qualitative evaluations. Negro educators have contributed to this aspect of the movement through working with schools as they prepared for accreditation, and have served on visiting committees of the various regional associations.

The instrument constructed by the cooperative study was developed for use in secondary schools. The Southern Association of Colleges and Secondary Schools subsequently sponsored the development of criteria applicable to elementary schools. A number of Negro teachers from schools throughout the South participated in its development. Charity Mance and Eunice Matthews, of Tennessee A. and

---

[29] William H. Brown, "An Instrument for Studying Viscidity Within Small Groups," *Educational and Psychological Measurement*, XIII (Autumn, 1953), pp. 402-417; and William H. Brown, "Potential Cooperation in Groups," *Phi Delta Kappan*, XXXIII (May, 1952), pp. 418-420.
[30] *Ibid.*, p. 416.

I. University, participated in the planning and in the experimentation associated with the criteria.

VI. Contributions Viewed in Philosophical Perspective

To what extent may the contributions made by Negroes be regarded as consistent with a philosophical point of view in our historical development? Have the ideas, practices, and principles which have guided Negro education been consistent, say, with John Dewey's theory of a democratic society?

Obviously, the Tuskegee idea could not have been influenced by the thinking of John Dewey, since the program at the Alabama institution was developed before his influence was felt in American education. The program was more directly related to Pestalozzianism and to what later came to be known as the manual labor school. Stuart Noble points out that after the failure of manual labor schools in other sections of the country, ". . . a few decades later Samuel C. Armstrong and Booker T. Washington found abundant success in similar institutions for Negroes in the South, and the agricultural and mechanical colleges, authorized by the Morrill Act of 1862, carried forward the manual labor idea under more favorable auspices."[31] Aside from the fact that Tuskegee as a type of institution probably could be associated with Pestalozzianism, some of the teaching principles applied were consistent with Dewey's point of view. Practices at Tuskegee reflected acceptance of the thesis that the psychological organization of subject matter is sound, as illustrated by the statement that students ascend to general principles by beginning with ideas that are related to their experience. Washington believed, as did Pestalozzi, that the school could regenerate the social order, a position which would not have been opposed by Dewey and his followers.

In addition to the fact that the Tuskegee idea seemed to reflect a particular philosophy in our historical development, there were threads of various philosophies running through other early school programs. Undoubtedly these early schools were influenced by the

[31] Stuart G. Noble, *A History of American Education,* New York: Rinehart and Company, 1938, p. 207.

kind of training many of the founders had received. The humanitarians obviously had been influenced by the classical training in vogue then in many New England schools. Such a point of view presented the organizing principles for most of the private schools and colleges. A philosophy that reflected an aristocratic ideal, therefore, led to a disproportionate amount of emphasis upon Greek and Latin in the early schools and to the belief that the purpose of the school was to discipline the mind. As an early graduate of Atlanta University, it is understandable that Lucy C. Laney, for example, would give priority to Latin in the curriculum of Haines Institute, while at the same time endeavoring to provide the student with industrial training.

It is not clear that Charlotte Hawkins-Brown espoused the cause of social realism in the founding of Palmer Memorial Institute, though it is true that the finishing school movement has been identified in history with this point of view and more specifically with the ideas found in the writings of Montaigne.

We may say, then, that the earlier schools were influenced in the main by Pestalozzianism and by classicism, as the latter existed in northern institutions. This latter influence was the source of considerable discussion among white Southerners who believed that Negroes should restrict their efforts to industrial education. The specific influence of Dewey's philosophy on Negro education has been limited undoubtedly in the same ways that Sidney Hook finds it to have been limited in the larger educational picture. Hook says:[32]

As important as this influence has been—and no recent theoretical influence has been more important—it has been limited. Limited by the way it has been interpreted, limited by the way it has been applied, limited by the absence of certain social conditions whose existence its ideal presupposed—and limited, above all, in comparison with the tremendous possibilities of educational reconstruction which would follow from a nation-wide experiment in carrying out its basic principles.

In particular, the Negro school has developed in a situation that is antithetical to the social situation implied in Dewey's conception of

[32] Sidney Hook, *John Dewey: An Intellectual Portrait*, New York: The John Day Company, 1939, p. 177.

a democratic social order. It is significant, however, that many ideas and practices in Negro schools are consistent with Dewey's ideas.

Within the last quarter of a century, elementary schools the nation over have taken seriously the idea that programs must reorganize in the light of relevant social, psychological, and philosophical principles. This trend has caught hold in Negro elementary schools, with the acceptance of the principles set forth by John Dewey and elaborated by William H. Kilpatrick, Boyd H. Bode, and others. The attempt has been made to develop elementary schools that represent democratic living at its best.

There is considerable evidence that the curriculum is thought to consist of all the experiences which children have under the guidance of the teacher. And, in observing the organization of learning experiences, one would be led to the conclusion that the teachers believe with Dewey that experiences should possess two dimensions, continuity and interactivity.

To implement these views, the learning unit has figured prominently in the organization of instruction. An examination of some programs throughout the country shows a tendency in thought, if not in actual practice, to reject conventional grades and to emphasize levels of achievement among elementary school children. Emphasis is placed upon providing situations in which the child progresses at his own rate and develops as a total person.

The programs at the secondary level have been influenced to a lesser degree than those of elementary schools. This may be accounted for, in the main, by the pressure exerted upon these schools by colleges and universities. Yet, from the secondary school programs examined in the preparation of this chapter, it is possible to identify practices that are consistent with the philosophy we are here examining. Specific practices include:

1. The organization of core programs designed to cut across subject lines and to deal with problems associated with daily living.

2. The tendency to effect good school-community relations.

3. The general acceptance of the need for a philosophy of education as a basis for organizing an instructional program.

4. The development of in-service programs for teachers based upon problems which they face in the classroom.

5. The emphasis upon continuous reorganization of the curriculum. Implied in such an enterprise is the fact that the social order is a changing one, rather than static and fixed.

In higher institutions, also, there are features which are consistent with Dewey's belief. And, in this connection, it would seem that these features are becoming more evident with the changing character of leadership in these schools. Thus, ideas, practices, and principles found in Negro higher institutions include the following:

1. Through programs of curriculum reorganization there exists a tendency to effect a unity in the students' educational development, to evaluate this development in behavioral terms, and to relate the program to a functional philosophy of education.

2. There is a tendency to organize programs of higher education on the basis of democratic principles. Negro colleges tend more and more to break with dictatorial administrative practices that were once a salient aspect of the program.[33]

3. There is a trend to break with the practice of restricting programs, and to provide broader experiences for students. This is especially evident in teacher education programs where emphasis is placed upon affording pre-service teachers an opportunity to have experiences with children, and upon organizing off-campus student teaching programs and internships.

4. The tendency to experiment with new ways of educating young people is reflected in current studies of general education and in new programs in teacher education.

5. The programs of early admission point the way toward eliminating the tremendous waste and lack of articulation mentioned in the writings of Dewey.

VII. The Education of the Negro in Transition

It is abundantly clear that uppermost in the minds of Negro educators has been an acceptance of the view that education is a potent

[33] For lucid statement of procedures utilized in one Negro college see C. L. Spellman, "Democratic College Administration in Action," *Association of American Colleges Bulletin*, XXXVII (October, 1951), pp. 349-353.

means of preparing children and youth to live competently in the democratic community. Through the years, Negro leaders have worked diligently toward making democracy a reality. Although many persons criticized Washington and his program, there is no denying the fact that he believed the end to be served by industrial education was the progressive democratization of the Negro.

The emphasis in the 1930's on adult education, and the more recent emphasis spearheaded by Ambrose Caliver and his associates, recognize that the democratic way of life tends to flourish exactly to the degree that an enlightened citizenry is developed.

We are now enmeshed in two epochs—one that looks back to a period in which the Negro developed against tremendous odds and another that promises to bring to fruition the Negro's fondest dreams. The Negro has labored to set the stage for a new social order that is emerging, since, beyond the important emphasis he has placed upon gaining educational opportunities for himself, the Negro has continued to examine bi-racial education.

Over the years, the *Journal of Negro Education,* published at Howard University, has done much to shape the thinking of Negroes and students of social thought with respect not alone to securing improved opportunities for Negroes but to advance the ultimate democratization of education as well. In reporting on the first conference on integration held at Howard University in 1952, Virgil Clift stated: "The deliberations and proceedings of the conference will determine in a large measure the course of action that will be taken by the Negro in the next few years in his attempt to eliminate segregated education."[34]

Prior to the 1954 decision of the Supreme Court Negro leaders worked valiantly to help others gain a sound point of view relating to democracy and education. They have continued since the decision. Statements by Benjamin Mays of Morehouse College, Rufus E. Clement of Atlanta University, and Alonzo G. Moron, formerly of Hampton Institute, point up the fact that Negro schools are looking forward to an era in which all students may attend on an integrated basis schools that were previously segregated. Speaking before the

[34] Virgil A. Clift, "The Attack on Segregated Education Continues," *School and Society,* LXXV (June 7, 1952), p. 361.

1953 convention of the Congress of Industrial Organization, Dr. Moron asserted:[35]

My faith in the future of America includes a belief that the legal barriers to the use of all our educational facilities by boys and girls, men and women, of all races will soon be destroyed by direct legal action, or by giving legal and social effect to the growing realization that as a nation we cannot afford the cost in money and prestige of segregation and discrimination.

There is general agreement among Negro educators that Negro colleges should be good colleges, qualified to serve all youth regardless of race, creed, or color. On this point Rufus E. Clement, President of Atlanta University and member of the Board of Education of Atlanta, Georgia, wrote:[36]

These institutions are working for the complete liberation of the human mind and the human spirit. When the day of abolishment of segregation is approached in America and the physical characteristics of a man's body cease to be paramount criteria upon which decisions respecting his training and future are made, these colleges will become centers of training of all the people and the resources will be used for the development of our human resources without respect to color, creed or race.

There is today positive evidence that Clement's forecast is being realized. Recently, Fisk University awarded an advanced degree in the field of race relations to a young white woman. Bethune-Cookman College, Daytona Beach, Florida, numbered among its summer graduates a white marriage counselor who took his degree with a concentration in psychology. Several Negro colleges that previously had all-Negro student groups have revised their admissions policies, with West Virginia State being a notable illustration.

Negro education is in a period of transition. Yet it has advanced rapidly from an inauspicious start and at this moment the Negro educator possesses important resources that he has placed at the disposal of the United States for making the idea of democracy more meaningful for all citizens.

[35] Alonzo G. Moron, "Higher Education for Negroes in an Era of Transition," *The Hampton Bulletin*, L (October, 1953), p. 13.

[36] Rufus E. Clement, "The Present and Future Role of Private Colleges for Negroes," *Phylon*, IV (Fourth Quarter, 1949), p. 327.

III

Anthropological and Sociological Factors in Race Relations

Ina Corinne Brown, Professor of Anthropology
Scarritt College

I. BIOLOGICAL AND SOCIOLOGICAL REALITIES

IN THE United States we operate within a Judeo-Christian, democratic framework, one basic assumption of which is the value of the individual. Consistent with—indeed necessary to—this conception are the ideas (1) that every individual has a right to be judged on the basis of his personal worth, and (2) that, for such judgment to be fair, each individual should be permitted the fullest development of which he is capable. It follows that in such a society every effort should be made (1) to provide opportunity for the maximum development of each of its members, and (2) to utilize to the fullest the contribution to the society each member is able to make. Furthermore, if the individual is to be judged solely on the basis of personal worth, factors such as race, sex, religion, and national origin would not appear to be relevant.

Actually, of course, not all members of the society are committed to Judeo-Christian or democratic goals, and numerous persons who claim to be so committed have, since the beginning of our history, sought to justify exceptions of one kind or another. Women, slaves, Negroes, Orientals, Jews and the foreign born have been, at various times, left outside the category, "every individual." There is often an attempt to justify such exclusion on the grounds of imputed biological difference; for, as someone has pointed out, this pushes the problem out of the social field, in which man is responsible, into the biological field in which God can be held responsible. Many students of society feel that these efforts to justify exceptions to the "American Dream" have produced a sort of collective schizophrenia.[1]

The most significant aspect of the Supreme Court's 1954 ruling[2] on segregation is its official and specific recognition of the individual's right to be treated as an individual, not categorized by the color of his skin or by the fact that one or more of his ancestors had a given racial origin. The Court has ruled that race is not a relevant factor in determining which public school an individual may attend. By implication, therefore, the Court has said that race is not a proper or relevant basis for classifying or categorizing individuals for the purpose of defining or limiting their rights as citizens.

Consciously or unconsciously both Negroes and white people have sensed that the issue is more than that of desegregation in education. The Court's action is seen, therefore, as a direct challenge to a long established way of life. It raises in the minds of many, questions that seemingly have nothing to do with education as such. "Letters to the Editor" in newspapers, the speeches of officials and candidates for public office, and conversations with all sorts of people indicate certain beliefs, confusions, and misunderstandings on the part of many white people. There is confusion of the biological with the social; a misunderstanding of what race really signifies; the belief in significant racial differences, specifically in the existence of innate inferiority or superiority; the fear that desegregation will lead to cultural deterioration and the lowering of educational standards; the confusion of the public, civic, and impersonal aspects of life with those that are individual, personal, and social in the narrower sense; the belief that practical problems of implementation are in-

[1] This question runs through the most ambitious study yet made of the American race problem: Gunnar Myrdal, *An American Dilemma*, New York: Harper & Brothers, 1944, 2 vols.

[2] The text of the ruling may be found in: Harry S. Ashmore, *The Negro and the Schools*, Chapel Hill: University of North Carolina Press, 1954.

surmountable; the cherished belief—or perhaps it is hope—that Negroes "really want to be to themselves;" and, on the other hand, the fear that white schools, churches, and other institutions will be "swamped" by Negroes. All of these beliefs, hopes, fears, and misunderstandings are a part of the social reality with which educators must deal, and they have been sharply accentuated and made immediate by the Court's ruling.[3]

Of particular importance at the present time is the fear that any breakdown in the segregation pattern will lead to social intermingling which in turn will lead to interracial marriage, the end result being "mongrelization" of the American people and the consequent deterioration of "Anglo-Saxon" culture.

There is, of course, no necessary relation between these actual or feared events. Purely social activities are everywhere voluntary and, therefore, are entirely within the individual's control. Moreover, little such interracial social activity occurs in areas in which there is no enforced segregation. No woman in the United States is forced to marry against her will, and in the states in which interracial marriages are permitted they seldom occur. As will be shown later, there is no evidence that when race mixture does occur it results in either biological or cultural deterioration.

Of major importance also is the confusion of learned behavior— such as language, religion, nationality, and culture—with racial traits. Many people assume that race is a major factor in determining the behavior of people and, consequently, that such behavior is inherited and not subject to change. They may believe that Negroes are "naturally" lazy or immoral or whatever a particular bias suggests. They often believe that "Negro blood" is different from "white blood" and many people accept without question the idea that anyone "having Negro blood," no matter how little, is properly to be considered a Negro and may be expected to have other "Negro traits."

These and numerous other such beliefs add up to what the term "race" suggests to many people. Such concepts, of course, bear little

---

[3] Although Negroes have generally welcomed the Court's ruling they, too, are not without their fears and anxieties regarding its consequences. This aspect of the situation will be considered briefly at the end of this chapter.

relation to the anthropological meaning of the term or to the biological reality for which it stands. They constitute, however, the sociological reality with which we deal when we speak of race prejudice, race attitudes, or race relations. In these areas we are dealing not so much with races in the biological sense as with what Robert Redfield has termed "socially-supposed races," that is, people who regard themselves as a race or who are so regarded by others.[4] The extent to which the socially-supposed race corresponds to biological reality is immaterial so long as there is a "believed-in" difference. What I believe is to me a fact.

Any useful analysis of race relations must take into account both biological and sociological realities and the fact that the two are commonly confused. From the practical point of view the significant difference in the two kinds of reality lies in the fact that the biological factors are inherent in the germ plasm and hence are relatively fixed, while the sociological factors are the result of learned behavior and are, therefore, subject to modification or social manipulation. The biological and sociological factors are, of course, interrelated and they cannot always be completely separated. In general, however, we may say that the biological factors involved are important to society mainly when and because people think they are significant.

It would, of course, be naive to assume that people can be changed by pointing out to them the fact that their beliefs and attitudes are out of harmony with objective reality. It is important, however, that the facts about race and race differences be known. Moreover, the educator would have little excuse for being if it were not possible to help people change the way they think, feel, and act about real or supposed facts through the utilization of appropriate educational and social processes.

II. BIOLOGICAL ASPECTS OF RACE AND RACE DIFFERENCES

Although anthropologists do not always agree on precise definitions of race or on the specific criteria to be used in setting up racial categories, there are certain broad areas of general agreement regarding race and race differences. Some of the more important

[4] Robert Redfield, "What We Do Know About Race," *The Scientific Monthly*, LVII, (September 1943), pp. 193-202.

facts, in terms of practical significance, will be set forth here in the form of generalizations. These statements must of necessity be over-simplified and limitations of space will prevent their full elaboration. References in the footnotes will indicate sources to which the reader may turn for more detailed information.

1. *There is no way by which all the individuals—or even all the populations—of the world can be classified into neat, orderly, and precise racial categories.* There are no "pure" races. Throughout human history wherever peoples have come in contact they have interbred and all populations represent varying degrees of mixture of peoples of different physical types. As Krogman points out, what we term races in man are poorly defined "because they are not—as in races in lower forms—homogeneous; they are intermixed, hybridized, diffused. That is why one man says 'no races', the other 'many races'. The first is appalled at the difficulty of disentangling intermingled varieties; the second holds that secondary or composite groups warrant racial status."[5]

The kind of racial categories established depends on the criteria selected, and such selection is always in some degree arbitrary. More-over, within any racial category, however established, there will be wide variations and the description of "a race" most certainly will not be a description of each individual belonging to that race. It is not possible to use a single criterion in establishing racial categories because the same characteristics may be found in several populations that are otherwise quite different.[6]

[5] Wilton Marion Krogman, "What We Do Not Know About Race," *The Scientific Monthly*, LVII (August, 1943), pp. 97-104. Theodosius Dobzhansky, *Evolution, Genetics and Man*, New York: John Wiley and Sons, 1955, says, "It cannot be too often emphasized that 'pure races' exist only in asexual organisms and are figments of the imagination as far as man is concerned," p. 347.

[6] The problem is actually much more complicated than is here implied. The difficulty lies not only in the limitations of our knowledge but also in the nature of the material with which we deal. Commonly accepted racial classifications are based on a combination of observable and measurable characteristics of the organism—the phenotype—which is determined partly by the genetic constitution and partly by the environment. We do not as yet have adequate techniques for studying the genetic constitution itself—the genotype—except as it is manifested phenotypically. Furthermore, several different combinations of genes may produce the same phenotype and we have no means of distinguishing these differently produced phenotypes one from another. For discussion of these problems see: William C. Boyd, *Genetics and the Races of Man*, Boston: Little, Brown and Company, 1950; Carlson S. Coon, Stanley M. Garn and Joseph B. Birdsell,

This problem is well illustrated in skin color which is one of the most noticeable of the characteristics by which races are distinguished and, also, the characteristic to which many people today react emotionally. Dark skinned peoples are found in Africa south of the Sahara, in the area of the Pacific known as Melanesia (the islands from New Guinea to Fiji), in Australia, in parts of India, in Ceylon, and in scattered areas elsewhere in the world. Shall we put all these people into the racial category of Negroids? If we do, we immediately find ourselves confronted with several major difficulties.

In the first place, these populations cannot, by any reasonable procedure, be assumed to be genetically related. We have no evidence that all of these peoples were derived from common ancestors or that they share a common gene pool. It is possible that differences in skin color may be the result of natural selection which occurred independently in different areas.[7] In the second place, to group these populations together requires that we ignore a great many characteristics. These dark skinned peoples vary greatly in both head and body hair, which are significant inherited factors. They also vary in facial features and in other less conspicuous ways.

The use of any other single criterion of race would plunge us into the same kind of difficulties. But the fact remains that people do differ in physical features and nobody would have much hesitation in saying a Congo Negro, a Chinese, and a blond Norwegian represent three different stocks or races. It is in this common sense way that one should accept present day racial classifications. They are based on the fact that a fair-sized portion of the world's peoples can be grouped into categories on the basis of certain combinations of inherited physical characteristics which set them apart from other peoples having other distinguishing combinations of inherited characteristics.[8]

Races, A Study of the Problems of Race Formation in Man, Springfield, Illinois: Charles C. Thomas, 1950.

[7] Boyd, op. cit. p. 20. See also: Julian S. Huxley and A. C. Haddon, We Europeans, New York: Harper and Brothers, 1936, p. 41.

[8] Strictly speaking we do not inherit characteristics but certain genes and chromosomes which in combination and under appropriate conditions produce particular characteristics. See: Lancelot Hogben, Nature and Nurture, New York: W. W. Norton and Co., 1933, p. 11 ff.

Most anthropologists agree on the establishment of the broad general categories of Caucasoid, Mongoloid, Negroid, and possibly Australoid, which are usually referred to as stocks or racial divisions and which may be thought of as sub-species of homo sapiens.[9] There is much less agreement regarding the subdivisions of these larger groupings into races, or varieties, and there are many populations that do not fit into any of the conventional categories. One group of anthropologists, who listed six possible racial categories, said the names of these stocks served as useful labels so long as one realized that they were "generalized, arbitrary, tentative, and in some respects misleading."[10] Boyd says that whatever races we choose to distinguish will be "almost entirely arbitrary,"[11] and Ashley Montagu goes so far as to call the concept of race "an omelette which corresponds to nothing in nature."[12] All in all, perhaps the most important thing the anthropologist can say to the non-specialist on the subject of racial categories is that none of them should be taken too seriously.

The racial position of American Negroes is a case in point. Definitions of race usually involve both the idea of common ancestry and of phenotypical likeness, that is, the sharing of a certain combination of inherited physical traits. Yet observation of the effects of race mixture shows clearly that common ancestry and phenotypical likeness do not necessarily go together. Neither does common ancestry guarantee likeness in genetic constitution.

Race mixture between whites and Negroes has occurred since the beginning of our history in this country. Legally, and by custom, the offspring of such unions are considered Negroes; and, in most parts of the United States today, any person known to have had a Negro ancestor is regarded as a Negro. The mechanism of inheritance, however, takes no account of marriage vows or of legal definitions

[9] Practically all specialists in the field agree that all living men belong to the same species. For a discussion of this point see: Boyd, *op. cit.*, pp. 9-13. Also: Wilton Marion Krogman, "The Concept of Race," *The Science of Man in the World Crisis*, edited by Ralph Linton, New York: Columbia University Press, 1945, pp. 38-62.

[10] Coon, Garn, and Birdsell, *op. cit.*, p. 115.

[11] Boyd, *op. cit.*, p. 207.

[12] Ashley Montagu, *Man's Most Dangerous Myth, The Fallacy of Race*, New York: Columbia University Press, 1945, p. 32.

which cannot alter biological realities. It follows that there are many persons in this country who are legally Negroes but who are genetically and phenotypically white; that is, they not only look white but they possess no genes for Negroid characteristics and cannot transmit such genes to their children.

Furthermore, it is theoretically possible for two mulattoes (mulatto here meaning an individual having one white and one Negro parent) to have entirely white or entirely Negro children. This possibility grows out of the fact that while a child receives one half of his chromosomes from each parent, he does not necessarily receive one fourth from each grandparent. In fact, as Boyd points out, there is "a distinct though small chance" that not a single one of your chromosomes came from a particular grandparent.[13] A brief reminder of the mechanism of inheritance will show why this is true.

Each individual has twenty-three pairs of chromosomes, each of his parents having contributed one of each pair. This individual in turn passes on one of each pair to each of his own children, the "partner" in each case coming from the other parent. There is a new deal of the cards as it were for each child (except for identical twins) and which one of each pair of chromosomes any child gets is apparently a matter of random selection. Since each mulatto parent has an equal number of "white" and "Negro" chromosomes any given child could, theoretically, receive all of his mother's "Negro" chromosomes and also all of his father's "Negro" chromosomes and thus be entirely Negro.[14]

Another child might receive all of each parent's "white" chromosomes and thus be, both genetically and phenotypically, white. It would, of course, be extremely improbable, and impossible to prove in any case, that a child would receive all forty-six of his chromosomes from only two of his four grandparents. As Dunn and

[13] Boyd, op. cit., pp. 57-58.
[14] The words "Negro" and "white" are put in quotation marks when referring to genes or chromosomes to indicate the difficulty in terminology. All that the terms mean here are genes or chromosomes received from a Negro or a white parent. The vast majority of human genes and chromosomes are held in common by all groups of men and have, so far as we know, no racial connotation at all. Coon, Garn, and Birdsell (op. cit., p. 12) say "all of the characters which we consider racial, when added together, make up but a small part of the total man. Human beings have far more genes in common than they have apart."

Dobzhansky point out, however, a grandchild inherits each kind of gene from only two, never from all four, of his grandparents since he receives only one of each pair from each parent. Therefore, in any given pair of genes that the child receives, two of his four grandparents are not represented.[15]

Only a small number of man's thousands of genes appear to be "racial." Krogman says, "We might almost go so far as to say that in 99 44/100 per cent of all basic physical characteristics all men are alike."[16] It undoubtedly occurs, therefore, with a fair degree of frequency that a child of mulatto parents receives all of his racially significant genes from either the two white or the two Negro grandparents.[17]

Glass points out that these segregants—the persons getting all the "white" or all the "Negro" genes—are really genetically what they seem. The child receiving a double dose of "Negro" genes is genetically, as well as phenotypically, a Negro and he can pass on to his children only "Negro" genes. Of course, a dark child of racially mixed ancestry can carry the recessive genes for blue eyes and blond hair, just as a brunette white person may carry recessive genes for blue eyes. The white segregant, however, could transmit only "white" genes and if he married a white person their children would be entirely white. The "Negro" genes he did not receive would, as far as he is concerned, be gone forever and could not possibly lurk

[15] L. C. Dunn and Theodosius Dobzhansky, *Heredity, Race and Society*, New York: Penguin Books, 1946, p. 47. The statement would not necessarily be true of chromosomes since there may be "crossing over" of genes. The number of genes found in the human chromosomes is not definitely known. Dobzhansky (*op. cit.*, p. 33), says estimates run from 10,000 to 100,000 genes in a human sex cell.

[16] Krogman, "The Concept of Race" *op. cit.*, p. 41 Krogman does not mean this figure to be taken literally. Estimates of the number of genes held in common by all men vary from 90-99 per cent. See Dunn and Dobzhansky, *op. cit.*, pp. 50-51. See also Bentley Glass, *Genes and the Man*, New York: Bureau of Publications, Teachers College, Columbia University Press, 1943, and Boyd, *op. cit.*, pp. 200-201.

[17] It is generally agreed that probably several pairs of genes are responsible for each of the traits used as racial criteria such as skin color, nasal breadth and lip thickness, and furthermore that the genes which influence these traits seem to be inherited independently. See Boyd, *op. cit.*, 308ff. See also Curt Stern, *Principles of Human Genetics*, San Francisco: W. H. Freeman and Co., 1950, pp. 250ff.

around somewhere in his blood stream to spring up in unsuspecting future generations.[18]

There does not seem to be the slightest possibility that such an apparently white person could produce a "black baby" unless the infant's other parent were black. In general, it can be said that if both parents are part Negro the children can be no darker or more Negroid than the combined qualities of darkness or Negroidness of the two parents. That is, the parents cannot pass on to their children more "Negro" genes than the parents possess. If only one parent is Negroid, the child can, generally speaking, be no darker than that parent. This is true, as Lawrence Snyder points out in *Medical Genetics* although, as he adds, "this fact spoils the effects of certain novels and short stories."[19]

It is, of course, generally known that a certain number—nobody knows how many—of these legally Negro, but genetically and phenotypically white, persons decide at one time or another to claim their actual biological heritage by passing into the white category. The number who do this is probably not so large as it is often estimated to be, since to do so involves cutting one's self off from one's family and former associates. It also involves the risk of being found out and perhaps having a carefully built world fall about one's ears. An element of guilt is probably a restraining factor, also, because many Negroes and most white people seem to regard such passing as a

---

[18] Glass, (*op. cit.*, pp. 172-173) referring to the genes for skin color, says that mulattoes may have completely black or completely white children. "Moreover," he continues, "these extreme types are both homozygous, and, therefore, not only appear pure black and pure white, but will breed pure black and pure white respectively." See also Stern, (*op. cit.*, p. 329). For a clear, non-technical discussion of the inheritance of racial and other characteristics, see: Amran, Scheinfeld, *The New You and Heredity*, Philadelphia: J. B. Lippincott Company, 1950.

[19] Lawrence Snyder, *Medical Genetics*, Durham: Duke University Press, 1941, p. 62. Dunn and Dobzhansky (*op. cit.*, p. 52), say that the stories of mulatto children born to white parents are "unadulterated humbug." See also Stern (*op. cit.*, pp. 329-330). In most of the characteristics in which Negroes and whites differ the Negro genes seem to be either dominant or additive, a fact which would prevent their being carried as hidden recessives in the way that the genes for blue eyes and light hair can be carried by persons having dark eyes and hair. Boyd, (*op. cit.*, p. 49). For some of the more complicated aspects of this problem see A. Franklin Shull, *Heredity*, New York: McGraw Hill Book Co., 1949, IV, pp. 113-114 and 192-196. See also Boyd (*op. cit.*, p. 318).

repudiation of one's race. Since in the nature of the case, however, such persons appear to have a larger inheritance from their white than from their Negro ancestors, it is not surprising that they sometimes decide to identify with their ancestral majority, regardless of the legal definitions which place them with the minority.[20]

2. *Most of the criteria used in determining racial categories have to do with physical characteristics that are of little or no consequence in human behavior except as they are made so by the way people feel about them.*[21] Color of the skin is primarily a matter of the degree to which various pigments are present and the same thing can be said for the color of the hair and eyes. Almost all other racial differences are quantitative, being in effect a bit more or less in this or that measurement or index. In practically any measurement or index used there will be not only great variations within any designated population but also great overlapping between populations. There is no evidence that differences in skin color, hair or features are in any way correlated with a particular kind of brain or with qualities of mind and character. Modern studies show no significant racial differences in brain size or structure. W. E. LeGros Clark, Professor of Anatomy at Oxford University, writes "—in spite of statements which have been made to the contrary, there is no macroscopic or microscopic difference by which it is possible for the anatomist to distinguish the brain in single individuals of different races. Now—if we accept the thesis that the brain is the material basis of mental activities, it suggests that the latter are also not fundamentally different in different races."[22]

[20] Some of these persons while phenotypically white and genetically free from those genes which determine Negro racial characteristics undoubtedly carry other genes of Negro derivation and thus represent a channel through which such genes flow into the white population. Thus a mutual exchange of genes that are non-significant racially has been in process a long time. See Stern, *op. cit.*, p. 566.

[21] Such factors as skin color may, of course, be important in relation to climate and geography; e.g., a white skin may be a handicap in the tropics. See Carleton Coon, *The Story of Man*, New York: Alfred A. Knopf, 1954, pp. 206ff. However, Coon, goes on to point out that "under the steam-heated, air-conditioned and labor-saving conditions of modern life all kinds of people can live nearly anywhere." *Ibid.*, p. 213.

[22] Quoted in Ashley Montagu, *Statement on Race*, New York: Henry Schuman, 1951, pp. 24-25.

3. *There are no known racial differences in normal human blood.*[23] The terms "Negro blood," "mixed blood," and the saying "blood will tell," all go back to a pre-scientific age when it was thought that one's characteristics were determined by the blood inherited from the parents. The idea in many people's minds seems to be that the blood of the parents is combined in the child and will in turn be passed on to his offspring. According to this notion, race mixture involves the mixing of white and Negro blood, which suggests something like the mixing of ink and milk. Actually, of course, each organism produces its own blood and, while blood types are inherited, there is no passing of the blood itself from parent to child. An Rh positive infant born of an Rh positive father and an Rh negative mother may in some cases need to have its entire blood supply replaced by transfusions from unrelated donors. Such a procedure would not alter in any manner the infant's genetic constitution, its physical appearance, or the characteristics it can later transmit to its own descendants.[24]

The ultimate absurdity in this connection was the establishment of separate war time blood banks for the blood of persons of different races. It is important that a person receiving a blood transfusion be of the same blood group as the donor but the race of the persons involved is of no consequence. The A, B, and O blood types are found in all races, and even in anthropoid apes. Children in the same family may have different blood types and hence a blond North European might be killed by a transfusion from his own brother but have his life saved by transfusions of matching type from a Hottentot, a Zulu, or an Australian aborigine.[25] He would run no more risk of turning dark or having dark children as the result of receiving such blood than he would risk losing his masculine

[23] There are differences in the frequencies with which different blood groups are found but there is no known way by which an individual's race may be told from his blood type or from the normal blood itself. A distinction may be possible when there is present the sickle cell trait found in a small percentage of Negroes. This, however, is a pathological condition of the blood cells and while it is inherited it does not produce other "racial" characteristics. See Boyd, *op. cit.*, p. 39ff. See also Ronald Singer, "The Sickle Cell Trait in Africa," *American Anthropologist*, LV, (December, 1953).

[24] For a discussion of the Rh factor see Shull, *op. cit.*, pp. 208-218 and 245-246.

[25] Boyd, *op. cit.*, p. 221.

qualities by receiving a transfusion from a female donor.

4. *There are no "child races" and there is no evidence that any one of the major races is more "primitive" or ape-like than another.* Many people hold to the idea that African Negroes (or for that matter American Indians or any other people whose culture is relatively simple) are a "child race," that is, they are backward or retarded and must go through a long developmental process before they can "catch up" with the more advanced peoples. Therefore, the reasoning goes, any individual of such a race must be backward, or primitive, or otherwise incapable of thinking, feeling, and acting "like a white man."

This construct is based on a number of misconceptions in which race is confused with culture and genetic equipment is confused with learned behavior. It is true that it would be difficult to teach African Negroes in an African setting to think, feel, and act like Americans. There is, however, no evidence that anything other than cultural factors would be involved. Man's cultural progress is recorded not in his germ plasm but in his social institutions. If this were not true, we should expect the present day Egyptians to be more civilized and "advanced" than Europeans or their American descendants. The Egyptians had developed a complex civilization many centuries before Europe emerged from the level of tribal cultures.

In recent years, increasing numbers of African Negroes born into simple cultures have later shown themselves quite capable of earning advanced degrees in British, European, or American universities. The causes of cultural advance or retardation are complex and obscure, but there is no evidence that race plays any significant role in the matter or that the individual's genetic endowment can be inferred from the culture into which he was born.

The facts do not bear out the notion that any one race is more "primitive" or ape-like than another. Negroes may be more ape-like in having flat noses and dark skin, but apes have thin lips, straight hair, and a great deal of body hair—all of these being characteristics in which Negroes are much farther removed from the apes than are white people. There is, of course, no evidence that these so-called primitive traits are of any significance in human behavior.

5. *There is no evidence that any serious biological evils result*

from race mixture as such. Most of the problems that arise from race mixture grow out of the way in which people think and feel about it; that is, the problems are social, not biological, in character. Common notions regarding race mixture are that the offspring of mixed unions are psychologically or emotionally unstable, that children of mixed unions inherit the worst of both parental stocks, or that the more "primitive" type determines the character of the offspring. Many people also believe that race mixture will result in "disharmonic crossings," and there is a common belief that if a population becomes racially mixed cultural deterioration is sure to follow.

The notion that people of mixed racial ancestry are unstable as a consequence of such mixture confuses biological and cultural factors. There is no evidence that skin color, hair form, or features are in any way related to personality or temperament; and to suppose that there is incompatibility in the genes of people of different races is to resort to pure speculation. When people of mixed racial ancestry are unstable—and it certainly is not true that they always are—sufficient explanation can usually be found either in the individual's particular make up, as with persons of any race or, more commonly perhaps, in the fact that the children of mixed unions frequently find themselves culturally rejected by one or both parental groups.

The notions that children of racially mixed parentage inherit the worst of both parental stocks, or that the more "primitive" type determines the character of the offspring, seem to be the result of ignorance, wishful thinking, or both.[26] The child receives one of each pair of chromosomes from each parent and, as far as we know, the particular chromosomes received are in each case a matter of random selection. The procedure is exactly the same regardless of the race of the parents or the fact that they may be of different races.

---

[26] Dunn and Dobzhansky, *op. cit.*, p. 114, say, ". . . contrary to the opinion vociferously expressed by some sincere but misguided people, such a trend [toward race fusion] is not biologically dangerous. Mixing of closely related races may even lead to increased vigor. As for the most distantly separated races, there is no basis in fact to think that either biological stimulation or deterioration follows crossing. The widespread belief that human race hybrids are inferior to both of their parents and somehow constitutionally unbalanced must be counted among the superstitions." The authors point out that it does not follow that race crossing leading to race fusion is necessarily desirable, since such a course would lead merely to the replacement of inter-racial variability by individual variability.

It is, of course, true that in certain individuals, whatever their race, are to be found certain genes that are deleterious in their effects, such as those which account for hemophilia, albinism, and other abnormalities, and if persons carrying such genes mate with one another a certain percentage of their offspring will show the defects. This, however, has nothing to do with race and to suppose that deleterious genes show a special affinity for one another in race mixture is to move into the realm of the fantastic.

Probably what most people who hold to these beliefs really have in mind is that the children somehow inherit the worst character defects of both racial stocks. The children do not, of course, inherit "character" at all but a specific genetic structure which is made up of particular genes and chromosomes, taken not from the races at large but from the genes and chromosomes of the two parents in question. When the parents are sound, healthy individuals there is every reason to expect sound, healthy offspring, whether the parents belong to the same race or to different races. It is true, of course, that when interracial unions are forbidden by law or are socially unacceptable, the majority of such unions may occur between individuals who are lacking in those qualities which would make them desirable parents, whether they were to choose partners of their own or another race.

Dunn and Dobzhansky remind us that "mankind has always been, and still is, a mongrel lot."[27] Many outstanding individuals of mixed racial ancestry, from Alexander Pushkin to Ralph Bunche, have achieved international recognition. It is a curious fact that many of the persons who hold to the theory that people of mixed ancestry inherit the worst of both parent stocks also insist that the achievements of such people are due to their "white blood."

The idea that the more "primitive" type determines the character of the offspring is reminiscent of the Nazi mythology about the "prepotency" of Jews or the belief that an "un-Nordic soul may lurk in a perfectly good Nordic body."[28] Such notions have no basis in fact. No race has any monopoly on the so-called primitive characteristics.

The idea that racial mixture may result in such "disharmonies"

[27] Dunn and Dobzhansky, op. cit., p. 98.
[28] Huxley and Haddon, op. cit., p. 73.

as large teeth in small jaws or short arms combined with long legs is based on such inadequate evidence and is in itself so inconsequential that it is difficult to see why it should ever have been taken seriously. Equal or greater differences are found in persons of the same race. In any case the consequences of these alleged racial disharmonies are minor compared with the consequences which may follow the union of an Rh negative woman with an Rh positive man of the same race. Ashley Montagu calls the whole notion of disharmonic crossing "pure myth."[29]

There is no evidence that racially mixed populations suffer cultural deterioration because of such mixture. Huxley and Haddon say bluntly ". . . we can assert without contradiction that genetic mixture of human types is certainly not harmful, and that it is to be found in every people which has achieved great things in history."[30] It is true, of course, that a too rapid influx of great masses of alien people could result in disorganization in the receiving culture. This disorganization, however would not be due to the foreign genes but to the alien habits and customs, the prejudices and resistances involved.[31] Present day American Negroes are not of an alien culture and the majority of them already possess varying numbers of non-Negro genes. Moreover, and more significant, they are not seeking further race mixture but access to publicly financed community services. There is no reason to suppose that any threat of cultural deterioration is involved.

6. *There is no evidence that there is any such thing as an inferior or superior race.*[32] Unquestionably, individuals come into the world with different potentialities but the evidence suggests that in any of the major racial groupings the whole range of individual poten-

---

[29] Montagu, *Man's Most Dangerous Myth*, p. 121. Stern, *op. cit.*, p. 569, says, "It may be assumed . . . that a developing human being during his embryogeny and later, in general, will form an internally adaptively balanced system, regardless of the origin of his genes from diverse races."
[30] Huxley and Haddon, *op. cit.*, p. 229.
[31] *Ibid.*, p. 232.
[32] Differences are "racial" only if genetically determined. Many characteristics that are often considered racial are the result of social and economic differences or of particular circumstances. It is assumed here that people are concerned primarily not with physical superiority but with mental traits. Physical superiority is in any case related to time and place (e.g., dark pigmentation in the tropics), to relative isolation and exposure, and to socio-economic standards.

tialities will be found. While Shull states that races "undoubtedly differ in their mental qualities just as they differ physically" he goes on to say that when "an attempt is made to assess these differences it is glaringly apparent that no reliable measure exists."[33]

The absurdity of trying to "prove" racial inferiority or superiority, given the present state of our knowledge, becomes apparent when the situation is examined dispassionately. For one thing, to what "race" do we refer when we speak of "racial" inferiority or superiority? A great many Negro populations show evidence of unusual musical ability. Shall we say that the Negroid peoples are superior musically? Many people do think so, but what about the Oceanic Negroids and other Negroid peoples who show no evidence of such ability? This does not mean that musical talent is not inherited. It does mean that one cannot assume that, given the genes which produce a dark skin, broad nose, and Negroid hair, one will also find the genes responsible for musical ability.[34]

The problem, however, involves more than deciding what constitutes a race or setting up a reliable measure to assess differences. Who is to determine what is meant by superiority and inferiority? As Shull points out, someone has to decide how to balance "literary ability against artistic; scientific bent against philosophy." He adds, "One can scarcely avoid the conclusion that estimates of racial worth are simply rationalization; someone is trying to brand as true that which he wishes were true, and acceptance of which as true would for the moment benefit him."[35] Huxley's conclusion is that "until we have invented a method for distinguishing the effects of social environment from those of genetic constitutions we shall be unable to say anything of scientific value on such vital topics as the possible genetic differences in intelligence, initiative, and aptitude which may distinguish different human groups."[36]

Many people will argue that there are objective measurements of

[33] Shull, op. cit., p. 275.
[34] For a discussion of the "passion for labeling and classifying large groups of people on insufficient evidence" see: Jacques Barzun, Race: A Study in Modern Superstition, New York: Harcourt, 1937, pp. 18ff.
[35] Shull, op. cit., pp. 275-276.
[36] Julian Huxley, Man Stands Alone, New York: Harper & Brothers, 1941, p. 126. For a discussion of varying points of view on this point see The Race Concept: Results of an Inquiry, Paris: The United Nations Educational, Scientific, and Cultural Organizations, 1952.

racial difference and they point to intelligence tests, particularly those given during World War I, to prove the racial inferiority of certain groups. Specialists now, however, are generally agreed that at present we have no tests that can reveal innate racial differences in intelligence.[37]

Other people point to cultural backwardness or inferiority as an evidence of racial inferiority. But, aside from the problem of definitions, one must ask when the judging is to be done, since people of different races have been in the cultural lead at different times. If the judgment had been made before relatively recent times (as man's history goes), the peoples of northern and western Europe would have had to be considered among the backward races. They were a thousand or more years behind the high civilizations of the Nile, the Tigris-Euphrates, and the Indus river valleys. Not one of the major discoveries and inventions on which civilization rests— the domestication of plants and animals, the use of metals, the wheel, writing, the alphabet, calendar, paper, printing, or the compass—can be credited to northern and western Europeans. As William Howells reminds us, ". . . empires had risen and fallen in Mesopotamia several times over; yet western Europe clung to tribal life and went uncivilized for many centuries more, down to the end of the Iron Age. Nothing remotely like a city-state appeared. Only gradually did the population . . . quite late, begin to live a rude town life of its own."[38] In other words, long after civilization was well advanced in the Nile and other river valleys, the Europeans were just "natives."[39]

Even if there were some way to prove that the people of one race were on the average superior to those of other races, or that some one race had in it an unusually high proportion of superior people— and there is no proof that either of these things is true—it would still

[37] For elaboration of this point see the following: Philip E. Vernon, "Recent Investigations of Intelligence and its Measurement," *Eugenical Review*, XLIII, (October, 1951), pp. 125-137. See also the statement in Carl E. Brigham, "Intelligence Tests of Immigrant Groups," *Psychological Review* XXXVII (1930), pp. 158-165, and Allison Davis, *Social Class Influences on Learning*, Cambridge: Harvard University Press, 1948.

[38] William Howells, *Back of History*, Garden City: Doubleday & Co., Inc., 1954, pp. 348-349.

[39] *Ibid.*, p. 117. See also Huxley, *op. cit.*, p. 114, and Coon, *op. cit.*, pp. 216ff.

be unrealistic and socially wasteful to use race as a criterion for determining who shall be permitted to do what. For we know that in every race there are people who are mentally deficient and incapable of normal social participation; we know, too, that in all the major racial groupings are to be found persons who have achieved distinction by standards recognized throughout the civilized world. The one socially useful criterion is the individual's personal worth.

In his presidential address before the Pacific Division of the American Association for the Advancement of Science, A. H. Sturtevant pointed out that while there seems to be evidence of "statistical differences" between racial groups one must avoid "the view that one race (usually that to which one himself belongs) is 'better' than another. All that can properly be concluded is that they are inherently different. It follows," he continued, "that society would do well to insure that as many people as possible, of as diverse racial origins as possible, get an opportunity to show what they can do to advance civilization. It may confidently be expected that individuals of various races will have the necessary genetic equipment to make unique contributions."[40]

On the practical level, it is not the average or statistical differences between races that matter but how particular individuals behave. For, however we may define them, "races" do not think, or imagine, or create. They do not work, or vote, or govern. They do not go to school, commit crimes, sing songs, or write books. They do not have a mentality, or a gift, or an I.Q. Only an individual actually functions in a society, and it is the individual's gift, his ability, and his contribution to society that counts.[41]

[40] A. H. Sturtevant, "Social Implications of the Genetics of Man," *Science*, CXX, (September 10, 1954), pp. 405-407.

[41] When people of the same race act as a unit, it can usually be demonstrated that they do so not because they are alike racially but because they have had like experiences. When people are treated alike, they act in response to that treatment. For example, other things being equal, Negro doctors, college professors, or business men are likely to think, act, and vote very much like white doctors, college professors, or business men. They are not likely to think, act, and vote like Negro porters, waiters, or day laborers unless all the Negroes in the community are lumped together and so discriminated against that this fact overrides all other interests and concerns.

III. The Sociological Realities

Racial attitudes, including what we call race prejudice, are best understood when seen as aspects of culture. Culture may be said to consist of the sum total and organization of a group's behavior patterns, and it is an anthropological axiom that any cultural phenomenon must be understood and evaluted in the total cultural setting.

Anthropologists assume that if an American white baby and a Chinese, or a Norwegian and a Congo Negro, were swapped about at birth and each were then fully accepted as "belonging" in its new home, each individual would grow up to accept the cultural patterns, attitudes, and beliefs of its adoptive, rather than its own, family. There is equal reason to believe that if in this country the positions of Negroes and white people had been reversed, Negroes would feel the way white people now feel and vice versa. The same thing would be true of Northerners and Southerners. In other words, there is every reason to believe that the present racial and sectional variations in attitude are not due to any inherent differences in the people of different races and sections but to the fact that in a country such as this one there are many sub-cultures.

To be sure, not all the people of either race feel alike about these things even when they live in the same community. There is a sense in which every man lives in a world of his own. Not only does each individual have his own unique genetic structure and his own inner environment (his blood pressure, his endocrine balance, and perhaps his allergy or his ulcer) but he has his own private external world as well. We are living in a land of unregulated books, newspapers, magazines, radios, movies, and television, as well as in a land in which there is free choice and great mobility. In spite of a great deal of standardization, therefore, we are not all exposed to the same stimuli, nor do we all have the same experiences even when we are members of the same family.

In spite of having many shared experiences, different people may perceive the same situation differently. As Julian Huxley points out, ". . . our perceptions are thus based on a mass of assumptions derived from what we have learnt by experience. This is why it is easy to construct illusions. They introduce false assumptions, which then make us alter our total perception."[42] It is the difference in the "mass of assumptions," as well as the difference in the positions from which the situation is viewed, that accounts for the fact that in the same society, and even in the same community, segregation may be regarded as wholly good or as wholly evil. A stratified society—particularly when the stratification is reinforced by observable physical differences and rigid legal and social barriers to certain types of association—tends to perpetuate not only its structure but the attitudes and values which are in part derived from the structure and which, in turn, support it.

In consequence of the stratification in our society, many white people, particularly in certain areas of the deep South, have never had any interracial contacts except in a relation of dominance and subordination with Negroes of a low social and economic level. These white people perceive not only these particular Negroes but the whole of Negro-white relationships in terms of the mass of assumptions derived from such experiences. Many Negroes once shared, to some extent at least, white people's assumptions about the appropriateness of their relative positions. Through the years the introduction of new experiences has altered the mass of assumptions and hence has made possible new ways of perceiving the situation. Circumstances have been such that the Negro in the South has often had more new experiences than his white neighbor (he was previously more restricted and had farther to go) and his position has changed more drastically. Thus the gap in the way many whites and Negroes perceive themselves and their relation to one another has widened to the point of constituting a social crisis—a crisis based on "the polar attitudes of the American white, who does not yet accept the Negro as his equal, and the American Negro, who is no longer satisfied with anything less."[43]

Many of the components of the sociological situation will be treated in other chapters in this volume and limitations of space do not permit their elaboration here.[44] A mere recital of some of the

[42] Julian Huxley, *Evolution in Action*, New York: Harper & Brothers, 1953, p. 107.

[43] Ashmore, *op. cit.*, "Introduction," p. xv.

[44] For an elaboration of these and related problems see Ina Corinne Brown, *Socio-Economic Approach to Educational Problems*, Washington: U.S. Government Printing Office, 1942.

major factors will serve as a reminder of the complexity of the problems with which we deal. There are population or ecological factors that make the situation quantitatively, if not qualitatively, different in different sections of the country. There are differences in socio-economic levels and in occupational distribution, in education and in cultural levels that are the result of generations of poor schools, job discrimination, and exclusion from cultural opportunities available to white people. There are psychological realities, such as the long established way of looking at the situation from the white or the Negro point of view, of thinking in terms of "we" and "they," of "my people," and "your people." There is the combined force of history, tradition, and habit which serves to maintain the status quo.

Finally, there are the supporting myths; the socially supposed and believed-in differences which do not exist in fact but which, because they are believed in, influence behavior as much as if they were actually true. Some of these myths come down as a part of history and tradition; others arise in the stress and strain of daily contact and are related to the fears that develop when established and familiar patterns are threatened. These supporting myths are allied to rumors, which are often myths in the making. Many of the notions about race and race mixture described in the preceding section persist as supporting myths. They are believed, not because there is objective evidence to support them, but because they lend credence and validity to things as they are or things as one wishes them to be.[45]

So much for those aspects of the social situation that tend to perpetuate existing patterns and to maintain the status quo. There are other social realities that facilitate change. Many of these factors are minor in themselves but they add up to impressive influences. There is the very passage of time itself which tends to modify the strength of past relationships, past bitternesses, and old stereotypes. There is the continuing redistribution of the Negro population, and

[45] For an elaboration of these points see Ina Corinne Brown, *Race Relations in a Democracy*, New York: Harper & Brothers, 1949. See also Howard Odum, *Race and Rumors of Race*, Chapel Hill: The University of North Carolina Press, 1943.

the mobility of both whites and Negroes in the process of which pressures are shifted and new patterns established. There is the changing socio-economic picture with Negroes increasingly distributed throughout the occupational hierarchy according to ability and training rather than race. There is the steadily rising educational level of the Negro population, with an increase not only in the number of Negro high school and college graduates but also in the number who hold graduate and professional degrees. There is the already successfully achieved integration of Negroes into the Armed Forces and into many previously all-white schools, colleges, and universities in the South and elsewhere. There is the better communication between whites and Negroes in many areas and the more favorable presentation of Negroes on radio and television, in the movies and the press. There is the growing awareness of their own strength and importance on the part of Negroes themselves, and the growing skill in the effective use of both the economic and legal means at their disposal.

An important factor in the Negro's favor is the fact that in recent years he has steadily gained legal support for his full rights as a citizen. It is true that the 1954-55 rulings of the Supreme Court have stirred up an enormous amount of latent race hatred and fear, and have strengthened resistance to desegregation in some sections. On the other hand, there are areas in which there has been a reduction of prejudice and an increased acceptance of Negroes as persons. Furthermore, having the law on his side is a powerful aid in the achieving of the Negro's aspirations. Laws do not of themselves change the way people think and feel, but laws can change the way people act and can make possible experiences that result in changed feelings and attitudes.[46]

There are in addition, four enormously powerful social forces that, barring some cataclysmic world upheaval, make practically inevitable a steady progress toward the full integration of Negroes into

[46] Two very useful volumes dealing with the changing position of the Negro in recent years are Eli Ginzberg and others, *The Negro Potential*, New York: Columbia University Press, 1956, and Lee Nichols, *Breakthrough on the Color Front*, New York: Random House, 1954.

American life.[47] These forces need to be examined.

1. *The pressure of world opinion* has become an increasingly powerful influence against all forms of discrimination in this country. World War II made several related facts very clear: first, that the American people, whether they like it or not, are "involved in mankind;" second, that approximately two-thirds of the world's peoples are colored; and, third, that the colored peoples of the world are determined to rid themselves of white colonialism at almost any cost.

The darker peoples of the world, therefore, look on race practices in the United States as a measure of the sincerity of our words and deeds in the rest of the world. Almost every serious traveller, whether government official, missionary, news commentator, or thoughtful tourist, reports that racial discrimination at home is one of our most serious liabilities abroad. Needless to say, news of our bad deeds is carried much faster and farther than news of our virtues. Communists at home and abroad have turned our failure to practice democracy in this area into a powerful propaganda weapon.

It seems unfair that Soviet mass purges and slave labor camps are ignored in the world's press while even minor racial disturbances in the United States rate headlines everywhere. An official in India explained this to Chester Bowles by noting "we have always had great expectations about your country, while we expected little from Soviet Russia." He pointed out that the United States had set very high ideals for itself and had led other peoples to believe in these standards. Any failure on the part of the United States, therefore, leaves them disappointed precisely because they have taken our idealism at face value.[48] Fortunately, an increasing number of

[47] For a discussion of changes which have taken place since the turn of the century, see Ina Corinne Brown, *The Story of the American Negro,* New York: The Friendship Press, revised 1957.

[48] Chester Bowles, Ambassador's Report, New York: Harper & Brothers, 1954, p. 215. Mr. Bowles lists among certain "intractable facts" the existence of "an Asian viewpoint held by half of all the people in the world" which condemns with vigor "American racial discrimination wherever it comes to light." *Ibid.,* p. 387. For other revealing reports from Americans abroad see J. Saunders Redding, *An American in India,* New York: Bobbs-Merrill, 1954; Carl Rowan, *The Pitiful and the Proud,* New York: Random House, 1956; and Richard Wright, *The Color Curtain,* New York: World Publishing Company, 1956.

Americans are uncomfortable about their failure to live up to the world's "great expectations" of the people whose forefathers left them the Declaration of Independence and the Bill of Rights.

2. The second social force, related in many ways to the first, is the *pressure of the "American dream."* James Truslow Adams called it "that dream of a land in which life should be better and richer and fuller for every man with opportunity for each according to his ability or achievement."[49] However imperfectly the American dream may be realized, it does exert a powerful influence over the lives of many people.

We are essentially a fair minded people and this country rests on the foundation of a Judeo-Christian, democratic heritage that places great value on individual worth. To exclude Negroes from the rights and duties of full citizenship solely because of race is in manifest contradiction to our cherished conception of ourselves as a people who judge a man by what he is. The plaintive insistence, now so frequently heard, that segregation is right because "God made the races different," is in itself an evidence of the conflict from which men try to escape by laying the burden of their dilemma on the Creator.[50] The Judeo-Christian tradition, nevertheless, plays an important role in the next social force to be discussed.

3. The third powerful social force, often underestimated, is that of *an aroused Christian conscience.* Religion has an enormous appeal to many American people. This is evidenced, among other things, by the sale of Bibles and religious books of all kinds. This is particularly true in the section of the country in which the majority of Negroes

[49] James Truslow Adams, *The Epic of America*, Boston: Little, Brown, and Co., 1931, p. 404.

[50] One of the curious arguments, by no means limited to the uneducated, is that only man tries to violate the laws of nature by race mixture; that animals stay each with its own kind and that man should do the same. This analogy overlooks the fact that animals that do not mix are for the most part of different species that are incapable of interbreeding, whereas all men are of the same species. See Dobzhansky, *op. cit.,* pp. 165-190. Furthermore, there are not now and probably never were any "pure" races. Dobzhansky says, "the gene pool of the now living mankind contains genetic elements which are present in many and perhaps in all major populations of the past." *Ibid.,* p. 334.

live. While white Protestant churches,[51] North and South, have been extremely reluctant to receive Negroes at the local church level, they have been by no means unmindful of the inconsistency of their position. In the past twenty-five years all over the country, in conferences and training schools, thousands of young people and adults have wrestled with the problem and with their consciences.

No person familiar with this quarter-century of activity was surprised when every major denomination in the South expressed official approval of the 1954 Supreme Court ruling. As a matter of fact, a number of denominations had taken official anti-segregation stands long before that decision. The International Convention of the Disciples of Christ called upon local congregations in 1949 "to make the inclusion of all races in their membership the first goal of the new century."[52] Two years earlier the United Lutheran Churches had stated that "Christian brotherhood is impeded by practices enforcing segregation." The Methodist Discipline of 1952 stated bluntly ". . . there is no place in the Methodist Church for racial discrimination or racial segregation," and indicated that this was not merely a verbal formulation by adding, "it is our business to help free our world and our nation from these evils."[53]

Following the Supreme Court's action, official bodies of Southern Baptist, Presbyterian, and Congregational-Christian Churches, along with various state and regional groups of the Methodist and Episcopal Churches, took action in support of the Court's ruling.[54]

Catholic and Jewish bodies have added their voices to this Protestant chorus. There is, to be sure, a wide gap between official pronouncements and local implementation, and some regional church groups have repudiated the stand taken by the national body to which they belong. Nevertheless, there is great social significance in

---

[51] One factor entering into the reluctance of Protestant churches to receive Negro members is the great emphasis which many such churches place on recreational and social activities, the areas in which people are generally slowest to let down racial barriers. In most areas of the South, Protestant church members are in the majority.

[52] "The Churches Speak," *New South*, IX (August, 1954), pp. 1-8.

[53] *Ibid.*

[54] *Ibid.*

the fact that almost every professedly religious person, whether of the Catholic, Protestant, or Jewish faith, knows that his Church has spoken out against segregation as a burden which the human spirit should not be asked to bear.

4. A fourth social force making for the integration of Negroes lies in *the American concern for practical efficiency*. It is becoming increasingly apparent that enforced segregation is economically unsound and socially wasteful, and that to categorize people by the amount of pigmentation they have, rather than by their qualities of mind and character, simply does not make sense.

One facet of the situation lies in the growing social and economic importance of the Negro members of the community and their increasing awareness of that importance. Many newspapers in the South that once refused to use courtesy titles for Negroes and found only their crimes newsworthy, now find it good business to cater to all their readers, and many business concerns have discovered that they need the dollars of their Negro customers. It is generally recognized that the threat of economic loss was an important factor in the success of the lunch counter sit-ins in various communities. Moreover, a number of formerly segregated cities have concluded that orderly desegregation is preferable to violent resistance and the unfavorable publicity and consequent economic loss that such violence evokes.

It has become increasingly apparent that anything which holds a large segment of the population to sub-standard levels increases the burden on the rest of the community. It is only beginning to occur to many communities that in segregating Negroes and excluding them from normal participation in civic life the community itself is extravagantly wasteful of its human resources. Many communities once assumed that the white people did things for Negroes. They then came to the point of assuming that Negroes might serve "their own people." Now there is a growing awareness that many Negroes have a contribution to make, not as Negroes to Negroes, but as citizens to the total community.

It is generally conceded that the integration of Negroes in the Armed Forces has been highly successful, has greatly increased the effectiveness of the Negroes involved, and hence has increased the effectiveness of the units of which they are a part. There is every reason to believe that with the lifting of "the burden on the human spirit" now laid upon them by segregation, Negroes will make increasingly greater contributions to our common life.

IV. THE SOCIAL PROCESS: STRATEGY IN RACE RELATIONS

Very few people in this country would take seriously any suggestion that a South African *apartheid* be practiced in the United States. This does not mean that there are not numerous people who wish to see segregation continued indefinitely; and since the Supreme Court ruling the positions of many people have become much more extreme. Perhaps the majority of people today would —with great variations within each group, of course—fall roughly into one of the following categories:

1. People who are in no way committed to the Judeo-Christian, democratic tradition and who would take almost any measure, however extreme, to maintain "white supremacy." These are the actual or potential members of the Ku Klux Klan, Silver Shirts, or other fascist or "hate" organizations. Although these groups were relatively quiescent preceding the Supreme Court action, they have since taken a new lease on life. Where they sense a permissive atmosphere they bomb homes and schools, burn buses, and commit other acts of violence. Recent German history should warn us not to underestimate the appeal of such groups, particularly in times of stress.

2. People who give at least lip-service to the Judeo-Christian, democratic tradition but see no conflict between this tradition and their insistence that Negroes should be "kept in their place." Many such people merely do not think clearly enough to see the inconsistency in their position. Others take refuge in the notion of racial inferiority. If Negroes are biologically inferior, this supposed fact offers a justification for discriminatory behavior.

3. People who do see the conflict between the Judeo-Christian, democratic tradition and the special categorizing of Negroes. Within this group will be found people of such varying shades of opinion as the following:

a. People who see the conflict but who are unable or unwilling to face up to its implications. They are caught in the "American dilemma" and see no clear way out.

b. People who cling to the notion that you really can have a "separate but equal" life, and that Negroes "really want to be with their own people."

c. People who see integration as inevitable but who would postpone it to sometime in the distant future when people are ready for it, which according to some of them won't be "at least for a hundred years."

d. People who see integration as inevitable but hope "it won't go too fast."

e. People who see integration as both inevitable and desirable, but who are mindful of the numerous problems and difficulties involved in its implementation.

f. People who want all barriers down right now and who do not think too much about consequences.

g. People who want all barriers down right now, regardless of consequences, even if it is necessary to force some sections of the country to conform.

Since the Judeo-Christian, democratic tradition does underlie the United States Constitution and the "American dream," and since the scientific facts eliminate race inferiority as a "way out," most educators probably fall somewhere within the third category. Many of them, however, will encounter in their communities numerous people who fall into the second category and, in some areas, persons in the first category are both vocal and influential.[55] In dealing with people in any of these categories, it is important to realize that

[55] The basic issue of the right or wrong of segregation has been obscured by conflict over questions of the function of the Supreme Court, the intent of the Constitution, and states' rights. The defiance of the Supreme Court by people in responsible positions has important ramifications in the breakdown of law and order. See Charles Fairman, "The Attack on the Segregation Cases" in the *Harvard Law Review*, November 1956, reprinted in *New South*, May 1957.

most of them are probably convinced of both the honesty and the rightness of the position they hold. If they change their views, they will do so not through denunciation but through circumstances and events which lead them to see themselves and the situation in a different light.

Perhaps this is the point at which some word should be said regarding the role of Negroes themselves in the social process. This chapter has been written for the most part in terms of majority attitudes and practices; yet it must be remembered that a great deal of the success or failure of this new step toward democratic living will depend on the way in which Negroes in each community meet the situation.

Although Negroes have generally welcomed the Court's decision, they, too, particularly in the areas of heaviest Negro population, are not without fears and anxieties. While Negroes in some communities have taken an active stand, others are timid and fearful, afraid of antagonizing the white community, or are reluctant to face the competition of the white world. It is not true that all people, either white or Negro, are eager to better themselves, to get better jobs, to live in better neighborhoods, or to go to better schools. Upward mobility is usually painful and many individuals, of whatever race, are unready or unwilling to pay its price. There is a kind of security in the known and familiar world with all its limitations. In many communities, certain Negro leaders enjoy favored positions which would be threatened by integration. It is unrealistic to suppose that all of them will voluntarily renounce an immediate and private gain for a future communal good that can be attained only at considerable personal cost and sacrifice.

Desegregation will not, of course, solve all the problems the Negro faces. He will still have to wrestle with prejudice and with the legacy of the past history and previous low status of his people. The majority of Negroes will still face all the problems and difficulties common to white people of limited education and economic opportunity. It is clear, however, that an increasing number of Negroes see in desegregation an idea whose time has come. To them, the 1954 Court ruling appears as a sort of second Emancipation Proclamation freeing them from the psychic bondage of segregation. These leaders, many of whom are ministers, have counseled their people against hate, violence, and revenge, and they have sought to keep the Negro protest within legal and non-violent channels.

Much will be gained if both Negroes and white people distinguish clearly between those things that are public and civic and those that are private and personal; between rights that are due all citizens and behavior which is a matter of personal privilege; between actions and programs that are enforceable by law and those that yield only to public opinion; between institutions, customs, and associations that are publicly supported, either directly by taxes or indirectly by tax exemption, and those things that are privately supported for private use.

Although the terms desegregation and integration are used interchangeably there is a distinction. Desegregation, which is enforceable by law, simply requires that public facilities be open to all. Such facilities become integrated to the extent that they are used by both groups. Desegregation does not affect personal choices and it does not take away from the individual the right of choice in the use of public facilities. He may use them or not as he chooses. What the law says, in effect, is that he may not claim double rights; that is, the right to use them himself and also the right to deny their use to other persons.

Good strategy would seem to lie in these directions: (1) recognition of the various factors, biological and sociological, that enter into the situation to make it what it is; (2) recognition and utilization of the factors which facilitate desired changes; (3) recognition of the psychological factors involved in changing the attitudes of people; (4) recognition of the complexities of the problem, for example, that the mere fact of desegregation will not in itself change people or solve all problems; and (5) recognition of the regional variations in the nature and complexity of the problems and, therefore, in the most effective ways of handling them.

IV

Culture and the Personality Development of Minority Peoples

Regina M. Goff
Professor of Education
Morgan State College

I. The Bio-Social Basis of Personality

As is generally recognized today, complex behavioral patterns are learned. Persistent traits and modes of responses, reflecting among other things an integration of interests, attitudes, capacities, and abilities, become associated in a totality referred to as personality. Individual modes of perceiving, culturally determined, are accompanied by dynamic mental functioning which activates bodily energy later discharged in response. Uniqueness in perceiving and responding gives meaning to individual personality.

The biological features of development make possible perceiving, feeling, and responding, all of which are aspects of experiencing. As Sullivan[1] points out, "Experience is in its last analysis, experience of tensions and experience of energy transformations." Personality functions as a correlate of those particular provisions or controls of the culture which determine for individuals how tensions may be reduced and energy directed toward the satisfaction

[1] H. S. Sullivan, "Multidisciplined Coordination of Inter-personal Data, in Personality and Culture," S. Stansfeld Sargent (ed.), *Wenner-Gren Foundation* (New York, 1949), p. 175.

of needs. Good adjustment, the product of a so-called normal personality, is best tested by noting the direction of energy exerted in tension-arousing experiences. A requirement is constant restoration of balance and continuous social equilibrium.

Behavior does not originate within the individual, subject solely to personal peculiarities. Motivation to act, as well as the goals toward which action is directed, are as much recognition of current social phenomena and demands as they are responses to inner drives and past experiences. When current demands and potentialities for meeting them are compatible, satisfaction and end product reinforce and finally establish the accepted pattern of action. When barriers produce failures in response to demands, dissatisfaction results in behavior often punishable as an offense against social requirements. Fortunately, in the constant interpersonal interaction of experience, there is capacity for adaptability despite the persistence of recurrent modes of response.

The aggressively competitive and stratified American culture places value on personal achievement, independence, liberty, and power. The esteem in which the individual holds himself is directly proportionate to his feelings of mastery of circumstances, power over events, and prestige and acceptance among man. Such cultural demands, established values, have direct bearing on personality, being, in fact, motivators of behavior.

From birth, events, people, and laws influence what is learned by way of response. Since there is no common environment, there are no specific learnings which are universally shared. Personality is a function of special features of individual experiencing, and childhood is a determining stage in establishing the basic features of personality. Davis[2] points out the relationship between class position, methods of training in early childhood, and emergent behavior patterns. Variations in method and cultural exposures result in differences in specific learnings, motivations, and responses to varying folkways. Further, as shown in a study by Davis and Havighurst,[3] differences in personality may be traced less to race

[2] Allison Davis, "American Status Systems and the Socialization of the Child," *American Sociological Review*, VI (1941), pp. 345-356.

[3] Allison Davis and R. J. Havighurst, "Social Class and Color Differences in Child Rearing," *American Sociological Review*, XI (1946), pp. 648-710.

than to class training. Cultural differences in personality in middle-class and lower-class children, according to the study, are more pronounced than differences between Negro and white children of the same class. It is thus conceivable that much behavior stereotyped as racial is in reality class-patterned. Similarly, Linton,[4] speaking of culturally determined differences in personality, draws upon the findings of several studies which illustrate the tie between techniques of child care and particular features of the "modal personality" or personality norms of societies.

In general, it is conceded that although new learnings may be incorporated into new or revised action patterns, the early formative years with their attendant experiences arc basic to the nature of maturity. In addition to the overt manipulation of the infant's body, which involves communication, there are intentional social practices on the part of the parent which, from the earliest awareness of the child, are for the latter the raw material out of which specific concepts develop: rudimentary understandings of preferences in social acceptance, codes of morality, and areas of freedom and constriction. For the Negro child, particular learnings come about because of the economic and social position of the family and of the social taboos of the South and the discriminatory designs of the North.

In childhood the individual begins to build meaning for his world. Impressions deepen and are extended as his interaction with the environment proceeds. His progressive socialization carries with it learnings the family prizes in compliance with the expectations and demands of superordinate members of the culture. In conjunction with this, of course, crystallization of feelings occurs in relation to the self. The future promises less need of conformance to deferential behavior patterns and, to the growing minority members, more by way of equalitarian reactions. But the ideals of the culture which appear visionary to minority members will remain so unless impregnable social barriers are removed. The initial motivation to achieve acceptable social goals will persist, however, if such goals appear to be attainable. Otherwise, a disheartening apathy may arise, or a useless dissipation of energy in socially unrewarding

[4] R. Linton, "Problems of Status Personality in Personality and Culture," S. Stansfeld Sargent (ed.), *Wenner-Gren Foundation* (New York, 1949), p. 163.

endeavor may follow. In either case, the bright promise of early growth will fade with serious consequences for the developing self.

II. The Emergence of the Self

Clark,[5] Horowitz,[6] and Lasker[7] point out that consciousness of the self for the Negro child develops in the pre-school years. Davis found that in the South children begin to learn caste controls which differentiate them before they enter school. In these and other studies, the special features of the wider culture, which impinge upon the Negro child and cause negative feelings that have a bearing on self-perception, have been identified.[8] These include direct ridicule, name-calling, disparaging or belittling statements, physical ill-treatment, threats of violence of white adults, aggressive behavior by white children, and the more subtle effects of discrimination and discourteous or ill-mannered treatment, and indirect disparagement reflected in mass media productions, from movies to publications.

The extent to which actual first-hand intergroup interactions have influenced the child to differentiate the self from others by pre-school age has not been established, however. Horowitz conceives of group consciousness and identification as an "intrinsic aspect of ego development. . . . Before the ego has been completely formed, in the very process of becoming, we find it subtly approximating a visible symbol that has been socially institutionalized to aid it in marking itself off from the not-self." According to this view, facial identification, culturally prescribed, is in essence a developmental feature accompanying other aspects of growth. Radke, Trager, and Davis[9] state that Negro children reveal most vividly

[5] Kenneth B. Clark and M. J. Clark, "The Development of Consciousness of Self and the Emergence of Racial Identification in Negro Pre-School Children," *Journal of Social Psychology,* X (1939), pp. 591-599.

[6] R. Horowitz, "Racial Aspects of Self-Identification in Nursery School Children," *Journal of Psychology,* XI (1940), pp. 159-169.

[7] B. Lasker, *Race Attitudes in Children,* New York: Henry Holt, 1929.

[8] R. M. Goff, *Problems and Emotional Difficulties of Negro Children,* Contributions to Education, No. 960. New York: Bureau of Publications, Teachers College, Columbia University, 1949.

[9] M. Radke, H. Trager, and H. Davis, "Social Perception and Attitudes of Children," *Genetic Psychology Monograph,* XL (1949), pp. 327-447.

and often the feeling of insecurity resulting from anticipated rejection and insult from white children and that "adult values and interpretations have a greater bearing on the child's attitude than his actual experiencing with other groups." Thus, in the absence of concrete experiencing, social thought, nevertheless, is a force of great power in shaping projected attitudes on personality development. Symonds,[10] in his discussion of the ego and the self, speaks of three distinct elements of the ego. He refers to the ego as a receiver of impressions, an organizer of impressions into action plans through symbolic processes, and a doer or activator of the plans toward satisfying ends. This view supports Horowitz' suggestion that racial identification is an intrinsic aspect of ego development. There is, of course, uncritical acceptance on the part of the child of the thought content of parental attitudes and, thus, the Negro child, as perceiver, may develop an early sensitivity to color meaning.

Rose,[11] in a thorough historical exploration of Negro group attitudes and reactions, points to the movement from the initial diversified and disorganized pattern of slave behavior, later welded into open group revolt and mutinous rebellion, to the positive protest patterns that are still current. All of this is indicative of the gradual trend toward strong group identification—a concomitant of sociological and psychological factors. Residuals by way of strains in attitudes are still present: group pride and loyalty or, negatively, shame because of membership. To the extent that these are operative and are generated in relationships with the child, they form part of his social heritage and contribute to his image of self and of it in relation to others.

Implications of Color

There always have existed interferences to complete unity in group identification. In this area skin color is prominent, as several studies have shown. Goodman,[12] in a study of Negro children aged

[10] P. M. Symonds, *Ego and the Self*, New York: Appleton-Century-Crofts, 1951.
[11] A. Rose, *The Negro's Morale*, St. Paul, Minn.: The University of Minnesota Press, 1949.
[12] M. E. Goodman, "Evidence Concerning the Genesis of Interracial Attitudes," *American Anthropologist*, XL (1946), pp. 624-630.

2-4 years, found expressions of uneasiness, tension, sensitivity, and gregariousness accompanying self-identification. The degree to which tension and sensitivity is due solely to color is difficult to isolate, however, since there are so many possible contributing factors. Clark and Clark,[13] working with children aged 3-7 years, found that a negation of the color brown was associated with the conflicting need of identification with this rejected factor. Attempts to resolve the conflict were achieved through wishful thinking and fantasies. Some indications of acceptance of identification were noted around the seventh year. If the growing individual receives no mature support in willing acceptance of his group identity, ambivalent attitudes toward the self emerge. The result is a vacillating adult personality—an individual who wishes to retain an unrealistic ego image, though the actuality of fact is inescapable. These studies make it clear that color connotations arise in the pre-school years.

The studies of Bovell[14] and Parrish[15] indicate that individual reactions toward one's own color are paralleled by in-group preferences and discriminations. Parrish reported that three out of every five persons approached considered black the worst color and associated it with low status. The dominance of white standards is reflected in the attitude. The assumed utility of specific gradations of color was investigated by Seeman.[16] His concern was with the operational importance or function of skin color in choices of friends and of reputation in the group. In two out of three all-Negro school classes, skin color was found an important variable, with light color leading in acceptability and reputation. In pointing to the emotional counterpart of reactions to color, a study by Meyers[17]

[13] Kenneth B. Clark, "Emotional Factors in Racial Identification and Preferences in Negro Children," Journal of Negro Education, X (1950), pp. 341-350.

[14] G. B. Bovell, "Psychological Considerations of Color Conflicts Among Negroes," Psychoanalytic Review, XXX (1943), ppp. 447-459.

[15] C. H. Parrish, "Color Names and Color Notions," Journal of Negro Education, XV (1946), pp. 13-20.

[16] M. Seeman, "Skin Color Values in Three All-Negro School Classes," American Sociological Review, XI (1946), pp. 315-321.

[17] I. M. Meyers, "A Study of Anti-Negro Prejudice," Journal of Negro Education, XII (1943), pp. 709-714.

supports that of Frank[18] and others which show that Negro psychotics are preoccupied with color. This fact, according to Meyers, may be attributed to their role in the community at large and to notions prevalent in the Negro community.

Warner, Junker and Adams[19] contend that, while skin color is not the most significant factor for every individual in the development of social personality, it is nevertheless definitely associated with social position and, as such, is the most potent single element determining the good or poor development of Negro character. Color, without doubt, figures prominently in both class and caste. It may prevent the emergence of feelings of belonging in chance social groups, as well as in primary groups from which one cannot easily escape. To the extent that feelings of isolation persist, ultimate adjustment is affected. A feeling of group acceptance is a basic psychological need, requisite to good adjustment.

Mechanisms to defeat group inclusion are not unusual. Brenman's[20] study on defenses against identification devised by a group of urban middle-class girls revealed three approaches—namely, conscious rejection of racial identification, awareness accompanied by in-group rebellion and pride, and awareness accompanied by deep anxiety.

Reactions toward this physical characteristic result from reflective processes in which images are perceived and categorized as acceptable or objectionable, followed by the inescapable placement of the self somewhere along the color continuum and the adoption of responses appropriate to the feelings elicited. Feeling becomes integrated in the total self-system and emerges in characteristic traits which distinguish the individual. It would be fallacious to conclude from the foregoing, however, that, solely from this basis, every dark skinned person develops lowered feelings of self-esteem. Consciousness of color may be absorbed by strong interpersonal bonds in

[18] J. D. Frank, "Adjustment Problems of Selected Negro Soldiers," *Journal of Mental Disease*, CV (1947), pp. 647-660.

[19] W. L. Warner, B. Junker, and W. A. Adams, *Color and Human Nature*, Washington, D. C.: American Council on Education, 1941.

[20] M. Brenman, "The Relationship Between Minority Group Membership and Group Identification in A Group of Urban Middle-Class Girls," *Journal of Social Psychology*, XI (1940), pp. 171-197.

the home and with later associates, as well as by motivation in areas where power and ability have been demonstrated through success. Since light skin as a value grows out of white dominance, desegregation in all areas of American life, with a subsequent leveling of the white-black hierarchy, should in time lead to the disappearance of the color factor as a status symbol.

White Attitudes

Present-day majority group standards and selection are reflected also in the attitudes of the young. Ammons[21] found evidence, in a study of white boys aged 2-6 years, of discrimination in skin color as early as the second year, and the existence of active prejudices at the fourth year. Melzer,[22] concerned with nationality preferences of white children, found that white children rank Negroes in twentieth place. Likewise, Blake and Dennis,[23] in an investigation of stereotypes held by children in grades four through eleven, found that young children attributed nothing favorable to the Negro. With increased age and experience, according to the latter study, adult stereotypes were acquired which, while predominantly unfavorable, did attribute some "good traits" to the Negro, such as religion, cheerfulness, and dancing ability.

In an attempt to distinguish individuals who change their attitudes from those who do not, Mussen[24] experimented with planned intergroup camp experiences. White and Negro boys were housed in the same dormitories and engaged in the same activities. The socio-economic level of the groups was considered comparable. Measures taken on each of the white boys before and after the exposure showed "no change in attitude in the group as a whole." Similarly, Meyers presented to a group of college students at the

[21] R. B. Ammons, "Reactions in a Projective Doll Play Interview of White Males Two to Six Years of Age to Differences in Skin Color and Facial Features," *Journal of Genetic Psychology*, LXXVI (1950), pp. 323-341.

[22] H. Melzer, "Nationality Preferences and Stereotypes Concerning the Negro," *Journal of Genetic Psychology*, LV (1939), pp. 403-424.

[23] R. Blake and W. Dennis, "The Development of Stereotypes Concerning the Negro," *Journal of Abnormal and Social Psychology*, XXXVIII (1943), pp. 525-531.

[24] P. H. Mussen, "Some Personality and Social Factors Related to Changes in Children's Attitudes Toward Negroes," *Journal of Abnormal and Social Psychology*, XLV (1950), pp. 423-441.

third and eighth meetings of the class fifteen statements designed to elicit ethnic attitudes. There were ten hours of lecture and assigned reading between the two periods. The second administration showed a change from more liberal to less liberal attitudes. The change was attributed to the increased honesty of the second reactions.

The findings of Mussen contrast with those of studies which have shown a positive influence of intergroup experience under favorable circumstances. Watson,[25] for example, studying means of changing prejudices, found that personal contact with out-group members was considered a major factor in the change in 81 percent of the cases and a contributing factor in 18 percent. Contrary to the findings of Meyers, the same study revealed that school and college teaching were considered a major factor in dispelling prejudice in 16 percent of the instances, and a contributing factor in 25 percent of the cases. The objects of prejudice in this study included, in addition to the Negro, the Jew, the white, the Protestant, and persons of other nationalities. The important fact revealed was that change occurred as the result of specific experiences.

III. Prejudice and Its Sources

Prejudice is no respecter of ethnic groups. This was illustrated in a study by Berdie[26] on attitude patterns accompanying infiltration by Negroes into white neighborhoods. Though there were few Jewish children in the block studied and contact with them was limited, newly arrived Negro children held more favorable attitudes toward non-Jewish white children than toward those of Jewish parentage. The reaction was attributed to ". . . unconsciously held but subtle and pervasive stereotypes." This differentiation between groups of the white world, carrying even greater negative feelings in one instance, intensifies already existing in-group consciousness because it narrows the field of outgoingness. As areas of contrast multiply, it appears that differentiation of the self sharpens.

[25] G. B. Watson, "Changing Prejudices," mimeographed data, New York: Teachers College, Columbia University.

[26] R. F. Berdie, "Infiltration and the Attitudes of White and Negro Parents," *Journal of Abnormal and Social Psychology*, XLVII (1952), pp. 688-699.

Attitudes evolve from perception and feeling. Feelings provide the motivation which eventuates in response and, hence, they give content and expression to the self. The individual, an embodiment of a particular self-system, must relate himself, of course, to the larger world of other persevering selves. Because of its negative emotional aspect, prejudice prevents the emergence of conjunctive forces in human relations. Since prejudice is a part of the total personality structure, much attention has been focused on the probable causes of its occurrence.

Bayton[27] holds the view that the psychological sources of prejudice are to be found in the quality of parental control persisting through the formative years; that coercive, authoritative, and capricious control creates personality problems which have their outlet in active prejudices. The source is thus not related directly to the object or group toward which prejudice is directed. An indication of personality features involved in prejudice is given in a study by Gough, Harris, Martin, and Edwards.[28] They found a relationship between traits of prejudice and intolerance and emotional factors of fear, veiled hostility, and insecurity. An exhaustive investigation of anti-Semitism by Adorno, Frenkel-Brunswick, Levinson and Sanford[29] reveals the roots of prejudice within specific personality needs. Subtle displacement veiled actual pivotal factors. Lack of free affiliative relations at home and unresolved and unadmitted hostility toward parents were found to be reflected in anti-Semitism. Among the many findings presented by Allport and Kramer,[30] in their intensive study of the background of prejudice, was the evidence that individuals who had unpleasant childhood experiences with members of a particular group held generalized prejudices toward the group as a whole. Incidentally, contrary to a popular supposition, religious training was not an active in-

[27] J. A. Bayton, "Personality and Prejudice," *Journal of Psychology*, XXII (1946), pp. 59-65.

[28] H. G. Gough, D. B. Harris, N. Martin, and M. Edwards, "Children's Ethnic Attitudes: Relationship to Certain Personality Factors," *Child Development*, XXI (1950), pp. 83-91.

[29] T. W. Adorno, E. Frenkel-Brunswick, O. J. Levinson, and R. N. Sanford, *The Authoritarian Personality*, New York: Harper & Brothers, 1950.

[30] G. W. Allport and B. A. Kramer, "Some Roots of Prejudice," *Journal of Psychology*, XXII (1946), pp. 9-39.

fluence in its elimination. Individuals holding church membership were the least tolerant group, while people with no religious affiliation were the most liberal. This is an interesting commentary on the discrepancy between belief and practice, not a reflection on religion itself. Prothro,[31] in an investigation of ethnocentrism, found a relationship in attitudes held by a single individual toward different minorities; those who were unfavorable toward Jewish people were unfavorable toward the Negro. A large percentage of those low on ethnocentrism, however, were definitely anti-Negro. This finding shifts the emphasis of the previous studies. Historical, cultural, and situational factors, rather than personality dynamics alone, must be viewed as of major importance by those who seek an answer to the American dilemma.

Watson has called attention to types of prejudices which are products of particular motives. These are referred to as conforming, projecting, generalizing, and profiting. In some instances, they may exist as unexamined or unattended remnants of early exposures to social attitudes and practices. Jersild[32] cautions that a child of any ethnic group, who is protective of the self and defensive toward out-group members who have injured him, holds realistic attitudes which should not be labeled irrational prejudices. Participation in a single group, the result of friendships growing out of normal events and circumstances, should not be considered as rejection of other groups. Prejudices involving attitudes of bias, hatred, and distrust, however, are projections indicative of personal difficulties which prevent relatedness with others and which reflect the limited esteem with which the self is held. This view finds support in the study by Trent[33] who, in an investigation of Negro children, found a relationship between self-acceptance and acceptance of others. Children who held themselves in low esteem, the result of barrenness, lack of warmth and sympathy in interpersonal relations, and who were the least self-accepting, were rejecting toward both Negro and white children. The reverse was true in the instance of children who were most self-accepting.

[31] E. T. Prothro, "Ethnocentrism and Anti-Negro Attitudes in the South," *Journal of Abnormal and Social Psychology*, XLVII (1952), pp. 105-108.
[32] A. T. Jersild, *Child Psychology*, New York: Prentice-Hall, Inc., 1954.
[33] R. Trent, "The Correlates of Self-Acceptance Among Negro Children," Unpublished dissertation, Teachers College, Columbia University.

These findings in general contribute to the understanding of the psychological basis of misanthropy and have wide implications for personality development and inter-group relationships. The person with irrational prejudices in any ethnic or socio-economic group is propelled by unhealthy mental states which lessen his capacity for equalitarian relationships. Prejudice shown toward the Negro lowers his self-esteem. It is probable that the major source of security against ego-deflation is within the individual himself. Latent features of personality may be developed and augmented by interpersonal relationships between family members and, later, by ever-widening positive experiences with others. The emergence of strength to offset socially mobilized anxieties is proportionate to the building of early security through affective relationships. It would be amiss to assume that psychological factors which prompt irrational prejudices are merely personal matters that are unrelated to features of the culture. Undoubtedly, a culture of stress and competition, one with the historical and social history of America, will have within it stresses which mobilize anxieties to which all members are susceptible. Insecure parents, disquieted because of their own unfulfilled needs, project their dissatisfactions in their children.

IV. PROBLEMS OF PERSONALITY FORMATION

The Role of Symbolization

In the course of on-going interactions with the environment, the individual learns specific responses to particular cultural features. Meanings attached to cultural forms evoke responses appropriate to the level of his understanding. The red signal of the stop light, the warning blast of an air raid siren, the badge and uniform of the police officer, the passing flag, and the national anthem evoke, after continuing exposure, immediate reactions. But such a function of symbols does not necessarily imply the blindness or lack of insight associated with conditioned responses. Nor does it refer to symbols as labels or marks of identification. These responses have a subjective, emotional aspect as well as an intellectual one. Overt manifestations, where there is no penalty attached to behavior, give expression to inner attitudes and conceptions which eventually become part of the personality structure.

The study of Lewin, Lippitt, and White,[34] for example, illustrates the operation of learning mechanism in social situations. Specific types of leaders—authoritarian, *laissez faire,* and democratic—became symbols that evoked specific and recurrent forms of behavior in members of the group to which they were assigned. In everyday occurrences, the presence of certain individuals, or knowledge of behavior expectations under certain conditions, elicit specific reactions out of a repertoire of many possible responses.

The concept of symbolization is found in several studies. Kardiner,[35] in his discussion of slave psychology, infers that the plantation owner or master was a symbol of protection, therefore to be revered; but he was also an obstacle to freedom and, therefore, to be hated. The "Uncle Tom" behavior was an accommodation to ambivalent feelings. Both Mandelbaum[36] and Stevens,[37] observing the effect of Army segregation on the Negro soldier, found that such arrangements were damaging to motivation and morale. "Perhaps the main reason for this is that the fact of segregation increases the lack of confidence in each other as Negroes, a distrust which is held and implanted by potent sections of the larger society. And under battle stress, when the demand for mutual support is greatest, this undermining of confidence sometimes collapses the strength otherwise engendered in the primary group." The observation in this study of the negative response of Negroes to all-Negro assemblages is significant. Paradoxically, a sharing of feelings was offset by an inability to generate a common confidence. We infer here, also, the power of the symbol of the white man which, since it has endured through time, evokes feelings of security rather than of suspicion and distrust in specific circumstances. These findings call attention to the situational aspect of

[34] K. Lewin, R. Lippitt, and R. White, "Patterns of Aggressive Behavior in Experimentally Created 'Social Climates'," *Journal of Social Psychology,* X (1939), pp. 271-299.

[35] A. Kardiner and L. Oversey, *Mark of Oppression,* New York: W. W. Norton & Co., Inc., 1951.

[36] D. G. Mandelbaum, *Soldier Groups and Negro Soldiers,* Berkeley: University of California Press, 1952, pp. 89-90.

[37] R. B. Stevens, "Racial Aspects of Emotional Problems of Negro Soldiers," *American Journal of Psychiatry,* CIII (1947), pp. 493-498.

reaction patterns, the lack of air-tight fixity in behavioral responses, and the occurrence of change in reactions in terms of current needs and satisfactions.

The acceptance of white standards as right and desirable is further shown in a study by Bayton.[38] In this study, 100 students in a southern Negro college were compared with 100 at Princeton University with respect to stereotypes. The Negro students assigned characteristics to themselves which were different from those they assigned to a typical Negro, with whom, therefore they did not identify. As a result, a high degree of similarity existed between these Negro and white students with respect to the stereotypes of various racial and national groups they possessed. The study emphasized, as did those of Negro troops, the absence of intragroup morale. Brunschwig[39] made an analysis of the listings of famous Americans by Negro students in a southern college. The number of whites listed exceeded the number of Negroes mentioned. Responses indicated majority group members as evident symbols of prestige. A parallelism is seen in the Jewish group. Lewin[40] refers to the tendency of underprivileged groups to accept the values of the dominant members of the culture. Jewish anti-Semitism results from sensitivity to in-group standards which are a departure from accepted values of the wider culture. Group denial may express itself in rejection of Jewish institutions, mannerisms, and ideals, but though the tension level may be strained, fraught with fear and inferiority, expressions of group and self-hatred are typically subtle. A further example of symbolization is seen in an analysis of the fictional character "Bigger Thomas" in Richard Wright's *Native Son*. Charles[41] characterized Bigger as a neurotic individual to whom the white man was a symbol of fear. Final responses on the part of Bigger were interpreted as the result, in part, of the

[38] J. A. Bayton, "The Psychology of Racial Morale," *Journal of Negro Education*, XI (1942), pp. 150-152.
[39] L. Brunschwig, "An Analysis of the Listings of Famous Americans by a Group of Negro College Students," *Journal of Psychology*, IX (1940), pp. 207-219.
[40] K. Lewin, "Self-Hatred among Jews," *Contemporary Jewish Record*, IV (1941), pp. 219-232.
[41] C. V. Charles, "Optimism and Frustration in the American Negro—Negro Literature," *Psychoanalytic Review*, XXIX (1942), pp. 270-299.

white man's low expectation of him by symbolizing him as an aggregate of primitive impulses.

The factor of previous conditioning is important to consider in describing learned reactions of this nature. Lower-class Negroes, according to Catharn,[42] because of their specific experiences, are more unfavorable in their stereotyped conceptions of white people than either the middle or upper classes, while middle-class members possess most favorable conceptions. Action patterns in the presence of white individuals vary in terms of the meaning attached or the nature of the conceived symbolization. Lack of security in self, revealed in practicing in-group discrimination, rejecting identification, and viewing the group as an alien division symbolizing weakness, is most likely a feature of a total pattern of insecurity. In its inception this pattern is related to decisive factors in the immediate environment but, as subsequent cultural pressures multiply, is enlarged and deepened.

The above studies illustrate the influence of subtle social learnings in the development of traits which become characteristic features of personality. In particular, the significance of symbolization in interpersonal relations is revealed. The social implications of the 1954 Supreme Court decision, however, foreshadow a psychological change in the designation of symbols traditionally deemed superior. As Rose[43] pointed out, recent concerted action for democratic practices, support of protest groups, and more widespread use of the ballot give evidence of an ever-increasing high morale within the Negro group. As the acceptance of the Negro becomes more general, as equal respect is shown, and as the Negro sees himself along with other groups engaged in the attainment of common goals of a democracy, black and white should eventually symbolize a common humanity.

The Influence of Role Assignment

The nature of the functioning of the individual in the culture is, of course, contributory to personality formation. What the indi-

[42] T. Catharn, "Negro Conceptions of White People," *American Journal of Sociology*, LVI (1951), pp. 458-467.

[43] A. Rose, *op. cit.*

vidual does influences his perception, and his subsequent structuring, of the world. The elements which contribute to initial feelings of self-worth and final self-acceptance or depreciation occur within the framework of anticipated functioning and actual role assignment. The Radke study[44] showed that as early as the pre-school years, white children ascribed to Negroes inferior roles and low status. Without doubt, the attitude persists to later years in many instances. Considering the attitude of the Negro toward himself and his proposed work, Lawrence[45] discovered that Negro youth in California exhibited a lack of realism between occupational choices and availability of training. In addition, but one-half of the group had confidence they could achieve their goals. Poor school counseling was blamed for the discrepancy between aspirations and probable attainment. It is important to note that, while goal setting was not tempered by reality in terms of training possibilities, it was nevertheless realistic in terms of cultural values. The common trait of ego enchancement, guided by what society dictates as respectable functioning, is apparent.

In a study of aspiration levels of two groups of Negro children in North Carolina, aged 8-10 and 14-16 years,[46] little similarity was revealed, particularly in the low-income group, between the occupations of parents and the ambitions of children. Children chose areas of respectability in which inroads are of comparatively recent origin for Negroes, such as big league ball players and movie, radio, or television performers. There was generally a decrease in the confidence level, however, with increase in age, with low-income girls holding least hopes of success. The discrepancy between early goals and later achievement attests not only to cultural controls which interfere with strivings but also to psychological omissions in training which result in timorous fibers in character structure and lack of strength in confronting barriers. It is conceivable, of course, that some individuals use the excuse of social restraints as a way of

[44] M. Radke and H. Trager, "Children's Perceptions of the Social Roles of Negroes and Whites," *Journal of Psychology*, XXIX (1950), pp. 3-33.

[45] P. F. Lawrence, "Vocational Aspirations of Negro Youth in California," *Journal of Negro Education*, XVI (1950), pp. 47-56.

[46] R. M. Goff, "The Influence of Rejection on Aspiration Levels of Minority Group Children," *Journal of Experimental Education*, XXIII (1954), pp. 179-183.

escape from serious endeavor. Incidentally, the study mentioned earlier that concerned emotional difficulties of Negro children, and the study by Trent, agree with the above findings in pointing to the greater sensitivity of girls to social pressures and to their tendency toward self-rejection.

McNeil and Easton,[47] presenting research on the urban Negro, speak of the interaction of fixed status and free competition. "Fixed status places the role of the Negro in certain spheres of social life; competition allows him to widen the area in which he participates." Participation is one avenue toward integration. Widened opportunities develop feelings of belonging and acceptance, and these advance reactions of personal worth.

It is clear that the pattern of segregation has resulted in in-group status roles which serve either to augment or further to depress feelings of esteem. In some instances, members of the small minority of the upper class find compensatory relief in roles of importance within the group and, from this status, reject lower-class members. Those at the bottom, suffering a two-fold rejection are often as distrustful and suspicious of the sincerity of the upper-class Negroes as they are of whites. The degree of reward or felt satisfaction accruing from top in-group status not only determines the power of the impact of rejection of the larger world, it is also a factor determining which role is most functional in total personality. Complete satisfaction may result in an insular personality which rejects integration. This will occur most likely, however, for a person in conflict, his security in one area being threatened by his lack of confidence in handling the other.

Culturally approved or assigned tasks reflect society's image and evaluation of specific group members. These evaluations projected in behavior are then internalized by the members themselves. They come to see themselves as the culture sees them, depending on their individual strengths. Some persons accept stereotyped notions of themselves; others reject them. Whatever the reaction, it becomes a part of the intricate complex of feelings and of one's final judgment of worth of self.

[47] E. O. McNeil and H. R. Easton, "Research on the Urban Negro," *American Journal of Sociology*, XLVII (1941), pp. 176-183.

V. Feelings, Attitudes, and Responses

It is evident from the preceding exploration that the Negro grows up in a symbolic world. This is perceived in terms of early learnings and meanings that are abstracted from continuous experiencing of a specific nature; learnings which involve group identification, status position, and meanings of cultural features. In a survey of opinions of social scientists[48] on the psychological effects of segregation, ninety percent agreed the effects were detrimental. Consequences by way of inferiority feelings, including shame and embarrassment and the negative emotions of hostility and fear, are revealed in a series of studies on the subject. McLean[49] gave great weight to the presence of fear, noting that psychoanalysis of the Negro revealed a deep unconscious fear of the white man and associated guilt feelings, which resulted in deprecating feelings of self-loathing and self-hate. Such intensity in self-reference, as stated in this view, may be appropriate to disturbed individuals; it would be fallacious, however, as a generalization applied to Negroes as a whole.

Johnson[50] found an absence of emotional security, resulting mainly from conflicts in areas of status and occupation, in his investigation of the effects of adolescents of growing up in the South. Atwood, Wyatt, and Davis[51] found economic status to result in a corroding frustration which penetrated, in a variety of ways, all aspects of living. Frazier points out that the comparative isolation of the Negro youth because of his restricted participation in the larger community has an influence on attitudes and behavior. The home becomes a focal point and, accordingly, personality is considered a response to the family situation. Davis and Dollard[52]

[48] M. Deutcher and I. Chein, "The Psychological Effects of Enforced Segregation, A Survey of Social Scientists Opinion," Journal of Psychology, XXVI (1948), pp. 259-287.
[49] H. V. McLean, "The Emotional Health of Negroes," Journal of Negro Education, XVIII (1949), pp. 283-290.
[50] Charles S. Johnson, Growing Up in the Black Belt, Washington, D. C.: American Council on Education, 1941.
[51] J. H. Atwood, D. W. Wyatt, and V. J. Davis, Thus Be Their Destiny, Washington, D. C.: American Council on Education, 1941.
[52] Allison Davis and John Dollard, Children of Bondage, Washington, D. C.: American Council on Education, 1940.

point to the rise of patterns of aggression. While granting, as earlier mentioned, significance to factors of caste, class controls make the greatest impact on personality development. The four preceding studies were concerned with youth in that stage of development where the normal growth process elicits conflict patterns. Additional tensions at this stage of development accentuate biological, emotional, and social problems and this is of crucial importance in terms of later adjustment.

The following abbreviated account is illustrative of cultural influences on intra-family relationships and subsequent feeling reactions.

Ten year old Ted was brought to a behavior clinic by his mother, who reported concern over his hostile, aggressive behavior toward all family members and his threat of committing suicide. Ted was medium brown, as was his mother. His younger brother was light. The father, the least Negroid in appearance, was obsessed with the idea of the possibility of white parentage. The mother had finished college, but the college career of the highly ambitious father was interrupted by the pregnancy of the young woman he later married. Interviews with the father centered, of his own accord, mainly around the subject of "passing" for white. "I try to be certain when I cross the line. I can't stand a rebuff. It makes me sick. Ice picks start jabbing at my heart. I have to go to bed because I'm really downright sick." When the mother accompanied him down town, she walked accommodatingly two blocks behind. When at home, she dutifully bathed him and catered to his every wish. The light son, William, was referred to as "my heart." Of Ted the father stated, "He has his limitations, he's just normal, not even above average. I'm frightened, really frightened. He makes me think of the ole Negro in the South who just sits on a box with his feet dangling down, doing nothing. He just can't do much. I don't think he'll ever amount to much." The mother, sharing the father's lack of enthusiasm, elaborated on the contrast between the two children, and high-lighted the intelligence and virtues of the younger child. Meanwhile, Ted spent his time going about chanting, "Everybody hates me. Everybody hates me. I wish I was dead." Later he changed to, "I hate William. I hate William. I wish he was six feet under."

The antecedent of the attitudes and behavior observed in the child, of course, was the dominant white world. The more decisive factor was the immediate home. The father attempted an unrealistic escape from a biological reality—the self which was Negro. He broke before the pull of the culture which designated him as both white and non-white, according to the situation in which he was functioning, but which punished him for either role. Restrictive measures placed on him as Negro were interpreted as punitive. When he escaped through "passing" or crossing the caste line, realization that the new world was fictional not only sharpened the prick of reality, but generated a constant fear of unexpected exposure. When goal-directed sequences were threatened, that is, when there was interference in achieving white status, negative emotions and concomitant physiological reactions followed. Emotional dangling and insecurity were partially compensated for through status demands in the home—particularly in requirements of the mother. The affectional needs of Ted were ignored and, in fact, there was probably an inability to meet them. The father stated, "I'm a very inadequate father. I'm a much better husband and that's the role I prefer."

The mother, born into a caste arrangement from which she could not escape, held the same goals, nevertheless, as her husband by way of status and prestige. The need of a feeling of worth of self was heightened by her awareness of her husband's depreciation of the Negro group. The need for her husband's affection induced the necessity of catering to his whims and desires and identifying with his choices. The end result was her rejection of the child toward whom the father evinced no paternal feeling.

The conscious or unconscious assignment of Ted to a subordinate position naturally resulted in feelings of rejection on his part. Inter-group conflicts, reported by him, created further sensitivity to color meaning. The arrival of a light-skinned brother did nothing to help him in his strivings for self-esteem. The family structure for him was reduced to a mere proximity of people who offered no satisfactions or rewards and from whom he wished to escape. The result of the total situation was family psychological disunity and maladaptive behavior on the part of the child. The entire situation was grounded in the fact that color makes a difference in feelings and reactions.

In some cases, responses are channeled in the form of in-group aggression and crime. Moses,[53] studying differentials between Negro and white crime rates in Baltimore, for example, found felony and juvenile delinquency rates markedly higher for Negro areas. All murder and manslaughter offenses during a given period were committed by Negroes. "Due to low socio-economic status accentuated by racial proscription, Negroes do not have freedom of wholesale expression comparable to that of a similarly situated white group." This situation is prevalent generally. It is probable that much in-group aggression is misdirected hostility, a blind striking back at available scapegoats in the face of an inability to handle the larger white world.

Compensatory behavior is further seen in obvious display of material objects and varying forms of out-group aggression. A New York columnist facetiously stated there were more Cadillacs in one square block in Harlem than in any other square mile in the world. The roar of a high-powered car, with muffler deliberately bent to increase the fractious noises, and the handling of brakes so as to screech to a halt at busy intersections, are but subtle methods of indicating equality, or even superiority, in this area of ownership and control. Power is demonstrated over a mechanical aspect of the environment, at least. While there may be relief in abandonment and release of aggressive drives, and temporary bolstering of the ego in an assumed position of importance, little disguise is thus effected of the deep-seated feelings of inferiority. The practical realist finds the behavior childish. The student of human behavior sees it as an immature pattern of adjustment; nevertheless, he understands the underlying motives.

The pervasive influence of class on the nature of responses is again noticeable. Yet it would be an error to interpret behavior in the light of one's particular position, to ignore the fact that values and standards are relative, and to condemn individuals for techniques of adjustment which may be the best they can devise with the knowledge and aids available to them. The lower-class Negro

[53] Earl R. Moses, "Differentials in Crime Rates Between Negroes and Whites Based on Comparisons of Four Socio-economically Equated Areas," *American Sociological Review*, XII (1947), pp. 411-420.

whose image of himself is in a descendent position to all others seeks only to exist. He is passive toward wider social goals and uses aggressive defenses toward a hostile world. Occasionally, one endowed with the virtues of humor gets rid of his hostility through good-natured attacks, as did the cook who told her employer with a half chuckle, "You all supposed to be good folks and keep the Commandments, but the Lord say six days you work, and the seventh, ain't no work. But I works every day and Sunday too, and that ain't right." When the employer left, she added, "Don't come throwing slop in my face and call it water." When time off for church was granted, she calmly smiled, "Thank you Jesus."

Middle- and upper-class individuals are sensitive to their position in the wider social hierarchy; yet, facing the problems inherent in limited participation and incomplete expression, they continue to strive for the attainment of larger cultural values.

The group studies reported here give general trends. All along the continuum individual reactions toward the self determine the designation of goals and the extent of continued push toward the achievement of them. Motivation may stem from feelings of self-confidence and esteem or may be compensatory simply, arising from felt inadequacies.

VI. Is There a Negro Personality?

Kardiner and Oversey,[54] in an extended treatise on the Negro, explain that continuous childhood frustration, plus pressures to adapt to a white culture, coupled with an inability to achieve standards, result in personality which, among other things, is devoid of confidence in human relations. It reflects a loss of efficiency, also, by virtue of its preoccupation with factors that have a prior claim to attention. These investigators believe there is a basic Negro personality, which is a caricature of the corresponding white personality. Realistically, of course, a liberal person or a bigot may be either black or white and, whichever is represented, we assume similarity in attitudes and action patterns. Certain feeling reactions, such as inferiority, and certain impulses toward the environment,

[54] A. Kardiner and L. Oversey, *op. cit.*

such as hostility, which end in response patterns of withdrawal, avoidance, or aggression may appear, if it is true, more frequently within the Negro, than within the white, group. Caste arrangements are not without effect. If, however, we use this basis to refer to a unit personality which is Negro (this may not have been the intent of the authors) there is the implicit assumption that expressed behavior is a reflection of personality.

Behavior may or may not with certainty reflect an inner self. It may be an accommodation to the particular field of operation. The northern-born and reared Negro, when in the South, conforms with the controls operative at the moment, but in the more permissive environment of the North the same individual is more free to behave in terms of the dictates of the true self-system. He may then be very unlike his southern-born counterpart who occupies the same status position. Sullivan refers to learned accommodations in behavior as the sub-personality. That is, there is an adjustment to the assumed demands of a specific group. Such adjustment may demand that consciously held convictions be held in temporary abeyance. Further, since there are greater class differences within the group than there are caste differences between comparable groups, reference to a generalized Negro personality is questionable.

VII. EDUCATIONAL SIGNIFICANCE OF THE FINDINGS

A social order which breaks the spirit and trammels the selfhood of any segment of its population implies that those so treated have nothing to contribute to its greater good and strength. The present movement toward modifications of pressures and reforms in antisocial practices promises control over previous circumstances which prevented all citizens from enjoying a full measure of democratic participation. The movement to integrate all pupils in public schools is a test of the concreteness of the theory we have espoused. If the test is met, democratic sharing, planning, and participation in purposeful classroom activities on the part of white and Negro children will become instruments for the development on the part of all of respectability of self and concern for the welfare of others.

Students of education, working within the framework of scientific method, have made certain assumptions concerning the nature of the organism, the learning process, and the nature of society. One assumption is that passing on of the cultural heritage, diffusion of knowledge, and the development of tools for clear communication will result in personal power and efficiency in interpersonal relationships. Realization of the goal is dependent upon capacity to profit from experiences designed to advance it. Many Negro children, however, are early subjected to traumatic emotional upsets by virtue of illegitimate birth and subsequent rejections, exposures to adult insensitivity to cultural mores, and growth in homes harassed by financial insecurities and attending deprivations. Their motivation toward the acquisition of prescribed learning is dulled; the demarcation between content of school subjects and actualities of personal pressures are too wide.

A slow learning child may or may not be retarded, just as a mentally ill person may be bright or dull. Many children work below their capacity because of distracting, often soul-breaking, experiences for which no relief has been granted. Marie, for instance, a fifteen-year-old girl, stuffed into a third-grade seat in a school located near a migrant camp area, sat motionless, listlessly gazing out of the window. The night before, her drunken father had kicked her pregnant mother to death and that morning had attempted to rape her on the front porch. Psychopathic personalities are privileged with fatherhood, but unless discovered, no defenses are developed against the anxieties and tragedies which they mobilize. School was the only refuge for the hapless girl. Yet the teacher went blithely on with abstract subject matter, later revealing no knowledge of social agencies she might contact nor even showing an interest in what would happen to the girl at the close of the school day. Such instances, equally tragic, could be multiplied. What all would reveal, however, is that neglect of the fundamental features of growth and of social and emotional problems, together with the setting of goals unrelated to basic pupil needs, result in an unhealthy psychological state, resistance to learning, and a conflict in pupil-pupil, as well as in teacher-pupil, relationships. The unwitting behavior of middle-class teachers in imposing their standards on lower-class children, who make up the bulk of the public school population, is clearly presented by Davis.

This does not suggest that we ignore the importance of diligence in the performance of tasks within the range of individual capacity. Mastery of abstract symbols and successful transformation of the environment through manipulation of aspects of the physical world, where appropriate to the developmental levels of children, and when congruent with their interests, nurtures a feeling of confidence in self. If we learn what we live, mastery of problems through attention to details, which makes for thoroughness of the whole, engenders a feeling of equality with situations. The Negro child, in particular, should be helped to realize his potentialities for the development of insights and understandings. He is in need of the support which may thus be given to a self that may, otherwise, too easily evolve into a suppressed promise of "what might have been."

A second assumption is that the biological basis which makes learning possible also provides for adaptation to change as experience warrants. The work of Axline[55] points to change in attitudes and behavior through social interaction in play sessions. In a group which included Negro, Jewish, and white children, an atmosphere was provided which permitted free expression of feelings and in which consequences of behavior were accepted as personal responsibilities. Changes in behavior in the form of respect for individuals as persons were noted. The permissive atmosphere provided opportunities for social learning that could not be achieved under conditions of repression and undue constraint. Unfortunately, not all teachers are secure enough themselves to follow the leads of the psychology they know. In some settings, therefore, rather tight initial control, moving to a gradual lessening of routine disciplines, may be necessary. However achieved, freedom within rules provides means for the growing individual to learn for himself the meanings of the language of the democratic creed.

The desirable teacher not only uses the classroom and recreation centers as laboratories for the study of behavior, he makes a constant appraisal of his relationship with pupils, also. Friendly communication, given by way of gesture, if not verbalization, and

[55] V. Axline, "Play Therapy and Race Conflict in Young Children," *Journal of Abnormal Psychology*, XLIII (1948), pp. 300-310.

exemplification of good will contribute substantially in changing aggressive, antagonistic behavior, in which bigotry and unkindness are rooted, to behavior that is outgoing and trustful of others. Sympathy, understanding, friendliness, are learned more from example than from maxim and command.

A third assumption is that critical thinking and values can be taught. A corollary is that reason should control human behavior and social action. Despite the most careful research, attention to truth, and accuracy in subject content, there yet remain bright people who retain the prerogative of emotionalized attitudes and who see as right social inequalities that are based on such abstractions as skin color and historical status. Not all Southerners, not even all political leaders of the South, are dull.

Democratic behavior does need the force of intelligence. But it needs more. Facts in themselves do not bring release from human tensions nor do they fulfill felt needs. Since social arrangements are as much a product of individuals as individuals are a product of society, it is important to consider the totality of factors which interfere with the emergence of democratic attitudes and practices. Critical thinking and reasoning on social issues are functional in social action and betterment when they are congenial to the total complex of the personality. Stereotypes and emotionalized, irrational attitudes control human behavior when they serve the purpose of satisfying psychological needs. Verbalization, the printed page, even well-planned experiences do not necessarily lift the individual to a sense of human values. A criticism of the Lewin study on the influence of various types of leadership is that it does not go far enough. After discerning group behavior which followed each type of leader—authoritarian, *laissez-faire,* democratic—inter-group interaction was not reported. Democratic members, however, were noted to have been hostile on some occasions toward members of other groups, as were those who had not had the "democratic" exposure. Emotional reconditioning, more easily attained when there is intelligent understanding of basic causes of reactions, is imperative.

Along with experience, there must be continuous appraisal of interpersonal relationships within the total situation so that insights may be gained into personal inner forces active in determining the nature of relationships. Critical observation and evaluation will disclose the acceptance of facts and knowledge as these arise and function in the context of living.

A fourth assumption is that continuous reevaluation of experiences and cooperative, intelligent planning in terms of the democratic ideal will eventuate in the good life for all. Bode[56] states, "The school is peculiarly the institution in which democracy becomes conscious of itself." It is also an institution which, by virtue of this consciousness, becomes critical of itself. If democracy is a distinctive way of life, if things learned "must be translated into terms of emotion and conduct if they are significant," the school must exemplify what it teaches. The Supreme Court decision in 1954 repudiated the fallacy that democracy can be taught in segregated settings.

In addition to present objectives, education should turn attention to the building of psychological strength—preventive therapy—in order to offset human entanglements. This need should have been apparent throughout this discussion. The roots of democracy spring from an inner potential; the potential of a congenial outgoingness to an ever-widening circle of persons. Such a potential emerges in response to the human environment which nurtures it and, paradoxically, is embedded in the same raw material from which aggression and hatred spring. The challenge before the school is to devise the best means of developing those latent qualities for decency, which if unawakened, remain doomed to obscurity.

The continuing task of education, then, is the encouragement of social emancipation, the restoration from morbidity of thought which yields to bigotry, and the advancement of liberalism as decreed by law that has as its sustaining ground the Constitution of our country.

[56] Boyd H. Bode, *Democracy As A Way of Life*, New York: Macmillan and Company, 1939.

PART II

THE PROBLEM

V

Education and Social Relationships in a Democracy

H. Gordon Hullfish
Professor of Education
Ohio State University

EDUCATIONAL institutions come into being because adults value some gains in knowledge and certain principles of social relationships sufficiently to desire their perpetuation. In turn, the individual comes into whatever degree of humanity he eventually possesses because of this concern. Thus it is that education, as Ralph Barton Perry has said, "is the cultural process by which successive generations of men take their places in history."[1]

Education, both informal and formal, is in the business of transmission from the outset, a fact that has misled some men of good will. They have equated education with the sole task of transmitting a selected portion of the past to advance their values. What happens when men of ill will, totalitarians and dictators, for instance, write the same equation, reveals the inadequacy of this conception. Such men attempt to hold their tailor-made culture firm, denying the legitimacy of that which envisages change, making the limits of their own vision the limit of growth for the individual citizen. This is a torturing process. It stunts the growth both of the

[1] Ralph B. Perry, *Realms of Value*, Cambridge: Harvard University Press, 1954, p. 411.

culture and of the individual citizens who, if they were but free of restriction, would, through their participation in the going culture, be steadily involved in the redesigning of its patterns. Education, in short, where men are more than slaves who do their master's bidding, is always involved in a task which reaches beyond transmission.

What is transmitted, of course, does establish a relationship to the past. But this will not be a passive relationship where individuals are free from the growth-denying forms imposed by the authoritarian. The past, functioning within the present to help the individual gain his relationships to a culture into which he must be initiated if he is to survive at all, serves as an instrument by which a future is fashioned. And in a democracy each individual is a potential contributor to the shape of things to come. Perry, continuing with his conception of education, properly suggests that the purpose of education has a three-fold character, "inheritance, participation, and contribution."[2] The future, if no torturing hand shapes it, will never be a mere duplication of the past. In the very act of learning, the individual is engaged, as John Dewey pointed out, in a "reconstruction or reorganization of experience which adds to the meaning of experience, and which increases ability to direct the course of subsequent experience."[3] Men do "take their places in history" and, if not moved there by an arbitrary authority which in the act denies them the opportunity to become fully human, they help create the places into which they move. "Because the future is only partially and uncertainly predictable, and because human faculties are inventive and resourceful," Perry contends that "education for the future implies education for a future which is of man's own making. This has been held to be the essentially democratic and American idea of education. . . ."[4]

One reason American education has seemed to many critics to have developed without direction is clear. It has developed in response to the need of a culture that has itself been seeking its di-

[2] *Ibid.*, p. 411.
[3] John Dewey, *Democracy and Education*, New York: Macmillan Company, 1916, pp. 89-90.
[4] Perry, *op. cit.*, p. 412.

rection amid a flow of change which has not only been continuous but which has been accelerating progressively. This fact neither gives warrant to the assumption that education may go forward without direction nor priority to the dogmatists who may wish to shape it to serve their selfish ends. What it does do is to give the educators of a democracy a two-fold responsibility. In the midst of change which foreshadows no firm ending they must find what it is that democracy today needs in its citizens to continue as a social conception worthy of devoted and loyal service by intelligent and sensitive men. Further, they must relate themselves to the culture in such educative ways that citizens generally are engaged in the same quest and approve of a public educational system which helps carry it forward. The problem before them is a larger one than that of selecting a "right content," important as content will always be, and of deciding upon "the right methods," necessary as it is to use the best that man knows at any given moment as to how learning occurs and, thus, to select means that are consistent with the ends of the process. The problem, thrust to the fore as it has been by the unanticipated successes of the totalitarians, is nothing less than the moral one of organizing an education that will serve all men equally and lead them to be sensitive to the interests of all with whom they build a common life. Our present moral imperative is the creation of an education that is openly dedicated to the advancement of the vision of a free life which all men, without regard to past or present conditions of birth or servitude, may share. No view less generous is good enough to serve humankind.

There are those who argue that democracy has not been achieved and who, in consequence, challenge those who write as if they were describing reality. Thus a thoughtful Negro may ask, "How am I to be a free man in a segregated society?" Others, admitting the existence of the democratic aspiration and, indeed, liking it, find no way in which to support the claim that it is better than other social forms man has thus far devised. Thus one of philosophic inclination, who, though he may live by the compulsion of his preference for democracy and be ready to fight in support of it, may nevertheless conclude that all which is at issue is a matter of faith, that no evidential case can be made out to give warrant to his choice.

Each group is right, though only partially so. The Negro cannot be free in a segregated society. But, and I say this with full recognition of the depth of personal frustration that underlies his question, he does not live in one. He is both given opportunities and denied them, as are other men—with the denials inexcusable in every instance. Yet the fact that the question may be raised (and to this should be added the further fact that the consciences of others will feel its hurtful lash) is evidence that our social relationships may not be described without qualification. Segregation there is, but there is also opportunity, including the opportunity to work for its elimination. What is overlooked in the question (and why should it not be by one who, though ready and anxious to participate with other free men in the fulfilling experience of sharing common responsibilities, is not always permitted to do so?) is that no blueprint exists to tell those who work to create democracy when the state of completion is at hand. This aspiration, like others, may flourish or decline. The proper query to put is as to the direction its movement takes within our complex social arrangements. On this score, the succeeding decisions of the United States Supreme Court reveal both movement and acceleration, as these decisions relate to segregation in particular human activities and in specific localities.[5]

In like manner, the other group is thwarted because it, too, wants its standard for judgment complete before it engages in the act of judging. It seeks a norm to use in measuring the "goodness" or "badness" of social relationships that neither springs from these relationships nor is affected by them, a norm it must know it is not to find. Each group, then, in its own way, gets trapped by its reach for completeness, for finality. This obscures, on the one hand, those gains in human relationships man does make and, on the other hand, the quality of the experience the aspiration has made possible.

It is within experience, as they have felt its releasing or restricting effects, that men have formulated the principles of democratic social

[5] Elsewhere in this volume the unanimous decision of the Supreme Court of May 17, 1954, that held segregation by race in the public schools to be illegal, is discussed. The decision did not solve the problem. It gave expression, however, to a running current of public opinion. See Frank P. Graham and Benjamin E. Mays: *Segregation and the Schools*, Public Affairs Pamphlet No. 209, June, 1954.

relationships. For democracy, in essence, is an aspiration (it is always more than a form of government, though the forms of governing bear directly upon its health) which guides men in their effort to create those conditions of social relationships within which men may know themselves to be equally free and free equally to extend the range of their vision. Its work is never done; complete ness is no part of its character; and, significantly for education, its work must be re-done generation by generation. One generation of callous men, or of fearful men, or of angry men, or of power-hungry men could leave the generation to follow with a human heritage so meager that it could not rise to democratic experience within its lifetime. This point is basic to the whole of our educational endeavor; yet, important as it is, we must note that for many, the democratic-denying generation has already arrived. Only where democracy exists in some degree are men now free to engage in the critical examination of the ideas by which their lives are shaped, to work towards the achievement of equality, to participate in building a common life.

We affirm democratic principles today because, in the first instance, we were nurtured where they were nurtured and, in the second instance, because the history written by the affirmations of our forebears has revealed to us that men are more truly men when these principles direct their choices. We believe in democracy because we were born among believers, but, equally, we believe because democracy has shown us in goodly measure what may yet be the character of civilization if we can but lift our eyes, and elevate our habits, to what its principles portend in human decency. It is because the democratic aspiration may answer those who cry, "Show me!" by pointing to the consequences in social relationships that result when its principles are used to explore their humane possibilities that John Dewey undertook to give the reason why we *should prefer* the democratic ideal, in contrast to why it is that we *do prefer* it. The following questions provide his answer. "Can we find any reason that does not ultimately come down to the belief that democratic social arrangements promote a better quality of human experience, one which is more widely accessible and enjoyed, than do non-democratic and anti-democratic forms of social life?

Does not the principle of regard for individual freedom and for decency and kindliness of human relations come back in the end to the conviction that these things are tributary to a higher quality of experience on the part of a greater number than are methods of repression and coercion or force? Is it not the reason for our preference that we believe that mutual consultation and conviction reached through persuasion, make possible a better quality of experience than can otherwise be provided on any wide scale."[6]

"Regard for individual freedom" and for "decency and kindliness of human relations"; belief in "mutual consultation and conviction reached through persuasion"—these are key principles to use in the democratic quest. They have been variously phrased and these phrasings have been caught up in the basic documents upon which our society rests and reflected in the legislation we, the people, have enacted. Each of us may try his hand from time to time at listing the principles we find central to our way of coming at life,[7] hoping thereby to secure for ourselves (and perhaps for others) a deepened understanding of the democratic aspiration. But the point to keep in mind is the nature of the principles, not the order of their listing. They serve, when they retain the elasticity characteristic of a principle and do not harden into dogmatic decrees or sink to the level of uncriticized routines, as the instruments by which we progressively reconstruct our social relationships. They serve us, in short, as the Constitution has served us, as a fount of human wisdom to which we repair to refresh ourselves as we seek anew to keep alive the hope expressed for man's future development by its framers. They serve a responsible and developing intelligence and sensitivity; they do not substitute for them.

It is our belief that we have sufficient evidence to give warrant to our continuing allegiance to these principles. It is our belief, further, that the intrusion into human affairs of Fascist, Nazi, and

[6] John Dewey, *Experience and Education*, New York: Macmillan Company, 1938, pp. 25-26.
[7] The author, for instance, in "The Nature and Function of Democratic Administration," *Democracy in the Administration of Higher Education*, Harper & Brothers, New York, 1950, stressed four principles: the principle of free intelligence, the principle of participation, the principle of individuality, and the principle of cooperation.

Communist have given this warrant further credibility. We come at our conjoint lives, therefore, in terms of what may be properly called democratic assumptions. These have been phrased succinctly by Charles E. Merriam.[8] He has said that the principal assumptions of democracy are:

1. The essential dignity of man, the importance of protecting and cultivating his personality on a fraternal rather than a differential principle, and the elimination of special privileges based upon unwarranted or exaggerated emphasis on the human differentials.

2. Confidence in a constant drive toward the perfectibility of mankind.

3. The assumption that the gains of commonwealth are essentially mass gains and should be diffused as promptly as possible throughout the community without too great delay or too wide a spread in differentials.

4. The desirability of popular decision in the last analysis on basic questions of social direction and policy, and of recognized procedures for the expression of such decisions and their validation in policy.

5. Confidence in the possibility of conscious social change accomplished through the process of consent rather than by methods of violence.

What these add up to in social relationships is a quality of interaction, an essential trust of man by man, which is expressed by the readiness of men to listen to what others have to say, to join with others freely at the points where their minds initially meet, and to share the confidence that their individual and conjoint lives will be enriched as they move beyond what each now comprehends.

Carl L. Becker summed up the principles of democratic social relationships in a simple sentence, saying, "A true democracy is an expression of the idea that men are, or ought to be in some sense, equal."[9] Minority groups suffer no defeating frustration from difference where this idea prevails; society, rather, gains in strength because of the contribution to shared action each group may equally and freely make.

[8] Charles E. Merriam, *The New Democracy and the New Despotism*, New York: McGraw-Hill Book Company, 1939, pp. 11-12.
[9] Carl L. Becker, *Modern History*, New York: Silver, Burdette and Company, 1931, p. 7.

Some years ago Albert Einstein suggested that man had moved beyond an earlier stage in human relationships when it was sentimentally right, at least, to think well of the other fellow, to want to consider him a full member of the human race. His point was that the advent of the A-bomb transformed what had been largely a matter of sentiment into a simple necessity for the survival of all. Since then the A-bomb has been succeeded by the H-bomb and the precarious future of man's hopes, and of man himself, has been made public through the testing of these nuclear devices (as the press releases call them, perhaps to make them less frightening). That men need to think differently of one another than has been their wont, and to act differently towards one another in consequence, is clear enough. The future of civilization ought not to rest on bases of ignorance, prejudice, habit, or misunderstanding. Driven as man may be towards the gaining of security, he can take but a small measure of comfort from his destructive stockpiles, knowing as he does, first, that when one resorts to his stockpile so will another and, second, that such acts and the retaliatory ones that will then follow may leave in their wake little more than remnants of our "stockpiles of security."

Perhaps this is to state the case on the low levels of fear and anxiety, crying calamity when naught but calm is needed. One may be calm in the face of fact, however, and the fact would seem to be that failure in social relationships today may lead to destruction that language has never before been called upon to describe. Immediate transformation of social habit and attitude, therefore, would seem to be the order of the day. But this is not to be, unfortunately, even where the spirit is right. The matter is not this simple.

Time will be required, as it always has been, to make the human gains man needs to make. Fission is not a principle that may be applied to habit, to attitude. What one early learns in the area of social relationships lingers long within behavior patterns. Often, indeed, these learnings undergo a minimum of change despite transformation on the face of experience which would seem to guarantee comparable transformation at its depths. Thus, men of good will may be detoured past the interracial problem by habits that were so fixed prior to a need to reflect upon them that they do not later arise as objects of reflection. As a further complication, some men whose reconstruction has led them to admit intellectually the rightness of the free association of man with man, with none barred on the arbitrary ground of difference in birth, may discover as they try to act in terms of the ideas they have newly gained that they are not up to it. They will find it hard to overcome a feeling that they deal with those who are somehow inferior. Yet it is only as they persist in acting to transform the social relationships they decide to be bad that they may give themselves the chance *to feel differently* about the behavioral consequences of the ideas they have reconstructed. It was within action that the initial feelings arose; it is there they will change.

It is often misleading, and frequently presumptuous, to treat a social problem of this nature in terms of the personal anecdote, seeming to conclude thereby that movement within one's own life may be equated with the movement that should occur within the lives of others. I must confess, however, that reflection upon my own experience, which included no relevant and serious reading until around the time of World War I, continues to provide an occasional luminous spot to enhance my understanding. I was born white and born where this made me privileged. I presume I "knew" Negroes as early as I knew anything. As I grew, I grew into an understanding of my "superiority" to them. Nor was this taught me in any formal sense. I took it on, so to speak, as I took in the food that sustained me; in a real sense, indeed, this attitude did sustain me as my social relationships, and my years, were extended. My "schooling" did nothing to call my "education" into question. I saw no Negroes in school, of course; nor were any problems discussed that could have been designated as "Negro problems." My work experience, which began early and replaced school, continued my education in discrimination. My work was meager in its immediate economic and intellectual returns. It was without limits, however. Obviously, Horatio Alger was white and the opportunity to follow in his footsteps was available to many, also white, of my generation. I understood in a dumb sort of way that this opportunity was not available to the Negro, having somehow learned that he was not basically educable and having observed that he did none of the work of the world (at least my world) an Alger ego would wish to do.

The details of these years are here unimportant (and they are not pretty, in any case). Suffice it to say that I entered an army mobilized for World War I, a war that was to make the world safe for democracy (and this purpose seemed meaningful to me) and was later separated from this army, without having my "education" called into question. It was only later, in a part of the country where the climate of social relationships at least made it possible for all who could enter higher education to enter together, that my attitudes were challenged. For a long time the challenge, though present, was not accepted. A matter of taste, and my habits took care of this, was all that seemed to be at issue. My life was going along progressively, however, in what was becoming an increasingly intellectual atmosphere and old habit, while not at first having to give way, did have to undergo occasional scrutiny. The occasion for what proved to be the critical scrutiny was contact with Boyd H. Bode, in person, and with John Dewey, through his writings. Each man was a philosopher of democracy and each saw in the shared experience necessary to make democracy work the opportunity to provide all men with a larger measure of decent and humane growth. The prospect was an exciting one, since, despite what appears to be a paradox, my "education" had elevated democracy to the status of a directing ideal. Yet my increasing insight and enthusiasm did not at first force me to a recognition that I was denying in one aspect of my social relationships, my attitude towards the Negro, what I affirmed in another, my attitude toward democracy. In time it did and, then, through a fortunate turn in my experience, a turn unplanned, I had the task of straightening out attitudes and beliefs that had previously had their being in separate compartments. It is not unimportant, in connection with the problem of this volume, to note that I had lived quite a few years before this task was recognized.

My experience points to some of the basic facts that bear upon our problem. The habits and attitudes that direct behavior in social relationships are formed early. This fact makes it clear that the task of building habitudes appropriate to democratic life is not primarily a school task. Nothing less than the entire community, as the late Joseph K. Hart always insisted,[10] can do the job required. Further, habits and attitudes are tenacious in character. Nothing short of *transformed action* which leads to their progressive reconstruction will break their power. Evidence as to how this works has come dramatically in recent years from the decision of the owners of professional baseball clubs to use the talents of the Negro player. The riots in the ball parks which many had feared did not occur, the morale of the teams was not lowered, and millions of television viewers have seen again and again that ability and character, not color, have been the test of an individual's opportunity to play. More and more of us now realize, therefore, that while color may often be an identifying symbol it is never by itself an evaluative one. Many schools and colleges could have predicted these consequences for the baseball parks; indeed, the reconstruction in habits and attitudes they have long fostered helped foreshadow this change on a national scale.

Meanwhile, thousands of Negroes, without benefit of television audiences or packed stadia, have moved quietly and effectively into the responsible activities that thoughtful citizens carry on. The services of Ralph Bunche to his nation and to the world, for instance, were related, not to a championship bunting, but to the issue of peace or war. His has been the contribution of a distinguished American to problems in whose solutions his fellow citizens had a vital stake. Finally, as I review my own experience, the simple fact that reconstruction of habit and attitude is possible stands forth. Men need not be forever confined to the limits which the conditions of their birth set down, nor need a culture spin forever on the bottom of a single rut. Reconstruction may just happen, in Topsy fashion to be sure; fortunately, however, the conditions that will accelerate it may be planned.

The fact that the conditions of my life involved me in the self-conscious act of reconciling elements within it that were in conflict, thereby sensitizing me to injustices that had earlier escaped me, has undoubtedly led me to conclude that improvement in racial relationships has been marked. I believe this to be so. I equally

[10] Joseph K. Hart, *Education in the Humane Community*, New York: Harper & Brothers, 1951.

know, however, that what may seem to me to be rapid change must seem to others, those who suffer because their own reconstruction is so often checked awaiting the manner of reconstruction I moved to so slowly, to be a veritable snail's pace. But, rapid or slow, the movement towards the improvement of social relationships, towards the inclusion of all in the responsibly shared concerns of citizens, has been with us since our beginnings. Ideas, as well as men, came to our shores. Improvement, however, is not written in the stars, much as it has been written into our history and is being written into our habits. Yet the gains we have made are not likely to be erased, apart from an atomic erasure that would void all speculation. Arnold J. Toynbee, has suggested that the twentieth century will be remembered 300 years hence as "the first age since the dawn of civilization . . . in which people dared to think it practicable to make the benefits of civilization available for the whole human race." He believes this "new social objective has probably come to stay," that we are now dealing with "a practicable objective instead of a mere utopian dream."[11] Toynbee, in effect, has placed his bet on the continuing spread of decency. It is not a bad bet. The problems which arise in social relationships today do so against a widened and deepened ground of common concerns which our citizens hold and, as Toynbee further suggests, when "once the odious inequality that has hitherto been a distinguishing mark of civilization has ceased to be taken for granted as something inevitable, it becomes inhuman to go on putting up with it—and still more inhuman to try to perpetuate this inequality deliberately."[12]

There is no reason to suppose, of course, even with this bet placed, that further progress will not be resisted, as it has always been resisted. The reaction of certain Southern states, and of some Northern communities, to the decision of the Supreme Court which holds segregation in the public schools to be illegal makes this fact clear. It is still significant, however, that a Southern reaction cannot be described. The South is not all of one piece on this issue. Not all states have reacted with official frenzy and border areas have shown a

---

[11] "Not the Age of Atoms But of Welfare For All," *New York Times Magazine,* (October 21, 1951), p. 15.
[12] *Ibid.,* p. 15.

degree of understanding which may be taken as evidence that the experience of the border has been, and is, an integrating one, even though official pronouncements have often suggested otherwise.

Karl R. Popper has said of philosophy that its rise "Can be interpreted . . . as a reaction to the breakdown of the closed society and its magical beliefs"; that "it is an attempt to replace the lost magical faith by a rational faith"; that it has founded a new tradition, "the tradition of challenging theories and myths and of critically discussing them."[13] In like manner we may say of democracy that its rise can be interpreted as the application of the philosophic spirit to the ways of the market place, where the impingement of man upon man degraded some and elevated others. Progressively the myths which supported the presumed superiority of one set of men over another have exploded, until, at last, man knows that whatever advantage over others he may enjoy (and at all times some men do enjoy certain advantages) is not to be traced to an inherent superiority which the future organization of society should perpetuate. Thus, though we may expect resistance to the continuing amelioration of man's relationship with man, we may anticipate equally that such resistance will help us create the social conditions in which the reconstruction of all relationships may more fruitfully occur.

This conclusion, of course, is predicated on the assumption that we maintain the democratic conditions of conference, consultation, discussion, and compromise in which each man and idea is respected as a potential contributor to the well-being of all; the very conditions, in short, which make for an open society. Resistance which arises as idea challenges idea, with the field of challenge a fair one and with no official dogma on hand to rule on the appropriateness of a given challenge, is a necessary condition to the stimulation of the rigorous thought upon which a lasting reconstruction of social habit and attitude will be built, if it is built at all.

Public education has played, and will continue to play, an important role in easing tensions between majority and minority groups in this country. In the majority of states the public schools have played their role, and met their responsibility, in the area of

[13] Karl R. Popper, *The Open Society and Its Enemies,* Princeton: Princeton University Press, 1950, p. 183.

social relationships *merely by being public,* thus serving as educational centers for all of the children of their communities. As they have, the children, not always of course unaffected by the differences their parents represent, have learned to study together, to plan together, and to play together; and, in the process, they have run the entire range of emotions which arise when young people are thrown together in large numbers. That the consequences of their associations have been generally good would seem to be beyond debate. This is not to say that they are always so, however. Young people can be as ruthless as adults in dealing one with another, especially when their actions ape those of the adults. Hitler youth knew quite well against whom to turn their unreflective hatred.

At its best, the American public school, by the simple act of being public, has encouraged friendliness rather than enmity; has encouraged the blurring of lines of difference, rather than their accentuation. Rabbi Morris N. Kertzer, in a discussion of the factors that have brought about an improvement in Jewish-Christian relations, has said of the American public school system that it is "possibly the single most potent influence for integrating amity."[14] The public school, on this score, is a specialized environment, within which "all of the children of all of the people" may learn to respect one another as they progressively build a sense of togetherness. All parochial movements in education, so far as democratic social relationships are concerned, should be measured by the contribution they make to amity within the nation. The only cure for whatever shortage there may be in public education is that its public character be extended.

In some of our states, of course, public education has been divisive, keeping the children of some citizens from associating in schools with the children of other citizens. In all fairness it must be said that in other states the private school has frequently served the same purpose. The simple fact is, of course, as these movements reveal, that the education of our children in social relationships is dependent upon much more than the schooling we may provide them, public or otherwise. The community sets the basic educational

[14] Morris N. Kertzer, *What Is a Jew,* Cleveland: World Publishing Company, 1953, p. 197.

pattern and, in doing so, may off-set the patterns which concern the schools. Bronislaw Malinowski, noting the accepted fact that democracy "lives and thrives by the principle of universal education," adds significantly: "It is clear . . . that as long as we have a discriminative birthright and a discrimination in citizenship, independently of the level of education, the freedom through education does not exist."[15] Where public attitudes of discrimination are dominant within a community individual schools are unable to do one aspect of their proper work. There is no final escape from this. The way a public thinks and feels does have meaning for a public school. Yet we need not accept this fact as the determining factor in the shaping of our educational thinking. Schools of the nation share the common responsibility of preparing citizens who can carry forward the heritage of free men with more of intelligence than did their forebears, as the parents of present-day children now carry on farming and manufacture more intelligently and effectively than did their parents. Each school must learn to help the other help its public comprehend the meaning of the democratic aspiration so that all citizens may be free citizens, so that equality in citizenship may be a fact within all lives and not merely a promise which some are not to realize.

In the long run our public schools will make a major contribution to the social relationships existing between the majority and minority groups of the country by being, as suggested above, steadily more *public*. But their contribution will be enlarged when in their central purpose they reveal a devotion to the achievement of as high a level of intellectual development as their ingenuity permits, for, as Irwin Edman put it, "The habits essential to intellectual freedom must be the central business of education."[16] To bring all of the children of all of the people together in a common educational undertaking is a social achievement of proportions, as history reveals. This is but a first step, however. We may bring children together to indoctrinate them in the ways of their elders, to tie the

[15] Bronislaw Malinowski, *Freedom and Civilization*, New York: Roy Publishers, 1944, p. 148.
[16] Irwin Edman, *Fountainheads of Freedom*, New York: Reynal and Hitchcock, 1941, p. 189.

strings of habit which guarantee their later smooth functioning as social puppets. We may bring them together, on the other hand, in order that each may grow to the limit of his intellectual capacity and that, together, they may grow continuously in their grasp of the humane implications of sharing ideas one with the other. This is the distinctive pattern of a democratic education.

Such an education will respect all individuals as potential citizens who may later share creatively in developing the social conditions that permit generations yet to come to achieve freedom within their lives in ever increased measures. It will also respect knowledge as this contributes to the shaping of such citizens. It is here, in fact, that we find a test for selecting knowledge for the teaching situation: that it enter functionally into the lives of those who learn, directing thereby the reconstruction of their experience. Our schools, then, will be involved at one and the same time in *the dual task of personalizing and socializing education.* In order to insure the effort which those who are to learn must exercise the teacher will need to reach or to excite the interest of the student. An effective education will be personalized necessarily, since it is within the experience of the student that the source of interest is to be found. Mere excursions through textbooks or mere recitals of memorized fact will not touch the individual as a person, a person of interests and concerns who is in need of knowledge in order to pursue and evaluate these more effectively. Teaching will turn primarily, therefore, upon meaning: the meaning of fact and of situation; the meaning of one choice rather than another; the meaning of past act and idea as these are reviewed within the present and as they imply consequences for the future. Thus, both because individuals will be involved in the learning situation as interested and concerned individuals and because the emphasis upon meaning will make a consideration of the social significance of decisions that arise as study goes forward a part of the learning, the personalization and the socialization of education may be realized in one and the same process. The one is not a purpose to be added to the other. "Habits of intellectual freedom" are habits that are directive within the lives of individuals; equally, they are habits shared by individuals because their meaning for both individual and social growth has been experienced as they were formed.

It will be no simple matter to create an educational situation which, in all of its parts, will advance the quality of social relationships our world now needs. Those to whom the educational responsibility is formally given, the school people, must work in close relationship to the overtones of the culture. Moreover, they are themselves products of the culture they serve and it is to be expected that whatever quality of social relationships their portion of the culture values will seem right to them. Some may see no reason to re-examine their values. Many are restive, however, aware of the need to square action with commitment. Having worked more and more with all of the children of the community, they have realized that none have a priority on intelligence or character, that all contribute to the enrichment of the common life of the school in unique and personal ways. They are discovering in school, in short, what others have discovered in offices and in unions, in stores and in shops, in the armed forces and in churches—indeed, in the whole range of human affairs. Thus it is, in school and out, that citizens are finding out that to take seriously the democratic principles they have cherished, even when they but vaguely comprehend them, is to add to the enhancement of life for all. Education may accelerate this process of self-examination where it is called for and, through the emphases suggested above, prepare the habits which will make the process a normal one in the lives of future citizens. It may, yet old habit and custom will not readily stand aside. We have moved to where we are, however, over roads that were rough and often uninviting, and against the roadblocks that old habit and custom have so assiduously fashioned.

The future will surely be different from the past but no future now envisioned suggests that the citizens of the free world can be anything less than unremitting in their efforts to keep their heritage a vital force in the lives of all. When it is blocked off from giving meaning to the lives of some, there is the always present danger that it may finally give meaning to the lives of none. Mr. Toynbee's bet is a good one, but only as those who are free to try "to make the benefits of civilization available for the whole human race" endeavor constantly to free more and more men for responsible participation in the undertaking. "We have advanced far enough," said John Dewey in 1939, "to say that democracy is a way of life.

We have yet to realize that it is a way of personal life and one which provides a moral standard for personal conduct."[17]

As we advance further we shall see that, basically, *democracy is a way of coming at life*. It is not a formula which determines the specific content of habit or attitude. It is not a formula which gives both individuals and schools a "right" answer for each situation. We need here only to recall that the principles of democratic social relationships are instruments we may use in each situation to find out what the "right" in a given set of human relationships should be. Democracy is not a completed conception and, for this reason, there is a sense in which it is not a way of life at all. Ways of living one with another democratically do emerge, however, as in our approaches to life, we use with understanding the principles free men have found good. When we come at life in these terms, we find our social relationships permeated by an ever-present sense that the lives of all are progressively enriched as men learn to link arms more freely and firmly in the quest for a shared humaneness. Thus we may move from what we know to be good to what our vision promises shall be ever better.

[17] John Dewey, *Freedom and Culture*, New York: G. P. Putnam's Sons, 1939, p. 130.

VI

Problems in the Achievement of Adequate Educational Opportunity

Charles H. Thompson
Dean, Graduate School
Howard University

It is not the purpose of this chapter to discuss the general problem of providing adequate educational opportunities in a democracy.[1] Our discussion, rather, will limit itself to the problems which the American Negro faces. It must be recognized, however, that the special problem confronted by the Negro in his attempt to obtain adequate educational opportunity is conditioned by the progress which has, or has not, been made in solving the larger problem of equality of educational opportunity in the country as a whole.

It is assumed for the purposes of this discussion that the minimum goal set by the President's Commission on Higher Education, namely, a high school education for all normal youth, is an acceptable and valid minimum objective.[2] Also accepted as valid is the

[1] Although statistics from the 1960 Census and 1958-1960 Biennial Survey of Education were not available at the time this manuscript went to press, interim estimates indicate a measure of improvement in the situation during the past decade. According to some of these estimates, by 1956 approximately 85 percent of the 14-17 age-group were enrolled in secondary school, and 32 percent of the 18-21 age-group were enrolled in college. It is probable that each of these percentages has risen several points by 1960. In spite of these shifts, the discrepancies between ideals and actualities noted in the text still exist.—Editor.

[2] The President's Commission on Higher Education, *Higher Education for American Democracy*, 1947, Vol. I, p. 37.

principle that higher educational opportunity should be limited only by individual capacity and the needs of our society in general. The Commission estimates that 49 percent of our population has the mental ability to complete two years of college and at least 32 percent is able to achieve "an advanced liberal or specialized professional education."[3]

INEQUITIES IN EDUCATIONAL OPPORTUNITY

It is probably unnecessary to observe in any detail that educational opportunity in the United States, as reflected by school enrollment, has not reached these minimum goals. In 1952, three-fourths of the high school population (ages 14-17) were enrolled in high school but less than two-thirds of them were graduated.[4] We have not yet approximated a median of 14 years of schooling for the population as a whole, nor four years or more of college and professional work for the upper third of the population. According to the 1950 Census, the median years of schooling completed by those in the age group 18 to 24 was approximately 12 years, and for the population 25 years and older 9.3 years.[5] Equally important is the fact that the educational attainment of the population varied according to the section of the country, and according to urban or rural residence. In the North and West, the educational attainment of the population was one to two years higher than the attainment of native whites in the South; and a similar higher educational attainment was found in the populations living in urban areas as contrasted with those living in rural areas.

One of the major causes of these inequalities is the fact that the public school system in this country is not one unified system but some 50 or more independent school systems, supported and controlled by the individual states and their minor sub-divisions. As a consequence of this decentralized support and control, there are

[3] *Ibid.*, p. 41.

[4] *Statistics of Public Secondary Day Schools, 1951-1952.* Biennial Survey of Education, 1950-1952, chap. 5, p. 7.

[5] U.S. Bureau of the Census, *U.S. Census of Population*, 1950, Vol. IV, Special Reports, part 5, chap. B, Education. Table 5.

wide variations in ability and willingness to support public education. Moreover, it frequently occurs that the states with the largest number of children to be educated have less money for that purpose. California, for example, has 4.5 times as much wealth behind each educable person as Mississippi, and New York has four times as much. Within any one state, there may exist the same sort of variation between counties and other administrative school divisions. Thus, irrespective of race, opportunity to obtain education is dependent upon the section of the country in which one lives, the state in that section, and the county or school district in that state.

In general, the Southern section of the country has relatively more children to be educated and less money with which to educate them. Unfortunately, two-thirds of the Negro population live in this section. Even if the ten million Negro residents in the South were white, they would still have considerably less educational opportunity than people living in the North and West.

A second major cause of disparity in educational attainment is the fact that educational opportunity is conditioned by the economic level of one's parents. Numerous studies have been made in the past 20 years which indicate that there is a high correlation between family occupation and income and the amount of schooling which children obtain. Summarizing a few of the results of these studies, Witmer and Kotinsky[6] noted: "Parents in the upper-income group in small cities in New England, the South and the Middle West send nearly all their children through high school and about 90 per cent of them to college. In the middle-income group, when these surveys were made, about 60 per cent of the children finished high school, but only 15 per cent went to college, while in the lower-income group only 30 per cent graduated from high school, and only one in twenty went to college."

The high correlation between family income and educational opportunity as measured by school attainment is further affected by the fact that the families with the largest number of children frequently come from the lowest income groups. In 1952, families

6 Helen L. Witmer and Ruth Kotinsky (eds.), *Personality in the Making*, New York: Harper & Brothers, 1952, pp. 116-117.

with one or two children had a median income of over a thousand dollars more than families with five or more children.[7] This phenomenon is subject to regional variations, the South representing the area with the largest proportion of families with low incomes and a large number of children. Since Negroes are so concentrated in this region, their educational opportunity would be affected by this factor to a greater extent than that of persons living in other sections of the country.

The basic problem which the Negro faces in his effort to secure "adequate" educational opportunity is not due entirely to the fact that he lives for the most part in the poorest section of the country. He is thrice penalized: first, for living in too large numbers in the wrong section of the country; second, for belonging to the poorest economic class; and third, for belonging to the wrong race. For the historical reasons sketched in Chapter I, the Negro too often has been relegated to an inferior position in the American social order primarily because he is a Negro. And this inferior status has militated against his obtaining as adequate an educational opportunity as the majority of the population.

THE EDUCATIONAL ATTAINMENT OF THE NEGRO POPULATION

The educational attainment of the Negro population in the United States is strikingly below that of the population as a whole. According to the 1950 census,[8] the median number of years schooling completed by the Negro population 25 years old and older was 6.9 years as compared with 9.3 years completed by persons in the same age group in the total population. Some 2,482,320, or 31 percent of the Negroes in this age group were "functional illiterates" (persons with less than five years of schooling) as compared with only 10.8 per cent of the population as a whole. Only 8.1 per cent of the Negroes in this age group had finished four years of high school as compared with 21.4 per cent of the total population, and only 2.1 per cent had finished "four or more years" of higher education as compared with 6 per cent of the total population. Even in

---

[7] U.S. Bureau of the Census. *Family Income in the United States, 1952,* Current Population Reports—Consumer Income, Series P-60, No. 15, Table 4.
[8] U.S. Bureau of the Census, *U.S. Census of Population, 1950, loc. cit.*

the 5-24 age-group, while the disparity was not quite so striking, the median number of years' schooling for Negroes was one to one and a half years less than that for the total population. A little less than half as many Negroes were enrolled in the fourth year of high school, and less than a third as many enrolled in the category of "four years or more" of higher education.

This disparity in the educational attainment of the Negro population is very striking at the high school level and above, and it is most marked in the area of professional training. An analysis of some 11 fairly typical professions reveals that the ratio of persons in these professions to the total population as compared with the ratio of Negroes in these same professions to the Negro population ranged from 1 to 1.2 for teachers to 1 to 35.6 for accountants and auditors. To put it another way, there were 35.6 times as many accountants and auditors in proportion to the total population as there were Negro accountants and auditors in proportion to the Negro population. Similarly, there were 17.6 times as many architects, 22.3 times as many designers and draftsmen, 34.2 times as many engineers, 16.4 times as many surveyors, 12.7 times as many lawyers, 7 times as many pharmacists, 4.7 times as many doctors and dentists, 3.1 times as many nurses, and 1.2 times as many teachers.[9] Moreover, current enrollments in schools training for these professions suggest that this disparity will not be reduced in the near future unless some drastic measures are taken to change the situation. For example, only a little more than a fourth as many Negroes were enrolled in medical schools in 1949-50 as one would expect on the basis of population. Similarly, only a third as many were enrolled in dentistry and pharmacy, one eighth as many in law, and a little more than one-twentieth as many in engineering.[10]

CAUSES OF LOWER EDUCATIONAL ACHIEVEMENT

There are several reasons which explain the inferior educational attainment of the Negro as compared with that of the population as a whole. It has already been noted that the concentration of two-

[9] *Journal of Negro Education*, Yearbook Number, chaps. XV, XVII, (Summer, 1953).
[10] *Ibid.*

thirds of the Negro population in the poorest section of the country explains this situation in part. It should be observed, however, that the Negro's educational attainment even in this section is proportionately as far below that of the total population of the section as his national attainment is below the population of the country as a whole. This fact is explained primarily by the inferior status which the Negro has occupied in the American social order in general, and in the South in particular.

One important factor has been the maintenance of segregated school systems. Seventeen states and the District of Columbia long required Negro and white pupils to be educated in separate schools. This arrangement made possible such gross discrimination in the provision of educational facilities in the Negro schools that they were invariably inferior to the white schools in the same communities. In 1900, the disparity in per capita current expenditures for white and Negro pupils was approximately 60 per cent. By 1930 this disparity had increased to 253 per cent.[11] It began to decrease after 1930 to 132 per cent in 1940 for nine of the 17 states, and to 43 per cent in these same nine states in 1952.[12] The disparities noted in current expenditures have been accompanied by even greater disparities in the provision of capital equipment, so that even in 1952 the disparity in this category was over 100 per cent. In fact, it has been recently estimated that it would take $350,000,000 to equalize the physical facilities of Negro separate schools with those provided for whites in 13 southern states.[13]

Prior to 1950, in the states providing segregated common school education, Negroes were excluded entirely from state-supported universities and no provision was made for their training in separate state-supported institutions. If a Negro in any one of these 17 states wished to study engineering, for example, he had to seek admission to an institution outside of the area. As a result of a decision of the U.S. Supreme Court in 1950, Negroes began to be admitted to the state universities in 12 of the 17 states. There are still five states

[11] Journal of Negro Education, IV (April, 1935), pp. 150-151.
[12] Harry L. Ashmore, The Negro and the Schools, Chapel Hill: The University of North Carolina Press, 1954, p. 62.
[13] Ibid., pp. 119, 156.

which do not admit Negroes to the state-supported higher institutions and little or no provision is made for their professional training in separate Negro colleges.[14]

Obviously, it is difficult to state exactly how much of the disparity in the educational attainment of Negroes is due to differentials in the provision of educational facilities. It is clear, however, that a considerable amount of the Negro's inferior educational status is due to this factor. And, what is equally important, the effect of these differentials has been cumulative.

In addition to lack of equal educational facilities, one of the most crucial factors underlying the inferior educational attainment of the Negro is his relatively low economic status. It has already been noted that there is a high correlation between economic status as represented by occupation and family income and the amount of educational opportunity which the children of such families enjoy. In general, the families in the lowest income groups have less educational opportunity than those in the higher income groups. Negro families almost invariably have lower incomes than families of other elements of the population. Moreover, they are most heavily concentrated in the section of the country where family incomes are the lowest and the number of children to be educated the largest.

Ever since Emancipation, the Negro has been the mudsill of our American economy. He has been employed in considerably greater proportions in the most poorly-paid and unstable occupations in the country, and has been, and is, forced to live at or below subsistence level even in normal times. In general, the average Negro family, despite the fact that it usually has had more members employed, has received only about half as much income as the average white family. Although Negro families constituted about 9 per cent of all families in the country in 1949, they received only about 5 per cent of the total money income. The median income of Negro families in 1949 was $1650, or 51 per cent of the median income of $3232 for white families. In urban communities, Negro family income was only 58 per cent of the white family median income of $3619. It was

---

[14] There has been some recent improvement in this respect. See Chapter X. —Editor.

44 per cent of the rural non-farm family income of $2851, and 39 per cent of the white rural family income of $1757.[15]

Using the criterion of "low" income families defined by a Congressional Committee in 1949[16]—those with income below $2000 in urban areas and below $1000 in rural farm areas—there were found to be approximately two and a half times as many Negro families as white families in this category. More specifically, practically six out of every ten urban Negro families, a little less than two out of every ten white urban families, almost seven out of every ten Negro farm families, and less than three out of every ten white farm families fell in this category. On the other hand, five (4.9) times as many white families as Negro had incomes of $4000 an above. In view of the fact that 59 per cent of all Negro families are in the lowest income group (two and a half times as many as white families), and five times as many white families are in the highest income group, it is not surprising that three to four times as many whites as Negroes are enrolled in higher and professional institutions and that the educational attainment of Negroes in general is one to two years lower than that of the population as a whole.

Even more important than the fact that Negro families are predominantly in the lowest income group is the fact that many of them occupy this position because of discrimination in employment and compensation. Negroes are not only employed less frequently in the higher paying jobs but, in many cases, receive lower rates of pay when they are employed. Most significant for this discussion is the fact that equality of educational attainment does not generally result in equality of compensation. The 1950 census presented data indicating the median incomes in 1949 of persons in various age groups according to the amount of schooling possessed. Table I presents the data for the total male population 25 years old and older and for the non-white male population in the same age group.[17] These data reveal a number of facts, but especially the racial bias which conditions employment in our American economy. While in

[15] George S. Mitchell and Anna Holden, "Money Income of Negroes in the United States," *Journal of Negro Education*, XXII (Summer, 1953), pp. 335-338.
[16] *Ibid.*, p. 334.
[17] Non-white population is 95 per cent Negro.

general income increased as the amount of schooling increased, wide disparities prevailed between persons with the same amount of training but of a different race. It will be observed that whites in every category received much more income than Negroes with the same amount of schooling. In fact, whites with only 8 years of elementary schooling received more income than Negroes with 3 years of college, and whites with one to three years of high school received more income than Negroes with 4 years or more of higher education. This condition is not a sectional phenomenon, since similar differentials obtain in all sections of the country.

In view of such facts, it is evident that Negroes do not have the same motivation to secure an education as whites or to continue it as long. Just how much this lack of motivation contributes to the generally inferior educational attainment of Negroes is not known. It is known, however, that it does have an important effect. And when it is added to the other factors which condition educational attainment, it assumes considerable proportions.

TABLE I. Median Incomes and Number of Years Schooling Completed by Male Persons 25 Years Old and Older in the Total and Non-White Populations, 1949.

| | POPULATIONS | |
Years of Schooling	Total	Non-White
No School Years Completed	$1108	$ 782
Elementary: 1 to 4 years	1365	1031
5 to 7 years	2035	1489
8 years	2533	1851
High School: 1 to 3 years	2917	1982
4 years	3285	2245
College: 1 to 3 years	3522	2255
4 years or more	4407	2633

SOURCE: U.S. Bureau of the Census. *U.S. Census of Population: 1950*, Vol. IV, *Special Reports*, part 5, chap. B. Education. Table 13.

PROBLEMS IN THE EXTENSION OF EDUCATIONAL OPPORTUNITY

This brief analysis of Negro educational attainment in the United States, and the discussion of the factors which condition it, both suggest some of the more important problems which must be resolved in obtaining adequate educational opportunity in this country. The Negro not only has the problem of securing "adequate" educational opportunity, but more immediately pressing, an "equitable" educational opportunity. And this problem is inextricably bound up with his attempt to improve his status in the American social order. Accordingly, this discussion is concluded with a brief summary statement of some of the things which he has attempted and is attempting to do to improve his status and the effect which they have had and might have in solving the problem of equitable, if not adequate, educational opportunity.

One of the most obvious steps which the Negro has taken to improve his status has been migration. Since the turn of the century some two or three million Negroes have moved out of the South to the large urban centers of the North and West, and several millions have migrated from the rural districts of the South to southern cities. For the first time, the 1950 census revealed that more Negroes were living in urban than in rural areas. This increased urbanization has had important effects upon his status, educationally and otherwise. The very act of moving has given the Negro more educational and other opportunities, although frequently these are not equal to those afforded non-Negro residents in the same areas. While migration and urbanization have improved Negro life considerably, they have not solved the problem of obtaining adequate or even equitable educational opportunity. There are too many Negroes still living in the poorest and most inhospitable section of the country; and the ghetto life which they are forced to live in cities, North and South, while an improvement over their previous condition, creates still another problem which they must face.

Changes in undesirable practices and the elimination of injustices in a democratic social order are effected by resort to the political machinery of the state—the ballot, the courts, legislation. Ever since Emancipation, and even before, the Negro has resorted to the political machinery of the state in an attempt to improve his status and secure the same treatment that other citizens receive. The history of his efforts has been encouraging, especially during the past quarter century. At the present time, he constitutes the balance of power between the two major political parties in a dozen or more border and northern states; and since the outlawing of the white Democratic primary some twenty years ago, he is becoming more and more a political factor in many areas of the South. It is estimated that there were more than a million Negro voters in the South in 1952, and that currently the number is nearly two million. Wherever the Negro vote has become an important factor, either because it is the balance of power or because it is large enough to influence elections, the Negro has been able to influence in varying degrees policies and legislation affecting his status. Even in the South, some dozen or more cities or states have either appointed or elected Negroes to school boards and other policy-making bodies. And their presence and voice on these boards have made possible the serious consideration, if not actual attainment, of greater educational and other opportunities. The Negro may well ponder how he might increase this influence.

It was noted earlier that one of the major factors which accounted for the Negro's relatively low educational attainment was his inferior economic status, and that much of his low economic status was due primarily to discrimination against him in employment. Negroes have felt that, along with pleas for fair play and the like, the problem could only be solved when there has been enacted some kind of general fair employment practices legislation, either at the state or national level, which could combat such discrimination. Experience with the federal government and some dozen states which have fairly effective legislation seems to bear out this theory. In any event, one of the most important problems facing the Negro in his quest for more adequate or equitable educational opportunity is the question of how he might utilize his political power, along with other means at his disposal, to combat discrimination in employment and compensation, thus attaining a higher economic status and greater educational opportunity.

In view of the Negro's minority status, he has often been forced to substitute the complex and expensive process of litigation for the ballot box. In many instances, the Negro's civil rights have been ignored or contravened in spite of laws to the contrary, and it has been necessary to resort to the courts as a last alternative. Consequently, numerous cases have been brought before the courts in an attempt to eliminate differential treatment based upon race.

It will be recalled that one of the important factors which explained the low educational attainment of Negroes was the legally-enforced separate public school, which almost invariably discriminated against Negro pupils. Negroes have resorted to the courts alleging that such segregation was unconstitutional, not only because unequal facilities were provided, but even more, because segregation itself was discriminatory. The U.S. Supreme Court handed down a unanimous decision on May 17, 1954, declaring unequivocally that such segregation was in fact unconstitutional.

Obviously, the problem of getting rid of segregated schools is not solved merely by the pronouncement of a decision. Since this decision and subsequent developments are dealt with in detail in Chapter VIII, they will not be discussed here. The theme of this chapter, however, does point up the significance of the decision. There is confidence that in the long run the decision will be obeyed, but there is recognition that the problem of implementation promises to be difficult. Although the legal atmosphere has been cleared so that the problem can be attacked with the law on the side of the Negro and his friends, it should be emphasized that the Negro separate school is not an isolated phenomenon. It is a symbol of the Negro's inferior status in the American social order in general. Thus, any realistic implementation of the Court's decision will involve not only the schools but other aspects of the Negro's life.[18]

It should be clear from this brief discussion that the problem which confronts the Negro in the realization of more adequate educational opportunity for his children is an integral part of his struggle for equal status in American life in general. The extent to which he will secure educational opportunity equal in any respect to that received by the population as a whole is dependent upon the extent to which he can achieve a status more nearly approaching that of Americans in general.

[18] The "sit-in" protests against lunch-counter discrimination are a case in point.—Editor.

VII

General Education: Its Problems
and Promise in the Education
of Negroes

Robert E. Martin
Associate Professor of Government
Howard University

I. THE NATURE OF GENERAL EDUCATION

A CONSIDERATION of the education of the Negro in American democracy would not be complete were the area of general education neglected. Its vital significance for the whole pattern of American education and modern democratic society and its role in majority-minority attitudes and relationships make imperative that its meaning be developed broadly and directly and related to the social heritage. This is the purpose of this chapter.

In making this analysis it will be necessary to consider some of the ideas of John Dewey. His philosophy has had a tremendous impact upon the development of American education. This is generally recognized. What may not be generally recognized, however, is that Dewey's philosophy has had, and still retains, crucial significance for both the conceptualization and practical resolution of certain special problems of Negro education. As will be pointed out,

183

the Negro in a real and special sense owes a debt to Dewey. For this our democracy is stronger.

While there are many varieties and philosophies, education may be divided broadly into general and special. Since there is no fully accepted definition of general education, it would be well to discuss this concept briefly and relate it to the broad problem with which we are here concerned. Approached negatively, general education is not concerned with preparation for a particular occupation. As the writer has said elsewhere, general education may be understood ". . . essentially as the broad training and educational experience without regard to specialized, vocational or professional work; its emphasis is upon broad understanding, knowledge or relationships, personality development, and effective living in a democratic society—in short, well-rounded preparation for the common life."[1] As the title of the Report of the Harvard Committee, *General Education in a Free Society*,[2] suggests, this type of education is concerned first of all with the individual's "life as a responsible human being and citizen."[3]

The basic idea involved in the concept of general education, especially as to its purpose, is very old, ". . . perhaps as old as formal education itself. Certainly it is inherent in the approach to education by the ancient Greeks, as evidenced by Platonic ideas."[4] While the schools of ancient Babylonia and Egypt were devoted to the preparation of students for specific professions—law, government service, priesthood, etc.—Greek education, especially among the Athenians, was concerned primarily with preparing youth for citizenship.[5] The essence of the idea of the proper training for free men has come down through the centuries enmeshed in the traditional concept of the "liberal education."[6]

---

[1] Robert E. Martin, "General Education: Challenge and Opportunity," *The Journal of Social Science Teachers*, I (May, 1951), p. 29.

[2] *General Education in a Free Society*, Report of the Harvard Committee, Cambridge: Harvard University Press, 1945.

[3] *Ibid.*, pp. 51-58.

[4] Martin, *op. cit.*, p. 3.

[5] Of course, this applied only to the approximately one-fifth of the population who were citizens. The others, being slaves or aliens were not affected.

[6] For a discussion of the criticism of liberal education, see *General Education in a Free Society*, *op. cit.*, pp. 51-53.

An important function of education is to transmit the social heritage, to form the connecting link between the cultural past and present. The social heritage includes, in addition to art, science, economy, and the like, also the things we believe in and for which we work—our ideals, values, and aspirations. Education, therefore, is a basic vehicle for passing on to the new generation the inherited conception of man and society, the nature of man and his relationship to society—its institutions, ideas, and purposes.

In America the carrying out of this function has posed, at points, serious problems and paradoxes, both as to relationships between the members of the majority group themselves and as to the relations between majority and minority groups.[7] There was no common ground which the equalitarian spirit of the Declaration of Independence could share with the status of either poverty-stricken poor whites or Negro slaves. Similarly in the twentieth century, the high purpose and principles of our democratic philosophy and Christian ethic have been strained and blunted in consequence of the harsh reality of the differential status of the underprivileged and, particularly, of the rigidly segregated and greatly handicapped Negro group.[8]

The internal conflicts involved in the process of transmitting the social heritage are highlighted by an examination of the history and problems of Negro education. The end of slavery and the extension of citizenship to Negroes did not bring an end to the widely differing views bearing on the extent and character of their education. Preconceptions as to the proper status and intellectual capacity of Negroes have crucially affected the kind of education provided for them.

[7] These conflicts have been described effectively in the writings of Alain L. Locke, late Professor of Philosophy at Howard University; see, for example, "The Negro Minority," Chapter IV in Group Relations and Group Antagonisms, R. M. MacIver, ed., New York: Harper & Brothers, 1944.

[8] While the exploitation of black and white labor has been characteristic of the developing industrialism, Negro labor has been marginal and more severely handicapped. See Charles H. Wesley, Negro Labor in the United States, New York: The Vanguard Press, 1927, pp. 254-306; S. D. Spero and A. L. Harris, The Black Worker, New York: Columbia University Press, 1931, especially Parts II-V; R. C. Weaver, Negro Labor, A National Problem, New York: Harcourt, Brace and Co., 1946, pp. 97-108.

Northern missionary societies, philanthropists, and the Freedmen's Bureau, in establishing institutions of higher education for the freedmen, tended to regard the Negro as being both worthy and capable of the best education that could be provided. Though differing among themselves, most white Southerners completely opposed these views.[9] Generally, they either opposed all education for Negroes or, if more generous, insisted on a particular type based upon certain negative conceptions of Negro ability and status.

Public education for Negroes in the South long was influenced by the assumption of Negro intellectual inferiority. The concept of racial inferiority was built up during slavery as a moral justification for this institution. This stereotype was developed further later, and then carefully reinforced, to disenfranchise Negroes— a campaign which ruthlessly embraced violence, trickery, and "legal" devices for bringing about Negro political impotence. The resultant elaborate stereotype of the Negro has continued to function as a severe and tragic limitation upon the acceptance and participation of this group in all reaches of American society, institutionalizing a markedly inferior caste-class status.[10]

The implications of this attitude for education are indicated by the following, and typical, statement of an influential Southerner. He called for text books ". . . which are especially adapted to the Negro mind, texts based on the most accurate and sympathetic knowledge of the characteristics of the Negro, which comprehend the peculiar needs of the Negro children, which are carefully planned and graded to teach the things fundamental in their proper education . . ."[11] The author, using the classic stereotype of the Negro as his ground, concluded that if good "results are to he hoped for, they must be obtained before the pupil goes beyond

[9] Dwight O.W. Holmes, The Evolution of the Negro College, New York: Bureau of Publications, Teachers College, Columbia University, 1934, pp. 68-70; see also Horace M. Bond, The Education of the Negro in the American Social Order, New York: Prentice-Hall, Inc., 1934, especially pp. 84-116, and Truman M. Pierce, ed., White and Negro Schools in the South, Englewood Cliffs, N. J.: Prentice-Hall, Inc., 1955, especially Chapter 2.

[10] Charles S. Johnson, Patterns of Negro Segregation, New York: Harper & Brothers, 1943; Gunnar Myrdal, An American Dilemma, New York: Harper & Brothers, 1944.

[11] Howard W. Odum, Social and Mental Traits of the Negro, New York: Columbia University Press, 1910, p. 47.

fourteen years of age; here the physical brain in the Negro reaches its maturity, and nearly all that can be done for a generation must be done by methods suited to children."[12]

The presumption of Negro intellectual and moral inferiority was widely held into the third decade of this century. The much publicized study of the Army Alpha tests came out in 1923, purporting to show scientifically and conclusively that black people were mentally inferior to white people.[13] This study, though soon critized by impartial scholars and shown to be basically unsound in its assumptions, its methods, and its conclusions,[14] circulated widely. It was often used as respectable documentation for anti-Negro attitudes and action.

Another limiting conception, related to the theory of mental inadequacy, grew out of the unquestioned acceptance of the belief that sharp racial differences existed—namely, the assumption that Negroes were morally irresponsible, particularly with respect to their work and sex habits.[15] As Gallagher points out, these ideas ". . . were [thus] used as a kind of frame of reference within which to construct the notion of what would be an education appropriate for this inferior people."[16] As late as 1926, a scholar, on the basis of an idea of "unequal stages of cultural evolution" among individuals and races, posed the need for "a system of unequal education."[17] This meant that "for the vanguard of civilization there must be provided an education commensurate with its cul-

---

[12] *Ibid.* In all fairness it must be noted that Odum, illustrating what can happen when the mind remains open, eventually repudiated his earlier views on Negro mentality, frankly acknowledging that scientific findings provided no evidence of inherent race differentials. For the last twenty years of his changed views see Odum's *Southern Regions of the United States,* Chapel Hill: University of North Carolina Press, 1936, and his *Race and Rumors of Race,* Chapel Hill: The University of North Carolina Press, 1943.

[13] C. C. Brigham, *A Study of American Intelligence,* Princeton, N. J.: Princeton University Press, 1923, pp. 191-195.

[14] See especially W. C. Bagley, "The Army Tests and the Pro-Nordic Propaganda," *Eductional Review,* LXVII (April, 1924), pp. 179-187.

[15] Daniel Katz and K. W. Braly, "Racial Prejudice and Racial Stereotypes," *The Journal of Abnormal and Social Psychology,* XXVIII, pp. 280-290.

[16] Buel G. Gallagher, *American Caste and the Negro College,* New York: Columbia University Press, 1938, p. 182.

[17] Francis C. Summer, "A Philosophy of Negro Education," *Educational Review* LXXI (March, 1926), p. 42. Here is an example of the Negro's acceptance of the stereotype created by the majority group.

tural status; for the rearguard an education likewise commensurate with its status."[18] Though earlier postulated upon a less sophisticated and less friendly base, this idea had long conditioned much of the education provided for Negro students.

Scientific evidence—psychological, sociological, anthropological, and medical—eventually repudiated the whole theory of inherent racial difference. It became clear that apparent differentials resulted from prolonged regional and cultural conditioning. In a broad and real sense, John Dewey made a significant contribution to this victory over superstition, bias, and the uncritical acceptance of old concepts and value judgments. This grew particularly out of his insistence upon the scientific method of thought, a process requiring that all conclusions be drawn only from tested data. Further, Dewey rejected the idea of the discovery of ultimate truth. Since truth was viewed as tentative, relative to the known facts at a given time, and subject to revision wherever new facts required it, those who claimed to possess the true views of racial superiority, views they held irrevocably, were confronted with a challenge that could not be ignored. And those who honestly sought the truth on this problem (and not all did, of course) reconstructed their earlier thought as Howard W. Odum did, placing it in relationship to a steadily widened horizon of knowledge.

This conception of truth as developing through a process in which closer and closer approximations are made, but in which finality is never attained, grew out of the readjustments resulting from the impact of the Newtonian synthesis on science. John Dewey performed a great service in doing so much to introduce this concept to education. Slowly but surely it contributed to the undermining of blind allegiance to tradition and reduced hostility to change—even where old biases and closely-held racial stereotypes were concerned. The resulting consequences of this advance in thought for conceptions of Negro ability and status, for race relations, and for restructuring Negro educational theory and practice were many.

The basis for a special, separate kind of education for Negroes, founded upon assumed mental and moral inadequacies, was de-

[18] *Ibid.*

stroyed with the emergence of a new intellectual climate within which to consider the problem. The elaborate stereotype of the Negro, built up by laymen and pseudo-scientists, was discredited. The outlook for education among Negroes, therefore, though by no means revolutionized, was brighter and more hopeful. Some people, of course, continued to think and act in terms of the outworn concepts; it takes a long time for new concepts to be accepted, especially when this necessitates giving up venerable biases and emotionally charged ideas. Thus, the old symbols could still be manipulated by unscrupulous persons for selfish ends. The important thing, however, was that the old stereotypes were no longer tenable as an objective basis on which to erect educational policies and practices.

This was especially significant for general education, which was now in a much better position to achieve its purposes and possibilities. As has been indicated, the most important purpose of general education is to prepare young people for the common life, those "spheres which, as citizens and heirs to a joint culture, they will share with others."[19] Patently, it was impossible even to approximate this great goal in a situation dominated by preconceptions of racial inferiority and a "special place" for the Negro in society.

As Dewey's approach became more influential in the determination of educational policy and planning, the basic objectives in Negro and white education gained more consistency and compatibility. Historic conflicts in educational thought, practices, and public policies, which had grown out of old racial prejudices and misconceptions, were largely resolved by the demonstration of their lack of validity. The democratic role of education, so vital and fundamental a part of the American Creed, could now develop more fully and the Creed itself be strengthened.

The extent to which this new insight produced meaningful change in the actual programs of Negro education has varied tremendously from region to region, North, East, West, and South. The speed of change has varied, also. Variation, indeed, has characterized the entire movement. Each region has been influenced by such variables

[19] *General Education in a Free Society, op. cit.,* p. 4.

as urbanism, size of the Negro population, presence or absence of segregated schools, the educational level (secondary or college) involved, the extent of public support, and the degree of white resistance to change, and the like. Prolonged research, involving considerable expense, would be needed to trace this development precisely.

Improvement did take place, however, as a result of the changing climate of opinion. New vistas of opportunity, challenge, and development opened up.

II. VOCATIONAL VERSUS LIBERAL EDUCATION

One of the factors that made it difficult to develop a satisfactory philosophy and effective program of Negro education was the controversy that raged around the relative merits of vocational or industrial education, on the one hand, and classical or liberal education, on the other.[20] This controversy grew in part out of the criticism of proposals to advance Negro higher education, a criticism that held this idea to be impractical.[21] Each side had a powerful spokesman: Booker T. Washington, the great apostle of industrial education, and W. E. B. DuBois, the brilliant champion of liberal education.

The conflict between the philosophies of these two leaders was neither as great as some of their statements appear to suggest, nor as irreconcilable as some partisans on each side believed. Both DuBois and Washington recognized merit in the other's position; the potentialities inherent in each posed the real problem. It seems clear that on this ". . . issue there was more heat and rivalry between the two groups than actual differences of opinion."[22] The full ramificatons of this controversy are well discussed elsewhere.[23]

[20] B. T. Washington and W. E. B. DuBois, *The Negro Problem*, New York: James Pott and Co., 1903. John H. Franklin, *From Slavery to Freedom*, New York: Alfred A. Knopf, 1950, pp. 377-396.

[21] Bond, *op. cit.*, pp. 116-126.

[22] Myrdal, *op. cit.*, p. 889.

[23] *Ibid.*, pp. 889-890, and 896-900; see also E. Franklin Frazier, *The Negro in the United States*, New York: The Macmillan Co., 1949, pp. 458-462. The reader will recall that a somewhat differing weighting is given to the sides of this controversy by the authors of Chapter I and Chapter II in this volume.

Of main significance here is the fact that Washington's views were supported by white Southerners and most northern philanthropy. This posed the danger.

As Frazier[24] and Myrdal[25] have pointed out, the attitude of the white South was not a product of the serious consideration of the "pedagogical advantages and disadvantages" of industrial education; rather "the political caste problem is always and necessarily involved. And the type of education to be given Negroes is always and necessarily connected with the amount of education and the financial obligations to be undertaken."[26] Gallagher states that ". . . the attitude of particular individuals and groups toward the problem of vocational education for Negroes will be determined largely by their beliefs as to the probable effects of the proposed education upon the status of the Negro within the caste system."[27]

The fear of DuBois and his followers was that usually the result of the industrial education provided for Negroes, whatever generous interpretations of the intent was made, would be the continued and further isolation of this group from the broad stream of American culture. It is clear that this danger was real, particularly in the formative period of Negro education.[28] While little effective industrial training was ever actually provided for Negroes, especially in southern public schools, the controversy had a negative effect upon the development of a well-rounded system of education for this group. A proper relative emphasis on preparation for individual careers and for full citizenship in the common life of a free society for them was delayed.

III. THE RENAISSANCE IN GENERAL EDUCATION

One of the most important developments in American education in the past few decades has been the expansion and growth of the movement for general education and, especially during the last

24 Frazier, op. cit., p. 460.
25 Myrdal, op. cit., pp. 897-898.
26 Ibid., p. 898.
27 Gallagher, op. cit., pp. 207-208.
28 Carter G. Woodson, The Mis-Education of the Negro, Washington, D. C.: The Associated Publishers, Inc., 1933, pp. 9-16.

several years, the increasing experimentation with special citizenship training programs. Few phases of our many-sided system of education have escaped the impact of this development. The basic idea of general education is rooted in antiquity. Yet, even though the purposes of general education have always been a major concern of the school, the movement dedicated to this broad training has undergone a renaissance since about 1930.

The volume *General Education, Its Nature, Scope and Educational Elements*[29] was published in 1934, and, in 1937, B. Lamar Johnson edited *What about Survey Courses?*[30] Interest increased and, in 1943, L. T. Benezet's *General Education in the Progressive College*[31] appeared; the widely read Report of the Harvard Committee, *General Education in a Free Society*,[32] was issued three years later. Begun in 1938, the reports of the Cooperative Study in General Education, sponsored by the American Council on Education, became available in 1948.[33] Voluminous periodical literature has been written on this subject. The pioneer intensive study of general education in Negro institutions of higher learning came off the press in 1947. This work by Irving A. Derbigny, *General Education in the Negro College*,[34] examined a representative sample of twenty of the 118 Negro colleges.[35]

The question arises as to why general education, with all its historic longevity, has received such tremendous and renewed

[29] William S. Gray, ed., *General Education, Its Nature, Scope and Educational Elements*, Chicago: University of Chicago Press, 1934.

[30] B. Lamar Johnson (ed.), *What about Survey Courses?*, New York: Henry Holt and Co., 1937.

[31] L. T. Benezet, *General Education in the Progressive College*, New York: Columbia University Press, 1943.

[32] *General Education in a Free Society*, op. cit.

[33] Findings were published in four volumes: *General Education in the Humanities; General Education in the Social Studies; Student Personnel Services in General Education;* and *Cooperation in General Education*, Washington, D. C.: The American Council on Education, 1948.

[34] Irving A. Derbigny, *General Education in the Negro College*, Stanford, Calif.: Stanford University Press, 1947.

[35] *The National Survey of the Higher Education of Negroes*, U.S. Office of Education Bulletin, Miscellaneous No. 6, III, Washington: U.S. Government Printing Office, 1942, gave only brief consideration to broad aspects of general education in Negro colleges; see section by L.E. Blauch and M. D. Jenkins, "Intensive Study of Selected Colleges for Negroes," pp. 42-46.

emphasis in the mid-years of the twentieth century. The main reasons, in brief, appear to be as follows:

1. An enormous growth of knowledge has occurred during the past half century.

2. Specialization and its resultant atomization and fractionalization of of knowledge has gone so far as to cause a growing reaction in the world of education. While the vital importance and legitimacy of specialism in a technical and technological world is recognized, there has been a rising feeling that something must be done to counteract the increasing tendency to forget or ignore, if not even to deny, the essential unity of knowledge, the common denominator of science, and the interrelationships of phenomena. The problem, of course, is taking new force and urgency under the rapid, and unexpected, Russian entry into outer-space in advance of the United States. Since Russia has obviously placed a major emphasis upon science in her educational program, the pressure to step up our emphasis has intensified. But this, when properly viewed, only keeps the need to avoid fragmentation to the fore.

3. The American system of education underwent great expansion, especially as a result of the increase in numbers of students with varying needs and their insistence on specialization.

4. The post World War I years, particularly, the prolonged depression of the 1930's and the coming of the Second World War, brought recurrent crises which necessitated a thorough-going reexamination of educational policies, curricula, and philosophy. Insistent current problems are sustaining this trend.

5. The conditions and needs of a complex, rapidly changing modern society, with its stresses and strains, have become such that they can no longer, if they ever could, be provided for effectively within the confines of the traditional system of education and the increasing specialization and professionalism of the last century.

IV. Significance of Recent Developments

The intensified interest in general education has made its influence felt in many basic areas of study: the humanities, biological scie..ce, physical science, social science, etc. In all of these, efforts are being made to improve the quality of the education intended to prepare students for living more effectively. For reasons which will become apparent, the role of social science[36] in general education will be given main emphasis here,[37] although the vital contribution of other disciplines is clearly recognized. Increasingly the democratic ideal is being given more emphasis and becoming more accepted in our society. General education can do much to broaden, perpetuate and add content to the democratic ideals in American life. As T. R. McConnell states, a basic objective of general education should be "an understanding of and devotion to those ideas and ideals which constitute the foundations of the central tenets of the democratic way of life and the acceptance of personal responsibility for the implementation and development of these concepts."[38]

The term "democracy" is too often used vaguely, as if all would understand its meaning on sight. The result is a familiar one. If we are to give specificity to the basic elements of the democratic aspiration, we should see to it that students come to grips with the following propositions:[39]

1. The conflicts of modern society, among which World War II and its after-effects loom large, have arisen not only as basic conflicts of values, but also because there are deep-seated maladjustments in our modern society.

2. The common good is paramount.

3. The basic dignity, worth, and importance of the human personality must be accepted.

4. The essential equality of persons of all races, religions, and nationalities must be recognized.

[36] Since the social sciences provide the data from which interpretative materials are adapted, and for other reasons, no differentiation is made here between social science and social studies.

[37] In terms of the purposes of both this yearbook on Negro education and the present discussion, the writer feels that the social sciences, by their very nature and interests, have a special obligation and an unusual opportunity.

[38] Quoted in Albert W. Levi, *General Education in the Social Studies,* Washington, D. C.: The American Council of Education, 1948, p. 6.

[39] *Ibid.,* pp. 8-9.

5. The method of compromise guided by intelligence, rather than the appeal to force, in the solution of political and social issues is indispensable.

6. All civil liberties must be vigorously defended and preserved.

7. All individuals in society have both the right and the obligation to work.

8. The stratification of American society into rigid social classes is undesirable.

In this process, it would be well to have the student examine carefully the four assumptions on which the Reeds based their study, *Preparing College Men and Women for Politics:*

1. That democracy is worth preserving.

2. That a truly democratic society in which individual freedom and initiative are steadfastly preserved is impossible outside the framework of democratic representative government.

3. That the two-party system is essential to the most effective functioning of representative democracy in the United States.

4. That the two-party system and government itself would be greatly benefited by more active and intelligent participation of college-trained men and women in them.[40]

It is important that students be encouraged to examine frankly the failures of our democracy in the past, as well as its present weaknesses, and to ascertain the causes and sources of the inadequacies. Equally important, of course, is to bring the student to an awareness of the strength and successes of democracy, "the achievements which it has made, the resources which it has, and the promise which it offers for the future."[41]

Always considered important, the vital need for effective citizenship is now being emphasized much more. There has been increasing experimentation, in high school and colleges, with special

---

[40] Thomas H. Reed and Doris D. Reed, *Preparing College Men and Women for Politics.* A Report to the Citizenship Clearing House, affiliated with the Law Center of New York University, New York: 1952, p. 1.

[41] Levi, *op. cit.*, p. 9.

courses and programs devoted to direct citizenship training.[42] Although there is considerable variety (and some conflict) in the aims, organization, content, and activities of these courses, they all share the common objective of providing more practical experiences and more direct contact between the student and the community, especially through opportunities for participation in the political process.[43] Efforts are made to generate among young people a continuing, constructive interest in public affairs.[44] The point of view of most of the supporters of this type of program is illustrated by the following comment of Judge Arthur T. Vanderbilt, who has been a pioneer in this field.[45] He states:

. . . I crave for young men and women of the rising generation a satisfaction similar to mine in helping to give their communities honest, effective government in the public interest. I am convinced that our college men and women, whose education has provided them a solid background for their activity, can supply the strongest possible constructive force in the politics of this country by working with their party organizations in their home communities.[46]

It is recognized increasingly that education for civic competence must begin long before college.[47] Thus, in 1950, the Commissioners of Education of the Northeastern States adopted the following resolutions:

Whereas, the Northeastern Commissioners of Education feel that the strains and tensions within our American and world society make it im-

---

[42] During the school year 1953-1954, the writer had an opportunity to visit and inspect several of the schools having interesting courses of this type. The project was made possible by a Faculty Fellowship from the Fund for the Advancement of Education.

[43] In addition to the descriptive materials provided by the schools, see Reed and Reed, *op. cit.,* especially Chapters II-IV and pp. 161-176.

[44] Some schools prefer to approach the problem of citizenship preparation differently. Columbia College, for example, uses broad courses like Contemporary Civilization, rather than special direct citizenship courses as such. This writer had a rewarding experience while teaching in the Columbia program in 1949-1950.

[45] Judge Vanderbilt was instrumental in the establishment of the Citizenship Clearing House at the Law School of New York University.

[46] Reed and Reed, *op. cit.,* "Introduction," p. V.

[47] This is important too, because of the large number of students who do not go on to college.

perative that education for democratic citizenship be an important part of every youth's education, and

Whereas, the school must redirect its efforts in civic education to the end that it shall provide the kind of experiences for its students which make for better living together in the democratic way while they are members of the school community, and that it shall seek to equip them intellectually and emotionally to make the best possible choices of the courses of civic action available to them as adults,

Therefore, be it resolved that an interstate committee be established to study the basic elements in American citizenship, subject matter for civic competence, and the educational activities which are appropriate for the schools of the several states.[48]

Regardless of the relative emphasis on direct participation in the political or other aspects of community life, the most fundamental function (and problem) of social science in general education is clear. It is to help students to obtain a practical, meaningful knowledge of the society in which they live and to increase their sensitivity to those social values which, because of the imperatives of the democratically oriented society, must be preserved and extended. The objective is to supply the knowledge of fact and value required as a basis for intelligent, constructive social action.[49]

This is crucial for all schools, Negro, white, and integrated. It takes on additional significance in relation to the education of Negroes.[50] Obviously, the minority status of the Negro and his resultant position of marked, though decreasing, disadvantage gives point and special urgency to the problem of education for dynamic citizenship. Discrimination and the walls of segregation present difficulties, yet they equally present a challenge to democratic development. Preparation for participation in the common life is basic; hence, the barriers to that participation must be analyzed, understood, and removed. As Derbigny states, attention must be focused upon ". . . the problems which face Negroes as they endeavor to live and work and make their contributions to the

---

[48] *Report of the Committee on Education for Citizenship*, appointed by the Commissioners of Education of the Northeastern States, Boston: April 1952, p. 1.
[49] Levi., *op. cit.*, especially Chapter 1.
[50] Space does not permit, and there is no need in the present context, for extensive discussion of this point.

development of a more satisfying, wholesome, and democratic way of life here in America and throughout the world."[51]

The implications for general education are clear. In the formal learning process, probably the most intimate contact with the great values underlying the democratic society takes place in general education. Here youth is first likely to examine systematically and critically the fabric of society—social organization and disorganization—the relative roles of various groups and their comparative status. Here the face of man and the community may first be viewed in the context of the historic struggle for justice, freedom, and dignity. Here social achievements and failures are analyzed, strengths and weaknesses assessed, and ideals and principles viewed in the light of social reality. Out of this process may come deeper insight and understanding, as well as the development of values and goals which give real meaning to life. Individual commitments leading to intelligent involvement in significant and constructive social action may also result.

The writer is convinced that herein lies great opportunity for the dynamic, creative powers inherent in our institutions and ideals. The schools have a special responsibilty in bringing about a transformation of society through bringing to it individuals whose increased intelligence makes possible progressively more effective choices on behalf of human decency. Dedicated to this high purpose, the schools can make a lasting contribution to the greater achievement of the American Dream. The 1954 decision of the Supreme Court which outlawed segregated public education removed another major impediment to the realization of this goal.

[51] Derbigny, *op. cit.*, p. 237. For a discussion of the broad objectives and organization of several of the general education courses in the social science area see William G. Tyrrell, ed., *Social Studies in the College,* Curriculum Series No. 8, Washington D. C.: National Council for the Social Studies, 1953. Note especially Emmett E. Dorsey and Robert E. Martin, "Introduction to the Social Sciences at Howard University," pp. 22-25.

PART III

THE CHANGING
SITUATION

VIII

The Supreme Court Decision and Its Aftermath

Guy H. Wells
Former President
Georgia State College for Women, Milledgeville, Georgia
Former Executive Director, Georgia Council on Human Relations
and
John Constable
Foreign Service Reserve Officer
U. S. Information Agency

I. THE LEGAL SITUATION

THE most decisive words in the history of Negro education in America were spoken on May 17, 1954. These historic words, written by a unanimous United States Supreme Court, maintain that:

> To separate [Negro children] from others of similar age and qualifications solely because of their race generates a feeling of inferiority as to their status in the community that may affect their hearts and minds in a way unlikely ever to be undone. . . . We conclude that in the field of public education the doctrine of "separate but equal" has no place. Separate educational facilities are inherently unequal.[1]

[1] United States Supreme Court, May 17, 1954, 347 U.S. 483, 74 S. Ct. 686, 98 L. Ed. 873.

On these words turns the future of the Negro in American public education. The decision not only is changing educational thinking and methods for the Negro in the southern area of the United States, but it is inspiring self-analysis and re-evaluation by educators in the North and West where extra-legal segregation has existed.

Although the school decision was not an abrupt change from then current trends, it did extend the principle of equal citizenship to persons living in the District of Columbia and 17 southern states. It also set the stage in law for a major revision of racial practices throughout the entire country.

The Supreme Court, in its decision, took into consideration the development of education and its importance today to American citizens. Thus the Court said:

In approaching this problem, we cannot turn the clock back to 1868 when the [Fourteenth] Amendment was adopted, or even to 1896 when the Plessy v. Ferguson ["separate but equal" ruling] was written. We must consider public education in the light of its full development and its present place in American life throughout the Nation. Only in this way can it be determined if segregation in public schools deprive these plaintiffs of equal protection of the law.

Today, education is perhaps the most important function of state and local governments. Compulsory school attendance laws and the great expenditures for education both demonstrate our recognition of the importance of education to our democratic society. It is required in the performance of our most basic public responsibilities, even service in the armed forces. It is the very foundation of good citizenship. Today, it is a principal instrument in awakening the child to cultural values, in preparing him for later professional training, and in helping him to adjust normally to his environment. In these days, it is doubtful that any child may be reasonably expected to succeed in life if he is denied the opportunity of an education. Such an opportunity, where the state has undertaken to provide it, is a right which must be made available to all on equal terms.[2]

The importance of education is clear to most citizens, but the key phrase in the above quotation is, "to all on equal terms." As John L. Childs points out: "If the young are to learn to become

[2] Ibid.

responsible members of our society, they must have opportunity to do more than to *learn about* the ways of their community, they must also have a well-balanced opportunity to participate in these ways of community life." And the Catholic Committee of the South put the idea in even plainer words:

There is a great difference between teaching and learning. We can teach principles of justice and charity in a racially segregated school. We can teach that there is no essential difference between the races, that God loves everybody, that we must love everybody. But the pupils do not really learn these principles. They give assent to them but they do not understand and accept them.

Although the May 17, 1954, ruling of the Court established the basic principles for future education in the United States, it was more than a year later when the court set down rules for putting these principles into practice.

Following the initial school ruling, some districts immediately began to convert their schools to a more democratic system; but for the most part, school boards and superintendents adopted a "wait and see" attitude until after the May 31, 1955, implementation ruling. This ruling, again unanimous, placed the responsibility for implementing the school ruling in the hands of the United States District Courts.

The key terms in the implementation ruling are: good faith, practical flexibility, prompt and reasonable start, deliberate speed, and equitable principles. According to eminent lawyers, these terms indicate that, although the decision is firm as to the constitutional principles involved, it allows a community to work out a solution in accordance with local conditions as long as the plan is in "good faith."

The plan laid down for compliance with the school decision is not a rigorous one. The Court allowed much leeway to the federal district courts although it need not have done so.

District decisions, while following for the most part the basic principles of the original rulings, have varied according to the community involved and the school plan submitted by education officials. Early rulings by district courts quickly indicated that the Supreme Court decision would be upheld in all future cases, but court processes have moved slowly in the intervening years. In 1960, nearly 50 school segregation cases were on the dockets of federal courts and desegregation penetrated the Deep South states for the first time in November of that year.

Both Supreme Court school rulings are couched in phrases which allow school officials to proceed voluntarily on a reasonable plan for more democratic school systems; but the rulings also make provisions for persons to seek court actions in areas where officials are reluctant to reorganize educational facilities in conformity with the "law of the land." The initial decision and subsequent rulings in the years following indicate that, although a satisfactory readjustment of the school systems in America might take a long period of time, eventually the democratic processes in education would be extended to all areas of the United States.

II. GENERAL REACTIONS

The initial reaction to the Supreme Court school decision was quite favorable. National and international opinion held that the United States finally had righted an old wrong; and, even in the South, reaction against the decision was extremely mild.

Some Southern politicians spoke out against the decision, but most public comment was restrained. Newspapers generally greeted the decisions as "inevitable," as did most private citizens. As one Southern daily put it, "No citizen, fitted by character and intelligence to sit as a Justice of the Supreme Court, and sworn to uphold the Constitution of the United States could have decided this question other than in the way it was decided."

The overwhelming majority of the major religious groups active in the nation and in the South endorsed the ruling as being in harmony with Christian and Judaic principles. Their statements are in the spirit of one adopted by the Southern Baptist Christian Life Commission: ". . . we urge Christian statesmen and leaders in our churches to use their leadership in positive thought and planning to the end that this crisis in our national history shall not be made the occasion for new and bitter prejudices, but a movement toward a united nation embodying and proclaiming a democracy that will commend freedom to all peoples."[3]

But the spirit of this and other endorsements have been slow in filtering down to persons on the local level. Various individual church leaders and ministers also called for "good faith compliance," but resistance slowly grew in some Southern areas until it sparked a revival of the Ku Klux Klan and other semi-secret societies dedicated to thwarting the Supreme Court school decision.

Organized Resistance

The initial organized resistance came from the National Association for the Advancement of White People (NAAWP), organized in Delaware by Bryant Bowles. Bowles and his organization were successful in Milford, Delaware, where their tactics were largely responsible for restoring segregation in the local high school. Although the NAAWP's success in Milford undoubtedly gave impetus to the resistance movement in the Deep South, Bowles failed in other places, notably Washington, D.C., and Maryland. The subsequent career of Bowles has been unnoteworthy; and at one point, he momentarily resigned leadership in the NAAWP, laying the blame on the apathy of white citizens.

As previously mentioned, the Ku Klux Klan also was revived soon after the Court decision, but its career has largely followed a course opposite to that of the NAAWP. The old Klan, with its program of terror and violence has largely been repudiated; and so the new organization found it tough sledding in its early stages. Its more recent development began under the leadership of the late Eldon Edwards of Atlanta, Georgia, whose initial efforts were in Georgia and South Carolina. Law enforcement officials and others spoke out against the Klan, and Edwards' early organizational attempts drew small audiences. As resistance to the Court decision grew, however, Klan activity increased.

Despite the growth and increase in activity, it is unlikely that the Klan can or will be permitted to grow to the strength it once enjoyed. Rivalry within the Klan organizations has resulted in splinter groups within the movement and has prevented a strong centralized organization. A good example is Georgia and its Klan

[3] "The Churches Speak," *New South*, XI (October, 1956), p. 7.

movements. Although Klan rallies during the sit-in activities of 1960-1961 in Atlanta drew sizable audiences, there were four separate Klan groups operating in the state. This number included two groups vying for followers of the late Eldon Edwards. During the same period, attempts made to organize all Klan groups into a strong regional Klan were ineffectual.

Coupled with the inability of the Klan groups to work cooperatively has been the growing reaction against the Klan, both by communities and law-enforcement agencies. Many white persons have spoken out against the Klan and a number of newspapers also have been outspoken in opposition. Officials have shown an increasing willingness to arrest Klansmen when they run afoul of the law. It would be unrealistic to assume that the Klan and its kindred organizations will not continue to be a problem in the South indefinitely; but it is quite unlikely that the South or the nation will permit the Klan, assuming it were capable, to grow as strong as it once was.

Although many fringe organizations have attracted an increasing number of followers, resistance to the school decision has been centered largely in the self-styled White Citizens' Councils (WCC). The parent group of this organization, which is also the strongest and most influential, is in Mississippi. The movement also is organized into an Association of Citizens' Councils of America with "national" headquarters in Greenwood, Mississippi. Greenwood also serves as headquarters for the state group.

Loosely affiliated units (WCC) were organized in Louisiana, Texas, Alabama, Arkansas, Florida, Georgia, South Carolina, Tennessee, and Virginia; and 15 other states have organizations of a similar nature. The WCC once claimed a combined membership exceeding the half million mark, but estimates early in 1957 placed the figure nearer 300,000. From studies in 1957, it was estimated that the WCC's collected well over two million dollars yearly from membership fees, donations, and from other sources.[4]

The WCC, according to their own official pronouncements, are dedicated to "the maintenance of peace, good order, and domestic tranquility in our communities and in our State and to the preserva-

[4] Paul Anthony, *Pro-Segregation Groups in the South*, Atlanta: Southern Regional Council, 1957.

tion of our States' Rights." The main object of such official statements appears to be an attempt to create an aura of respectability around the entire WCC movement. And although the movement attempts to embrace all "sufficiently respectable" groups, leaders strive to free the central organization of responsibility for utterances and actions of the local groups.

A decentralization program by the WCC enables the central office to disclaim credit for any violence or economic threat or pressure which may be undertaken by WCC units or individual members. This was done in the case of the North Alabama Citizens' Council headed by Asa Carter. This group, once loosely affiliated with the other WCC units, was disavowed by other Alabama WCC leaders and by regional leaders.

WCC leaders with few exceptions publicly decry any resort to violence; but it is apparent that if, as the WCC claims, the "best" people of the community make up their leadership and lend respectability to flouting the law, it is not surprising that cruder elements in the South are encouraged to try mob action.

Economic Pressure

The WCC initially publicized the fact that its chief weapon against desegregation would be the use of economic pressure; but after this tactic was condemned by newspapers and met by counter-pressure from Negro groups, the WCC disavowed organizational responsibility for economic reprisals. WCC leaders now claim that economic pressure by white persons arises "spontaneously" in areas where the segregation system is threatened.

Regardless of the degree of direct responsibility which may be attributed to the WCC, both economic and social pressures have been widely used against advocates of desegregation. The hardest hit have been the Negro farmer and small businessmen. Negroes have been denied credit and sometimes white retail merchants even refuse to sell them goods for cash. Negro merchants have been boycotted by wholesale distributors, and Negro teachers and other employees have been discharged with no reason other than their support of desegregation, membership in the National Association for the Advancement of Colored People, or registering to vote for the first time.

Although to a lesser degree, white persons also have been subjected to economic threats and pressures. White families have been ordered to move by angry groups of neighbors. Whites also have lost jobs or have been threatened with the loss because of their support of desegregation.

Little coverage was given by Southern newspapers to economic pressure campaigns in the early stages; and often, no weapon was available for the Negro to combat such tactics. Now, however, Southern newspapers are more zealous in covering such news; and white businessmen have learned that economic pressure is a two-edged sword.

Merchants in Orangeburg, South Carolina, cooperated in a White Citizen Council inspired economic squeeze against certain segments of the Negro community when desegregation was threatened. The merchants in turn were boycotted by Negro students of two colleges in the area and by other Negro citizens in and around Orangeburg. A total boycott by Negroes against any one merchant in the South can play havoc with individual profits.

The world also is aware of the now-famous bus boycott in Montgomery, Alabama, and there are other examples of Negroes employing their buying power to combat economic pressure against them or as a protest against discrimination itself.

The 1960-1961 student "sit-ins" and subsequent "selective buying" campaigns aptly demonstrate the importance of the Negro buying power on desegregation.

No one can accurately foretell just how widespread economic reprisals will become in the South's fight against desegregation or what effect this ultimately will have on the Southern economy. Two facts are clear at this point, however: Negroes are not the only ones to suffer and such reprisals cannot preserve segregated facilities indefinitely.

Violence

Violence in connection with the desegregation movement has increased steadily since the May 17, 1954, decision of the Supreme Court.

In 1955, approximately 50 cases of violence and threats of violence were reported in the 12 Southern states most directly concerned with desegregation in the schools. These cases included at least three murders; to date, no one has been convicted of the crimes.

By the first of January, 1959, the list had risen to 530 incidents of racial violence, reprisal, and intimidation. The incidents listed were only those which could be attributed to increased tension because of the Supreme Court's decision. The list included beatings, murder, the bombing of houses, churches, and Jewish synagogues, and riots such as the ones occurring in Little Rock, Arkansas, and Clinton, Tennessee.

During the 1960-1961 term of school, the world press trumpeted the violence which accompanied school desegregation in New Orleans and the brief rioting at the University of Georgia. Violence also accompanied a related effort in desegregation—the Freedom Riders—in Alabama.

Recently, however, the number of convictions of white persons involved in such incidents also has risen sharply although convictions still lag far behind the crimes.

Violence likely will continue to plague efforts to desegregate schools, but recent preventive efforts by law enforcement officers and increased convictions in court have lessened the danger of such occurrences.

Propaganda

Propaganda, in addition to economic pressure and violence, has been a weapon of the pro-segregationist. An abundance of literature is available from the groups ranging from vulgar diatribes distributed by handbills to articles in national magazines. Much of this literature is based on a foundation of half-truths and distortions, and some of these propaganda exhibits have been proven to be downright frauds.

The White Citizens' Councils also have their own radio programs which they peddle to local stations throughout the South. The WCC also makes speakers available to groups both in the North and the South.

Following the initial spurt in growth of the militant pro-segregation groups, membership has waned and ebbed according to local crises. Today, although all the pro-segregation groups are still quite vocal, it is unlikely that, with the possible exception of some areas in Alabama and Mississippi, any one such group enjoys a large dues-paying membership if it is not in a community facing imminent desegregation. Membership swells, however, when a community faces a desegregation crisis.

Political Action

Pro-segregation groups for the most part are political action groups which exert strong pressure on office holders and candidates for office. In four of the Deep South states, the government has been in the hands of persons who are wholly sympathetic with resistance groups. In Georgia, for example, leading politicians were among the top organizers of the State's Rights Council of Georgia. In the four additional states, pro-segregation groups exerted strong influence on the legislatures and public officials; and even in such states as Arkansas and Tennessee, which moved very slowly toward an official pro-segregation program, the public cry of resistance organizations inspired new segregation legislation.

Although WCC units and other pro-segregation groups have brought about an extended delay in the desegregation process, many of the resistance leaders admit that their efforts are at best merely delaying tactics.

It is now generally conceded that resistance tactics are doomed to failure. The problem is how much damage will be done to education in the South and the nation before the air is cleared. Little Rock, Arkansas, and some Virginia localities are now aware of the folly of all-out resistance to school desegregation. Their examples have served as a lesson to other forward-looking communities.

On the political front, an impressive number of new segregation laws have been passed since the May 17, 1954 decision to help buttress delaying activity by pro-segregation groups. In fact, several states anticipated the Court's action and passed new segregation laws prior to the school decision.

Although many of the pro-segregation laws have fallen before the courts and most, if not all, of the others will fall in due time, it is worthwhile to look at the general types of such laws and their effect on the educational system of the South.

The most serious aspect of the laws has been the threat to public education in general. Most of the recalcitrant states have made some provisions to close schools threatened with desegregation, and this has been done in Little Rock, Arkansas, and in some Virginia localities. Academic freedom of teachers in several states has been threatened and this tends to add to the weighty problem of the shortage of educators.

State pro-segregation measures have been both large in number and varied in approach, but they have fallen roughly into the following categories:

1. *Abolition of public schools.* As mentioned, school closing laws not only have been passed by a number of the states but have been put into effect in Arkansas and Virginia. The federal courts have ruled that a state cannot close one school or a portion of a school and allow other schools in the state to remain open. This leaves the alternative of an entire state without public schools or some desegregation.

Various "private school" plans have been formulated to take the place of closed public schools. Most of the school closing laws make some provision for "private" education usually based on tuition grants. As yet, no effective court test of the tuition grant has been made; but lawyers generally agree that the "private school" plans generally will be held unconstitutional as long as the state provides finances and/or buildings for them.[5] A federal court did prevent the turning over of the Central High School physical plant in Little Rock to a private school group. Prince Edward County in Virginia closed its public schools in 1959 and the community established private schools for white children. The private schools operated on purely private funds until the 1960-61 term of school when state and local tuition grant fees were utilized. This situation is expected to provide the first real test of segregated

[5] Florence B. Irving, "Segregation Legislation by Southern States," *New South,* XII (February, 1957), p. 3ff.

facilities with the use of state grants. The matter is now before the federal courts.

2. *Pupil-assignment laws.* This type of law has become the chief weapon of Southern states, not necessarily to delay desegregation, but to minimize the total effect. Pupil-assignment laws vary from state to state, but generally are based on such intangible factors as character, health, and welfare. Pupil-assignment laws in Virginia and Louisiana were struck down by the courts soon after their enactment,[6] but an Alabama assignment law was held to be valid on its face. During the 1960-1961 session of school, the Little Rock School Board, operating under a pupil-assignment plan, was ordered to speed up desegregation; but this was not a clear rejection of the pupil-assignment device. Pupil assignment in regard to the Negro likely will be before the courts for many years to come unless dedicated educators finally are allowed free decisions as to the educational systems.

Many educators look at the assignment law, as applied in the South's desegregation cases, with a skeptical eye. It is generally admitted that pupil assignment tests within a particular school to determine learning levels have merit, but only since the Supreme Court decision has the device been widely used for the general admission of students to a particular school plant.

3. *Non-support of desegregated schools.* This type of law was designed to enable the state to forestall desegregation on the local level by a willing school board. The law was declared unconstitutional in 1960 as it was applied by the state to two New Orleans' schools.

4. *Coercive measures.* The Deep South states and Virginia took the lead in this field with legislative attempts to punish persons advocating desegregation. Laws of this type generally have been aimed at teachers and other state employees who are members of the NAACP. Although federal courts generally have ruled out such coercive measures, some of these laws are still being fought out in the courtroom.

5. *Interposition and nullification.* The doctrine of interposition was originated in the nineteeth century on the theory that a state

[6] *Southern School News*, III (February, 1957), p. 2.

had the right to challenge a court decision which it felt violated the constitutional division of powers. This measure generally has been a propaganda device since most students of constitutional law have held that interposition has no legal force. Little Rock, Arkansas, was a clear answer to the question of the effectiveness of interposition and nullification. Despite mob action and moves by Governor Orville Faubus, federal court orders are being observed.

It should be reemphasized that the massive resistance, either legal or otherwise, to the Supreme Court decision was by no means spontaneous or complete. Resistance even in the Deep South was slow; and immediately following the Court decision, many schools moved quickly toward desegregated systems.

III. Patterns of Acceptance and Resistance

The "Desegregating" States

At the time of the Supreme Court decision, there were 17 states and the District of Columbia which had policies of segregation in the schools. Five of these states—Kentucky, Maryland, Missouri, Oklahoma, and West Virginia—and the District of Columbia early adopted school desegregation as a matter of official policy. The five "desegregating" states moved with varying speeds toward a single school system, but all five demonstrated "good faith" in instituting programs of desegregation.

West Virginia moved rapidly toward a program of desegregation. Local school boards had the backing of state officials in implementing the Court's decision; and so during the 1956-1957 school term, only three small eastern counties retained school segregation. The Charleston *Gazette* aptly stated, "Segregation is about over in the Mountain State."[7]

Missouri also moved quickly toward a desegregated public school system. Here, school officials had an excellent foundation on which to build since color barriers had been tumbling in the state for a number of years. St. Louis parochial schools were de-

---

[7] Harold C. Fleming and John Constable, "What's Happening in School Integration," *Public Affairs Pamphlet*, No. 244, p. 5.

segregated as early as 1947—seven years prior to the Court decision.[8]

St. Louis is a good example of a city laying the proper groundwork for desegregating public schools. Not only were parochial schools in the city desegregated in 1947, St. Louis University and Washington University both successfully concluded five-year desegregation plans. Both schools were completely desegregated by 1952. Students and teachers in the St. Louis public schools had varied interracial experiences prior to full desegregation of the schools. Interracial student activities had included The Intergroup Youth Organization, athletics, the city-wide student council, musical groups, and the Central High School Centennial Pageant. Teachers' activities included the Intergroup Education Association, training in human relations, and desegregated activities such as official committees, teachers' organizations, and administrative staff and meetings.[9]

The policies and actions of school board officials in St. Louis greatly contributed to the success of public school desegregation. The Board of Education made it clear that desegregation was a fixed policy to be followed firmly on the scheduled plan laid down. The superintendent told the teaching staff, ". . . This problem is different from any which we have faced in that *failure cannot be thought possible*. Integration is a fact. The time has come when we must submerge all of our personal feelings if we are to maintain our high standards of conduct and achievement."[10]

Preparations for desegregation varied from community to community. School officials and teachers prepared for desegregation as they thought best for their particular school. "In some areas there was intensive and extensive preparation, in others there was little or no preparation."[11]

The desegregation process in St. Louis has been highly successful

8 *Ibid.*, p. 6.
9 "St. Louis Integrates Its Schools," League of Women Voters of St. Louis, (January, 1955).
10 Bonita H. Valien, "The St. Louis Story: A Study of Desegregation," Anti-Defamation League of B'nai B'rith, 1956.
11 *Ibid.*

and is fulfilling the 1954 prediction of the *St. Louis Globe-Democrat,* which editorialized, "Another few years will find, we predict, segregation's end has produced a better democracy, a notable eradication of prejudice, generally improved and cheaper education for St. Louis children."

As early as the 1955-1956 school term, 85 percent of Missouri's Negro school children attended desegregated schools, and the remainder of the state's schools were moving rapidly toward desegregated systems.[12]

Transition to desegregated education in Oklahoma was delayed until the 1955 implementation ruling; but once the change began, the pace was rapid. Public opinion in the state, once very Southern, has shifted to a more westward outlook. This, coupled with court-ordered desegregation in higher education in the state, aided greatly the Oklahoma transition to a desegregated public school system. The change also was quickened when school boards were advised that, beginning with the 1956-1957 term, state funds would not be paid for the extra expense of maintaining separate Negro schools.[13]

Although Maryland has had one of the most challenging tasks in desegregating public schools, the state has maintained its unity under strong leadership and moved positively toward full desegregation. Some communities in the state have strong identification with the South due to economy and racial make-up. For instance, more than 40 percent of the population of Baltimore is Negro—a larger percentage than many Deep South cities.

Baltimore desegregated its public schools in the fall of 1954, prior to the Supreme Court implementation program. As in St. Louis, groups had been at work for several years trying to prepare the community for a smooth transition.

Unlike St. Louis, however, resistance was built up in Baltimore by a few individuals and groups until it appeared that the city's schools were headed for serious trouble. Picketing began at School 34 on September 30, 1954, and the next day spread to a half-dozen elementary schools in or close to the South Baltimore area. Offi-

[12] Harold C. Fleming, *op. cit.,* p. 6.
[13] *Ibid.*

cials believe that the spark that set off this demonstration came from Milford, Delaware, and the campaign by Bryant Bowles. The demonstrations found active support at less than a dozen of the 48 desegregated schools in the city and 97 percent of all pupils remained in classes during the troubled period. Reports indicate that even a portion of the three percent who stayed away from school did so because of fear of violence and not because they were in favor of the boycott.[14]

A firm policy by school and law enforcement officials ended the demonstrations in Baltimore. The School Board made it clear on the first day of the demonstrations that no schools would be closed and issued a statement that all children would be safeguarded. The Baltimore police force spent the first two days keeping the picket lines in order and preventing violence; but on the third day, Police Commissioner Beverly Ober took a firmer hand. He issued a statement, which was broadcast by radio and television, that the police would enforce two of Maryland's laws, one against inducing or attempting to induce a child to absent himself unlawfully from school and the other against disturbing any public school session. Commissioner Ober warned the citizens that any pickets appearing at the schools the following day would be arrested. This broke the demonstrations.[15]

Again public opinion was important—

. . . it was rallied to the support of the School Board to an extent that was quite unusual in amiable, imperturbable Baltimore. Civic, fraternal, religious and labor organizations publicly decried the picketing and mob actions. Newspapers called editorially for law and order. Ministers in South Baltimore were mobilized to appeal from their pulpits for an end to scare tactics and to school disturbances. Representatives of welfare and human relations agencies went into the troubled area to talk to the people, and the principal of Southern High School, John H. Schwatka, made a moving appeal via television to all South Baltimore pupils and parents.[16]

---

[14] "Desegregation in the Baltimore City Schools," The Maryland Commission on Interracial Problems and Relations and the Baltimore Commission on Human Relations (July, 1955), p. 20ff.
[15] Ibid.
[16] Ibid.

And so Baltimore continued its transition to a desegregated system. After the first year of desegregation, a study by two human relations organizations revealed that in Baltimore "there are no school or classroom problems inherent in integration. The problems that arise, whether they concern behavior, personal habits, learning speed or group participation, are problems encountered in all schools with children of all races and religions."[17]

The transition in Baltimore and Maryland has been made smoother through the use of the free-choice method, whereby pupils are permitted but not required to transfer to schools formerly closed to them. This has led to a markedly gradual transition in the state although Maryland has been moving steadily toward full desegregation.

Kentucky officials affirmed the intent to comply with the desegregation decision from the beginning; and, as in other states, community planning usually preceded actual desegregation. Kentucky's first step toward desegregation was taken in 1948 when the state law was changed to permit white and Negro nursing students to be trained in the same institutions. Since 1948, all higher education institutions have been opened to Negro students.

Louisville, Kentucky, also, presents an excellent example of how planning pays off. The late Omer Carmichael, superintendent of Louisville public schools in a *New York Times Magazine* article outlined the highlights in the preparation for desegregation.

Mr. Carmichael listed these highlights as:

1. Factors in the community's background made the transition easier. These factors included the fact that Louisville had always had desegregated street cars and buses; the city's police department employed Negro policemen; the Louisville Free Public Library was desegregated in 1948; the public golf courses were opened to Negroes in 1952; the bus terminal was desegregated in 1952, and civic groups had promoted good race relations.

2. Before and after the Court decision, the schools were busy with general human relations.

3. It was constantly reiterated that the Court decision must be

[17] *Ibid.*

accepted as the law of the land. This principle was impressed upon the faculties of the various schools.

4. After teachers were reasonably at home with the problem and questions involved, the program was fanned out into the entire community. This was done principally through the Parent-Teacher Association.

5. From the opening of the 1954-1955 term, all teachers worked with their children on desegregation.

6. The simplicity and permissive nature of the plan was greatly appreciated by parents by both races. Under the plan, the city was re-districted without regard to race. A card was sent to the parents of each elementary and junior high school child indicating the school to which each child was assigned. The card also told the parents, if they preferred another school, to indicate first, second, and third choice. For high school, no re-districting was done; but cards were sent to parents indicating they could choose any high school in the district for their children.

Transition in Louisville was smooth; but elsewhere in Kentucky trouble hit three of the state's schools. Mobs harassed students in Clay and Sturgis and a school in Henderson was boycotted. Protection was provided for colored students by the National Guard, and the interracial Henderson Ministerial Association broke the school boycott there with a truth campaign. Although some Kentucky schools have been harassed by resistance groups, the firm policy by state officials is beginning to assure Negro children of "equal" educational facilities.

Desegregation in the nation's capital also has been under attack. The pro-segregation activities here have been more subtle, however, in that they took the form of an investigation by a Congressional sub-committee, a group composed principally of admittedly pro-segregation Southerners.

Although records of the sub-committee hearings have been used to delay desegregation in other Southern communities, the hearings did little actual harm to the movement in the District of Columbia toward a more democratic school system. According to Carl F. Hansen, assistant superintendent in charge of senior high schools in the District of Columbia, "the integration . . . program . . . has been a miracle of social adjustment."

Although critics claim that the District of Columbia schools were desegregated too quickly, records show that this process did not take place overnight as many persons believe. As in other communities mentioned previously, school officials in the District of Columbia had taken several major steps in planning for the change. In December, 1952, the Board of Education opened up to public discussion the question of how desegregation should be processed if it were to take place at all. At subsequent meetings, it was suggested that interested individuals and organizations submit their suggestions in writing.

Early in 1953, the superintendent of schools developed a desegregation plan which was to be put into effect if and when the Supreme Court invalidated segregation. In December, 1953, the superintendent of schools informed the Board of Education of a plan to conduct intercultural relationship workshops for teachers and officers. An intergroup education committee, appointed by the superintendent, suggested a plan for a series of meetings for members of the Board of Education, the top-level staff, and all administrative and advisory personnel. On March 3, 1954, the first seminar was held for the purpose of creating "a climate for general understanding and improved relationships among the various segments of our population."[18]

As soon as the Supreme Court order was handed down, the program of desegregation was instituted. Desegregation in the District of Columbia schools was completed in September, 1955.

Again, the community had other factors which worked in its favor. The capital is under the direct control of the federal government; and for several years prior to the school decision, the government's policy had been aimed at the elimination of segregation. Racial barriers fell in hotels, parks, public housing projects, and in government operations. It has been demonstrated that, when other community barriers fall, school desegregation becomes much easier.

[18] Carl F. Hansen, "Miracle of Social Adjustment: Desegregation in the Washington, D.C. Schools," Anti-Defamation League of B'nai B'rith, 1957, p. 37ff.

The Superintendent and the Board of Education of the nation's capital set a primary objective of "the maximum development of every pupil, regardless of race, creed, cultural and economic status, and supposed capacity of learning." Mr. Hansen has said that "the concentration of effort upon this fundamental objective is now possible because the obstructive effect of school segregation has been removed, and the first distractive stages of desegregation have been passed."[19] The entire community, according to Mr. Hansen, is united in an all-out effort to improve public education in the District schools, which is being done under a broad and inclusive program drawn up by the superintendent.

The "Divided" States

Five of the 17 states with segregation laws concerning schools fell into a category generally labeled "divided." In these five states—Arkansas, Delaware, Tennessee, North Carolina, and Texas—the contrasts to be found in a single state were often extreme. Just as there no longer is a "solid" South due to geographical, economic, and cultural diversity, individual states are "divided" as to acceptance of the Supreme Court decision.

All 17 states have internal varieties in racial attitudes, but most of the state governments settled on racial policies that could be imposed statewise, at least for the moment. However, in the "divided" states, differing areas within their boundaries have moved in opposite directions.

Arkansas has been the most puzzling of the divided states. Even before the events at Little Rock, the state already had experienced both peaceful and difficult desegregation programs. Two communities, Fayetteville and Charleston, enrolled Negroes in formerly white schools soon after the Supreme Court decision. These communities apparently encountered little adverse reaction to their desegregation program. However, when the community of Hoxie desegregated the white high school, the school board was subjected to extreme pressures by pro-segregation groups, spurred and assisted by "outsiders."

It was the events at Central High School in Little Rock, Arkansas,

[19] *Ibid.*, p. 69.

that further served to muddle the picture in the state. Almost everyone is familiar with the major events of the struggle in the Arkansas
capital.

Briefly, a Federal Court approved a plan of desegregation submitted by the school board. When school opened, Governor Orval
Faubus, until then considered moderate on the desegregation question, called out the Arkansas National Guardsmen and prevented
the Negro students from entering Central High School. Following
a subsequent court order, Governor Faubus removed the troops
but tempers had been built up to such a pitch that a mob gathered
around the school and at least one Negro was physically attacked.
President Eisenhower sent United States troops to Little Rock to enforce the court order and federalized the Arkansas National Guard.
The Negro children were subjected to a type of "guerilla warfare"
while attending Central for the remainder of the year.

Subsequently, Central High School was closed for a year and was
reopened by orders from a federal court. The school board is now
controlling desegregation through pupil assignment. Negro students
are still attending Central and desegregation has spread to neigh-
boring Hall High. Central now has had several Negro graduates.

Regardless of the final outcome of things in Little Rock, the
action at Central High School during the 1957-1958 school terms
seems to have had two major results. It spurred court action by
Negroes attempting to break down segregation in schools, and it
slowed up voluntary action toward desegregation by school boards.

Delaware is divided by a canal which separates the industrial
county of New Castle from the southern, agricultural counties of
Kent and Sussex. Wilmington, in New Castle, began integration
soon after the Court decision and proceeded according to plan, and
the remainder of New Castle has presented no special problems.
Only Dover in the southern portion of the state had approached
desegregation as late as spring of 1957, and the program there was
an extremely cautious one.

As mentioned previously, Milford, Delaware, was hit by widely
publicized disorders which greatly dimmed the prospects for desegregation on a statewide basis. After Bryant Bowles and his
National Association for the Advancement of White People suc-

cessfully forestalled integration in Milford in 1954, political leaders in Delaware adopted an uneasy middle ground between the northern and southern areas of the state. Subsequently, the Delaware Board of Education adopted a state-wide, stairstep desegregation program beginning with the first grade. In 1960, a federal court invalidated this plan and left Delaware to come up with a more intensive program. Regardless of the outcome of the controversy over the method, it is now unlikely that Delaware will again be plagued with the desegregation troubles it experienced earlier.

Texas, too, has a split personality where desegregation of schools is concerned. In the rice, cotton-growing eastern section of Texas, old South restraints still remain. This area has a heavy Negro population compared to western sections and little inroads have been made in the segregation system. Then, too, the state political powers have advocated continued segregation.

Western Texas, on the other hand, has little in common with the cotton-growing section. Its outlook and economy is Western rather than Southern, and its Negro population is small and scattered. Desegregation in this section has proceeded rapidly as evidenced by the fact that 100 school districts had begun school desegregation by the 1956-1957 term. Houston began desegregation with a stairstep plan during the 1960-1961 term; and Dallas's court-ordered plan was for the 1961-1962 session.

Tennessee is an excellent example of geographical and economic diversity, and this diversity extends to race relations and attitudes. In general, resistance to desegregation is strongest in the western area and lessens perceptively as one travels eastward. The pro-segregationist flare-ups in Clinton, therefore, were an enigma to most people. It seems certain, however, that the trouble in Clinton came from the "have-nots" in the community who jumped at the chance to discredit current leaders. These persons again were spurred on by "outsiders," chiefly White Citizens' Council leaders from north Alabama and Washington, D.C., who came into the area in a last-ditch stand to keep all of Tennessee's public schools segregated.

Tennessee state officials refused to yield in the Clinton case, but the local board finally felt compelled to ask the federal courts for aid. Clinton High School has remained desegregated despite the fact that most of the original school was destroyed by a bomb. Credit for continued desegregation goes to the Negro children who refused to surrender and to Federal District Court Judge Robert Taylor who made it clear he intended his original desegregation order to stand.

The Nashville school board, in the 1957-1958 term, launched a limited desegregation program approved by the court; and the city, as in Clinton was hit by mob action and violence. Local police handled the situation; and although the school board has not been at all firm in its policy toward desegregation, it is expected to continue to adhere to the policy set forth by the federal court. Other Tennessee communities, such as Knoxville, are cautiously following Nashville's policy toward desegregation.

Three North Carolina cities moved toward limited desegregation during the 1957-1958 term. These cities—Charlotte, Greensboro, and Winston-Salem—enrolled a few Negroes in formerly all-white schools under the state's pupil assignment law. Other North Carolina cities have followed the lead of these three pioneers; and "token desegregation," as this program has come to be called, is spreading slowly. "Token desegregation," as practiced in the state, was designed to minimize the extent of desegregation, to lessen the chances of violence, and to keep North Carolina in the column of "progressive states" in the eyes of the nation. Public school desegregation in North Carolina has been on a voluntary basis, but it is likely that, unless more Negroes are admitted to desegregated schools under the pupil assignment plan, the state's school systems will be plagued with court cases for a long time to come.

The "Resisting" States

Two Southern states—Florida and Virginia—were classified as "resisting" states following the Supreme Court decision. The two gradually moved from "wait-and-see" positions to the "resistance" column. Since then, however, the histories of the two states in regard to desegregation have been quite divergent.

Political developments were largely responsible for this stiffening of attitudes, and the state governments in both states were more or less committed to delaying desegregation although Governor Collins of Florida did take the stand that the decision is the law of the land.

Florida continued in the "resisting" column with a dubious example of desegregation occurring for the first time in the state in 1959. In Dade County, the Orchard Villa School, in a transitional neighborhood, had 490 Negro children with eight whites.

As the legal attack from the NAACP became more concentrated in Florida in 1960-1961, Florida showed evidence of moving toward the policy of North Carolina and its "token" desegregation. Two Negro girls were assigned to two white schools in North Miami Beach in 1960. In 1961, the University of Miami announced it would desegregate. Peaceful examples of desegregation such as this can be expected to pull Florida into a more progressive position. Earlier indications pointed to the fact that many state officials hoped to avoid the experiences of Little Rock and New Orleans.

Conversely, leadership in Virginia swung from a merely passive resistance program to that of "massive resistance." Virginia was the first state to defy the federal government and close its schools rather than desegregate.

Leadership in the state was given over to the "black belt" counties, and thus the government took a strong stand against desegregation. The federal court ruling against closing a portion of Virginia's school system, combined with a strong rallying of moderate and liberal forces in the state for open schools, broke the back of the "massive resistance" policy. Now, employing the pupil-assignment plan, the more industrialized areas of Virginia are instituting "token desegregation."

Before leaving Virginia, it is well to note that, during the 1959-1960 school term, Prince Edward County, Virginia, was the only school system in the South not operating a public school due to the desegregation controversy. The county's white citizens operated private schools without assistance from the state. During the 1960-1961 term, students in the private schools utilized state and local tuition grants. The use of the grants, as well as the continued non-support of public schools in Prince Edward, is now under legal attack on constitutional grounds.

The resisting states should be distinguished from their more reactionary Southern neighbors, labeled here the "hard-core" states. In the two states just reviewed, there were enough dissenters from official state policy to give hope of an eventual solution to the desegregation problem. Few persons in the "hard-core" states braved opposition to official policies in the early stages of the desegregation controversy. Even by 1960, it was only in the large metropolitan centers such as Atlanta and New Orleans that intensive opposition to "massive resistance" had developed. Early in 1961, however, Georgia did break away from the "hard-core" states as will be shown in the next section. And in Louisiana, although the state tried almost every legal device in the segregationist book, it was unsuccessful in closing down the two schools under court order to desegregate.

The "Hard-Core" States

South Carolina, Georgia, Alabama, Mississippi, and Louisiana are classified here as "hard-core" states. Stretching through these states is the band of counties commonly known as the "black-belt." The Negro population of these counties range from 40 percent to as much as 80 percent, and here change comes slowly.

This band of rich, dark soil is the heart of the old plantation system, where its planter-aristocracy put down its deepest roots. Leaders in this section controlled the Southern political arena in the Civil War days; and although much of the rest of the South felt little loyalty to this cotton-producing and slave society, the plantation South used its political and economic power to build the solid South of the Confederacy.

Now the South has changed greatly in economy and population; but little change in the political structure has occurred. Industries have sprung up in the Piedmont South, and modern cities have drained away much of the "black-belt" population. Despite the heavy population loss and economy change, however, the "black-belt" portions of the "hard-core" states still retain political control. In many cases, the distribution of seats in the state legislature remains virtually unchanged since the turn of the century. "Devices like Georgia's county unit system serve to keep the center of political power in those areas where the after-effects of slavery are most strongly felt."[20]

It is in these five states that the future of desegregation has been exceedingly dim, but the picture is somewhat brighter today. Here, pro-segregation groups mushroomed and the governments firmly committed the states to last-ditch stands against desegregation in any degree.

As has been shown, however, Louisiana declined to utilize last-ditch methods when its legal maneuvers proved powerless against the federal courts. Although only a handful of white children attended a public school with one Negro child in a New Orleans school in the 1960-1961 term, the state and the segregationist elements in Louisiana failed to prevent the beginnings of public school desegregation in the state, meager though these beginnings were.

Georgia is another example where "massive resistance" apparently has become too great a price to pay for segregation. Following brief riotings at the University of Georgia in 1961 when two Negro students were admitted to the school, the state legislature struck down the state's segregation laws and instituted local option, pupil assignment, and tuition grant plans. This action was an historic reversal for the state which, at one time, was expected to close public schools to forestall desegregation.

In both New Orleans and Georgia, there have been organizations for continued public education. Uniquely, Atlanta has the first such group organized to save public schools before its schools were actually closed. Examples of other cities, the apparent determination of the federal government, and, last but not least, the increasing race for industrialization all affected Georgia's decision to swerve from its "massive resistance" program.

With desegregation in New Orleans in 1960, and Atlanta's court-ordered desegregation beginning in 1961, the desegregation picture does become much brighter. It is unrealistic, however, to expect voluntary desegregation in the Deep South states, at least for the next few years. The prospect for the "hard-core"

20 Harold C. Fleming, *op. cit.*, p. 13.

states for desegregation is a long, slow process with cases being fought out in the courts, system by system. It is probable, however, that court-ordered desegregation in other Deep South areas will be more easily accomplished as experiences are built up; and many students of race relations in the South think it probable that voluntary desegregation will proceed more rapidly in other Southern areas once a firm foothold is established in the "hard-core" states.

IV. THE FUTURE

What then is the future for desegregated schools? Although in some states the future seems dark, the overall picture has improved tremendously since the Supreme Court school decision. A survey by the Southern Regional Council, revealed at least 1,100 instances of desegregation in the Southern states in the two-year period immediately following the Supreme Court school decision. ". . . The results of the survey suggest that beneath the surface turmoil of Southern resistance, deep-running currents are steadily eroding the undemocratic patterns of the past. The causative forces are many —moral, economic, political, and international—but not the least of them is the insistent stirring of a broader conception of human dignity among Southerners, white and Negro."[21]

Further evidence of this "broader conception" is revealed in a 1956 survey of public opinion in the South which indicated that one in seven Southern whites then favored desegregation as compared to one in 50 in 1942.[22] In 1961, a Gallup Poll asked the question, "Will desegregation ever come?" Seventy-six per cent of Southerners answered, "Yes." Nineteen per cent now said, "Never," and five per cent were undecided.

The Negro Teacher

A greater worry today among many educators is the fate of the

[21] David Loth and Harold Fleming, *Integration, North and South,* New York: Fund for the Republic, 1956, pp. 49-50.

[22] Herbert H. Hyaman and Paul B. Sheatsley, "Attitudes Toward Desegregation," *Scientific American* (December, 1956), p. 38.

Negro teacher under the newly instituted desegregated systems in Southern communities. Pro-segregation politicians and groups loudly asserted that the bulk of Negro teachers will lose their positions when schools desegregate.

It is still too early to foretell the final results, but it is undoubtedly true that some Negro teachers are losing jobs when schools are desegregated. More will be dismissed as desegregation proceeds. It is unlikely, however, that there will be a wholesale discharge of Negro faculty members for several reasons. First, the teacher shortage is so extreme today that neither the South nor any other region can afford wholesale discharge of teachers, regardless of race. Second, tenure laws in some states protect teachers' rights; and if these tenure rights are allowed to go by the board as they concern Negroes, then white persons too can expect to suffer.

Kentucky offers the best example of a successful beginning to teacher desegregation. A 1956-1957 survey revealed that 112 Negro teachers in six Kentucky school districts were in schools with white teachers. In contrast, the loss of only 27 Negro teachers could be traced directly to desegregation; and of these, most found teaching jobs in other states.

Comment from school officials who had desegregated faculties were quite favorable and included: "According to all observations, the situation here is excellent. There has been no adverse reaction from either pupils, parents, or other teachers. . . ." "Students and teachers are happy over the success of integration of their schools." "The principal and supervisors are pleased with the job that she (the Negro teacher) is doing." "The five principals are enthusiastic about the teacher assigned them."[23]

Of course, Kentucky's experience cannot be expected to be repeated immediately in other areas in the South although many educators believe that the South will eventually make full use of Negro teachers in desegregated schools.

The conclusions the Kentucky Council on Human Relations drew from its survey on teacher desegregation paints a good picture of future prospects. The Council said:

23 "Kentucky Successfully Begins Teacher Integration," *Toward Integration*, Kentucky Council on Human Relations, 1956, p. 10 ff.

The successful beginnings of teacher desegregation have aided Kentucky's progress toward the goal of equal opportunity for all peoples. The desegregated pupil will not be integrated until he has an equal chance for employment. He will not be inspired to be a better pupil if he witnesses the dismissal of his qualified teachers just because of their race or color. Experience to date with teacher desegregation, even though limited, shows that pupils, teachers, and parents can accept teacher desegregation. Most encouraging of all is the knowledge that several other districts plan to begin teacher desegregation at an early date. The Kentucky school superintendent, who said, "In time, Kentucky and other border and Southern states will use a far higher proportion of Negro teachers in integrated schools than the Northern states have even done," can already begin to see his prediction come true.[24]

Northern and Western States

What effect, if any, does the Supreme Court school decision have for the non-South? Legally, the decision applied only to the 17 states and the District of Columbia which practiced segregation by law. However, it is clear that the spirit of the decision must and does extend to all states.

Segregation in the non-South generally has been accomplished in three ways. The chief cause of segregated schools in the non-South is segregated housing patterns, but it also is accomplished by overtly racial policies and by gerrymandering school zones. Some of these patterns have been discussed in a preceding chapter.

As racial barriers fall in housing, they automatically fall in schools and in other areas of community life where there are no state laws to hamper desegregation processes. Segregated neighborhoods are still prevalent in the non-South, but efforts are being made in some areas to eliminate this. Public housing has been newly desegregated in some areas and some private developments have begun accepting persons of all races.

The Effect of Segregation

What are the characteristics of a segregated school and what is being done about such schools?

[24] Ibid., p. 14.

In a memorandum, the American Jewish Congress cited a list of characteristics prevalent in schools where the Negro enrollment is 90 percent or more of the total school population. The characteristics, based on several different studies, were listed as:

1. Inadequate or obsolete buildings and classroom facilities.
2. School buildings are not well maintained; less money is spent on maintenance.
3. A higher proportion of classes for the mentally retarded than of classes for gifted children.
4. The rate of teacher turnover, of the use of substitute or inadequately trained teachers, is generally higher in segregated schools.
5. Class size is frequently larger in segregated schools.
6. Faculties tend to be less experienced; fewer teachers have tenure.
7. As a result of the above factors and their cumulative effect, educational standards and expectations are lower; pupil achievement drops below standard.[25]

The American Jewish Congress also made a list of recommendations to help dissipate segregated facilities in the non-South. These include:

1. The creation of a commission on integration within local school boards.
2. Rezoning of school districts and site selection of new schools based on the official recognition of integration.
3. Improve the quality of integrated schools.
4. Enact and enforce district residence requirements.
5. Drop racial designation from school enrollment reports and other official records.
6. End segregation in facilities for handicapped children.
7. End segregation in educational and welfare facilities provided by public and sectarian agencies—in children's shelters, detention homes, reformatories, etc.
8. Prepare to manage the community relations problems that may accompany plans to integrate the community's schools—school officials, parent and teacher organizations and community relations agencies.[26]

[25] From the report, "Desegregation in Northern Areas: the Public Schools," American Jewish Congress, XIX (March, 1957).
[26] Ibid.

New York City is one of the non-South cities that has undertaken an intensive self-survey concerning segregated facilities. New York took the lead in the use of state legislation and administrative action in breaking down segregation in housing, and New York City also instituted a program designed to bring its schools into conformity with the Supreme Court School decision.

In November, 1955, the Public Education Association reported to the Integration Commission of the Board of Education of New York City that the city's schools were "in fact segregated." In turn, the Board of Education unanimously adopted the following resolution:

Public education in a racially homogenous setting is socially unrealistic and blocks the attainment of the goals of democratic education whether this segregation occurs by law or by fact . . . the Board of Education of New York City . . . is determined to accept the challenge implicit in the language and spirit of the U. S. Supreme Court. . . . It is now the clearly reiterated policy and program of the Board of Education of the City of New York to devise and put into operation a plan which will prevent the further development of segregated schools . . . only in this way will the City of New York be able to provide for its children that type of democratic education which will enable these children to contribute their skills to the preservation of the greatness of our city, our state and our nation. . . .

Seven subcommittees in the city began investigating specific areas of responsibility for the purpose of making recommendations for desegregated schools. These subcommittees were: (1) zoning; (2) educational standards and curriculum; (3) educational guidance and stimulation; (4) teacher assignments and personnel; (5) physical plant and maintenance; (6) community relations and information; and (7) liaison.

The New York City Board began implementing its program as soon as recommendations were made. Similar self-surveys and programs have been sought in other non-South communities.

Higher Education

How has desegregation worked in higher education and what does the school decision mean for higher education? Positive answers can be given in both cases.

The admission of Negroes to formerly all-white colleges and universities in recent years is one of the most impressive examples of desegregation on record. In a 26-year period beginning in 1935, at least 131 accredited tax-supported colleges and universities in the South and border states and the District of Columbia opened their doors to Negroes. Desegregation at the University of Georgia in 1960 brought the total number of desegregated formerly all-white colleges to 117. This is out of a total of 199. Of 38 predominantly Negro tax-supported colleges, 14 are now desegregated. With private schools included, the total number of desegregated facilities is well over 200. The adjustment, with the exception of the University of Georgia, was made without difficulty.

The answer to the second question is demonstrated in even simpler terms. Of the more than 200 schools listed as desegregating their facilities by 1961, only 70 did so in the 17 years prior to the court decision. The remainder came in a seven-year period following the court order.

Some of these schools opened their doors to persons of all races because of court orders, but many desegregated on a voluntary basis. The University System of North Carolina is a good example. The University of North Carolina opened its doors to Negro graduate students and later to Negro undergraduates, but only after being ordered to by the federal courts. Later, Women's College of the University of North Carolina and North Carolina State College, units of the University System, opened their enrollment to all persons on a voluntary basis. (These developments at the level of higher education are so important that a more detailed account is provided in the next chaper.—Editor)

Many groups now are looking to officials in higher education, both private and public, to re-evaluate their programs in the light of the Supreme Court decision. Student groups, faculty members, and related organizations are more and more becoming cognizant of the move toward a more democratic educational system. This is in keeping with a resolution by the 13th National Congress of the National Federation of Catholic College Students, representing 150

Catholic colleges. The resolution read, in part: "The Thirteenth National Congress recommends and exhorts student governments, in whatever section of the country they be, to examine their campus situations, to work for the abolition of all discriminatory practices, and to support the Catholic hierarchy of their areas in implementing integration."

Conclusion

The future of desegregation in public schools is still unknown, but one can at least predict that the movement toward full desegregation will not easily be forestalled. Tremendous international, national, and even local forces support the Supreme Court Justices' conclusion that "in the field of public education the doctrine of 'separate but equal' has no place."

As has been demonstrated, the desegregation process is being pushed in all areas of the United States, and a variety of forces are expected to continue this push. Successful school desegregation has become a proven fact in many communities, and numerous others are beginning to try desegregated systems. The transition period is expected to continue for many years; but a simple listing of some of the groups and causative forces working toward the goal of integration demonstrates the bright future in store for the movement.

1. International forces, which call for free, democratic societies, influence leaders in the United States.
2. The United States government, itself, is committed to a policy of full citizenship for all people.
3. Actions by Negroes through the National Association for the Advancement of Colored People and other organizations will help bring the movement to its logical conclusion.
4. Human relations organizations are working for the elimination of prejudice and discrimination in all fields.
5. Civic groups, both on the national and local levels, support the principles of integrated schools.
6. All major religious organizations ask for equality of treatment.
7. Many public officials, national and local, have a growing realization that democracy means full participation for everyone.

8. And, last but not least, the spirit of the Supreme Court decision is growing; evidence supports the thesis that the decision is indeed the turning point for the Negro in American public education.

As the World Council of Churches puts it, one simply "cannot approve of any law which discriminates on the grounds of race, which restricts the opportunity of any man to acquire education to prepare himself for his vocation, or in any other way curtail his exercise of the full rights and responsibilities of citizenship and to share in the responsibilities and duties of government."[27]

[27] "The Churches Speak," op. cit., p. 3.

IX

Desegregation in Institutions of Higher Learning

Nelson H. Harris
Head, Division of Education
Shaw University

THE purpose of this chapter is to present a brief summary of the status of desegregation in institutions of higher learning in the Southern and border states with primary emphasis on formerly all-white, tax-supported institutions. The walls of segregation in the South were beginning to crumble even before the May 17, 1954 U. S. Supreme Court decision. Changes in segregation policies were taking place partly through court order and partly through voluntary action. For example, non-segregated travel in interstate coaches, pullmans, dining cars, and buses had become commonplace in many sections of the South, and more than fifty public and private colleges and universities in the area had opened their doors to Negroes.

Twelve Southern and border states and the District of Columbia had initiated desegregation in some of their institutions of higher learning to a limited degree prior to the U. S. Supreme Court ruling. These areas or states may be listed as follows: District of Columbia, Missouri, Oklahoma, Maryland, West Virginia, Kentucky,

Texas, Arkansas, Delaware, Louisiana, Tennessee, North Carolina, and Virginia. Desegregation was started in the graduate and professional schools of universities and has been gradually extended to the undergraduate level since the 1954 decision.

I

States that have proceeded with the desegregation of their institutions of higher learning at the most rapid rate are the District of Columbia, Missouri, Maryland, West Virginia, Kentucky, Oklahoma, and Delaware.

DISTRICT OF COLUMBIA

All colleges and universities in the District of Columbia area were open to Negroes without discrimination by 1957. Catholic University, American University, Trinity College, Dumbarton College of Holy Cross, and Gallaudet College admitted Negroes from four to twenty years before the 1954 U. S. Supreme Court decision. George Washington University enrolled its first Negro students in the fall of the academic year 1954-1955. Previous to the 1954 U. S. Supreme Court decision, Minor Teachers College and Wilson Teachers College were operated for the training of Negro and white teachers, respectively. By order of the District Board of Education, these two colleges were merged in the fall of the academic year 1955-1956, and persons of both races attend Wilson Teachers College. Howard University from its beginning in 1867 has always admitted white and Negro students alike. The enrollment has been predominantly Negro over the years, but for the last five years the University has been enrolling an increasingly large number of white students in all of its departments and schools.

MISSOURI

Negroes were admitted to the University of Missouri at Columbia, by court order, as early as 1950. Except for the university, all fourteen tax-supported colleges and universities desegregated voluntarily, and as of 1960-1961, Negroes were enrolled in practically all of these institutions. In addition, private colleges and universities were substantially integrated, with St. Louis University and Washington University taking leading roles. Lincoln University, formerly an all-Negro institution, admits both white and Negro students. No serious racial disturbances have arisen in these institutions, and all reports indicate that students have made excellent adjustments to school, classroom, campus, and community conditions.

MARYLAND

The University of Maryland admitted a Negro to its law school, by court order, as early as 1935. In 1954, following the Supreme Court decision, the Board of Regents of the University of Maryland opened all of its schools and departments to Negroes. Segregation in all other formerly white and Negro public institutions of higher learning was abolished as of June 22, 1955. This means that all of the state's eighteen tax-supported colleges and universities operate under desegregation policies. It is estimated that between 300 and 400 Negro students were enrolled in formerly all-white institutions of higher learning in the state at the beginning of the school term, 1960-1961.

Some years prior to the 1954 U. S. Supreme Court decision Negroes were admitted to such private colleges and universities as Johns Hopkins, St. John's College, Loyola College, Goucher College, Peabody Conservatory College of Music, Wesley Theological Seminary, Woodstock College, and the College of Notre Dame of Maryland, and other Catholic colleges.

The traditionally Negro colleges in Maryland are Morgan State College, Baltimore; Maryland State College, Princess Ann; Coppin State Teachers College, Baltimore; and Bowie State Teachers College at Bowie. A few white students were enrolled at Morgan State College, Coppin State Teachers College, and Maryland State College during the 1960-1961 session. There were no white students matriculating at the other colleges.

It may be observed that the public junior college movement is advancing rapidly in Maryland. For example, Anne Arundel County became the ninth Maryland school district to establish a two-year junior college program as an integral part of its public school system when, in September 1961, it opened the Anne Arundel Community College. The college is open to both races, as are other colleges (in practice or principle) in the city of Baltimore, and Charles, Baltimore, Frederick, Harford, Montgomery, Prince George's, and Washington counties.

WEST VIRGINIA

Negroes were admitted by West Virginia University to extension classes in the mid-1920's, and the University's graduate and professional schools were opened to Negro resident students in 1938. In 1950, Marshall College, the only other state institution with a graduate program, opened its graduate facilities to Negroes.

Within a few days after the 1954 U. S. Supreme Court decision, Governor William C. Marland issued a directive calling for an end to segregation with as much dispatch as possible. Following Governor Marland's directive, the State Board of Education, which has charge of nine state colleges, and the University Board of Governors, ordered an end to segregation and, in the fall of 1954, Negroes and whites began enrolling at previously all-white or all-Negro colleges. A large number of white students enrolled at West Virginia State College, traditionally an all-Negro school. During the fall of 1960-1961 approximately 60 per cent of the enrollment at West Virginia State College was white. This is an excellent example of desegregation in reverse. This college meets the needs of hundreds of white students who are within commuting distance of the campus, and many who reside in other areas of the state. The number of white students enrolled at West Virginia State College in 1954-1955 was 182, and the Negro enrollment was 801, whereas the white enrollment in 1957-1958 was 1107, and the Negro enrollment was 1107. Since 1957-1958, the white enrollment has been consistently larger than the Negro enrollment. The white enrollment has been increasing so rapidly that the West Virginia General Assembly in 1957 amended statutes governing the business and educational affairs of West Virginia State College, eliminating reference to it as a Negro institution. The president is a Negro, and the staff is integrated with respect to both teaching and office personnel.

Bluefield State College, a previously all-Negro school, had 65 white students in a total enrollment of 337 in 1957-1958, and it is estimated that the number of white students enrolled in 1960-1961 was close to 100. All of the eleven state institutions have white and Negro students enrolled with the exception of Glenville State College. This college is located in an area where the Negro population is very small. Practically all private colleges are open to Negroes with the most notable exception being Morris Harvey, the state's largest private college.

KENTUCKY

In 1949, by court order, the University of Kentucky opened its graduate and professional schools to Negroes, and after the U. S. Supreme Court 1954 and 1955 desegregation rulings, the eight tax-supported colleges and universities in the state dropped racial barriers, and opened all phases of their offerings to Negroes. In the fall of 1960-1961, the Negro enrollment at the University of Kentucky and the University of Louisville was approximately 150 and 250 respectively. It is interesting to observe that during the fall of 1950-1951, Berea College, three Catholic colleges in the Louisville area, Presbyterian Seminary, and the Southern Baptist Theological Seminary began admitting Negroes to all of their offerings. It is also important to remember that the doors of Berea College were open to Negroes from its beginning in 1855 until 1904 when the Kentucky Legislature enacted a statute known as the Day Law which forbade Negroes and whites to attend school together in any type of institution whether public or private.

Kentucky State College, the only previously Negro institution, reported an enrollment of 53 white students for the first semester of the academic year 1957-1958, and it is estimated that the enrollment was more than 60 in the fall of 1960-1961. It is predicted that formerly all-Negro colleges like Kentucky State which maintain high standards will increasingly serve the needs of students irrespective of race or national background.

It may be noted that with the exception of the University of Kentucky and Paducah Junior College that all of these colleges and universities desegregated voluntarily.

OKLAHOMA

The first Negro was admitted to an all-white institution (University of Oklahoma), by court order, in the fall of 1948-1949. The pattern during the early admission of Negroes to previously all-white institutions was to enroll them in graduate and professional schools and in undergraduate courses not offered at Langston University, the state college for Negroes. However, on June 6, 1955, the Oklahoma State Regents, the over-all policy making board for higher education in Oklahoma, adopted this policy: "The governing boards and the respective presidents of the state-supported institutions within the State System of Higher Education are hereby authorized to accept qualified Oklahoma resident Negro students for admission effective at the opening of the fall term of 1955."

The number of Negroes enrolled in formerly all-white state and private colleges and universities was 143 in 1955-1956, 446 in 1957-1958, and approximately 800 in the fall of 1960-1961. As of the fall of 1960-1961, Negroes were enrolled in nine of the eleven state-owned senior colleges, in six of the seven state-owned junior colleges, and in four of the six municipal junior colleges. In addition, it was reported that most of the independent colleges and universities were desegregated. Thus, the trend has been toward both a constant increase in the number of Negroes enrolled and in the number of institutions involved.

DELAWARE

Delaware maintains two institutions of higher learning, one predominantly white, and the other predominantly Negro. In the past, the University of Delaware was an all-white institution, and Delaware State College was an all-Negro college. Negroes, by court order, were admitted to the University of Delaware for the first time in the fall of 1950. For the school year 1960-1961, University officials reported that Negroes were enrolled in the graduate and undergraduate schools, and that no attempt had been made to count the number enrolled. The Negro enrollment in the graduate school was estimated to be several hundred whereas the number enrolled in the undergraduate school was said to be comparatively small. The larger graduate enrollment may be partly attributed to the matriculation of Negro teachers at the University for advanced degrees during the summer and (on a part-time basis) the regular academic year. Delaware State College has remained practically an all-Negro college with only a comparatively small number of white students enrolled. All phases of the University of Delaware's offerings were reported to be open to Negroes without discrimination.

II

Texas, Louisiana, and Arkansas rank next to the District of Columbia, Missouri, Maryland, West Virginia, Kentucky, Oklahoma, and Delaware with respect to progress made toward the desegregation of their institutions of higher learning.

TEXAS

The principle of desegregation in tax-supported institutions of higher learning in Texas began in 1950 when the U. S. Supreme Court directed that Herman Sweatt be admitted to the law school of the University of Texas. The decision of the court reads as follows: "What is important, the University of Texas Law School possesses to a far greater degree those qualities which are incapable of objective measurement but which make for greatness in a law school. Such qualities to name but a few, include reputation of the faculty, experience of the administration, position and influence of the alumni, standing in the community, traditions and prestige."

This decision represents one of the early attacks on the validity of the "separate but equal" doctrine, and very probably had a tremendous impact on the May 17, 1954 U. S. Supreme Court decision. As of the first semester of the academic year 1960-61, 27 of the state's 52 public colleges and universities had both races enrolled. It was estimated that during the first semester of 1960-61, the Negro enrollment at the University of Texas, the state's largest university, was 150, and that the number enrolled at North Texas State College and Lamar State College of Technology was 238 and 140 respectively. North Texas State College was considered to be the most integrated institution of higher learning in Texas with respect to enrollment and participation of Negroes in athletics and general student activities. The total Negro enrollment in previously all-white institutions of higher learning in Texas during the fall of the academic year 1960-1961 was between 1,100 and 1,200.

During the month of September 1961, Texas Tech and Texas Woman's University became the twenty-eighth and twenty-ninth public institutions of higher learning in Texas to desegregate when their facilities were opened to Negroes.

It may also be observed that Abilene Christian College, operated by members of the Church of Christ, is reported to have opened its graduate courses to Negroes as of September 1961.

The traditionally Negro public colleges are Prairie View A. and M. College and Texas Southern University. As of October 15, 1960, Prairie View was completely segregated, and Texas Southern University had five white students in a total enrollment of 3,260.

LOUISIANA

The first Negroes entered a tax-supported school in Louisiana in 1950, when, by court order, they were admitted to Louisiana State University at Baton Rouge. At present, Negroes are attending the following state-supported institutions: Louisiana State University at Baton Rouge; McNiese State College at Lake Charles; Southwestern Louisiana Institute at Lafayette; and Southeastern Louisiana College at Hammond. Louisiana State University's branch at New Orleans was reported to have had more than 250 Negroes in its 1960-1961 fall enrollment, and has been integrated since it was opened three years ago. Southwestern had more than 200 Negroes enrolled, the second highest registration at a desegregated school in the state. It should be observed that Negroes were admitted to these four state institutions through litigation. There were five tax-supported colleges that admit only whites.

The two Negro state institutions, Southern University and Grambling College, did not have any white students enrolled in 1960-1961. Xavier and Dillard, Negro private colleges at New Orleans, have had white students, at intervals, for a number of years. The traditionally white private colleges and universities have not fully desegregated. Loyola University since 1949 has admitted Negroes to its extension classes, Law School, Evening School, Institute in Industrial Relations, and graduate divisions. However, Negroes have not been enrolled at the undergraduate level. The New Orleans Baptist Theological Seminary has enrolled Negroes in its graduate program, and the St. Mary's Dominican College at New Orleans has had a few Negro students.

ARKANSAS

The University of Arkansas has been admitting Negroes to its graduate and professional schools since 1948 by order of the Board of Trustees. However, it is very likely that the action of the trustees was attributed largely to court actions in other states. As a rule, Negroes were accepted at the University for graduate or undergraduate work not otherwise available in the state.

In policy all of the seven state-supported colleges in Arkansas have been desegregated since the U. S. Supreme Court decision of 1954. The total Negro enrollment in formerly all-white institutions in the state was estimated at forty for the fall of 1960-1961. The enrollment of Negroes on the main campus at the University of Arkansas was much higher during the summers when large numbers of Negro teachers matriculate for graduate work. During the summer of 1951, only seven Negro graduate students were enrolled on the main campus of the University of Arkansas. In subsequent years the number of graduate students enrolled was as follows: 1952, 9; 1953, 29; 1954, 66; 1955, 97; 1956, 128; and 1957, 134. In addition, Negroes were enrolled in desegregated graduate courses at various centers in the state (usually on Saturdays) during the regular academic year. These graduate facilities have helped many Negro teachers to qualify for the master's degree. For example, between June, 1950 and January, 1959, 434 master's degrees were awarded to Negro students by the University of Arkansas.

Of the eight private colleges in the state, three church supported colleges, namely, College of the Ozarks at Clarksville, Arkansas College at Batesville, and Philander Smith College at Little Rock admit any qualified student. The first two institutions are predominantly white, and the last is primarily Negro.

III

The following states have made some but limited progress toward the desegregation of their colleges and universities: Tennessee, North Carolina, Virginia, Florida, and Georgia.

TENNESSEE

Negroes, by court order, were first admitted to the University of Tennessee as graduate students in January, 1952. In the fall of 1959-1960, all but two of Tennessee's state-supported institutions of higher learning had desegregated to some degree. During the first semester of 1959-1960, sixty-nine Negroes were enrolled in the various graduate and professional divisions of the University of Tennessee. It has been the policy of the University to admit Negroes for graduate and professional training only, with the understanding that Tennessee A. and I. State University, the traditionally Negro institution, would meet all of the undergraduate and some of the graduate needs of the Negro population. However, Negroes through suits were constantly seeking admission to the undergraduate divisions of all state-owned colleges and universities. Finally, in 1957, through pressure from the federal courts, the State Board of Education adopted a policy that removed race as a factor in admissions to the six institutions under its control. The board voted to accept all applicants who qualified for admission subject to each school's enrollment capacity and other admission policies. Testing as a screening advice was also approved by the board. During the fall of the academic year 1960-1961, 46 Negroes were enrolled at the University of Tennessee, 34 at Memphis State College, 8 at Austin Peay State College, and 33 at East Tennessee state College. On January 3, 1961, three Negroes became the first of their race to enter the undergraduate division of the University of Tennessee.

Tennessee A. and I. State University at Nashville, formerly an all-Negro school, has enrolled a few white students in the past. Scarritt College in Nashville (Methodist) and the University of the South at Sewanee (Episcopal) were the first all-white private institutions of higher learning to admit Negroes. However, there were no Negroes enrolled in these two colleges at the beginning of the 1959-1960 school term. Vanderbilt and George Peabody College, private institutions, had Negroes enrolled in their graduate programs during the 1960-1961 session. Fisk University and Meharry Medical College, private institutions, have had white students in their enrollments.

NORTH CAROLINA

The first Negroes, by court order, were admitted to the University of North Carolina at Chapel Hill in the summer of 1951. There were five in this group and each matriculated in the University Law School. Negroes entered North Carolina State College at Raleigh, a division of the University of North Carolina, for the first time during the fall of 1953, and they were first admitted to Woman's College (an undergraduate college) at Greensboro during the fall of 1956.

The first Negroes, again by court order, were admitted as undergraduates to the University in 1955-1956. The previous policy of the trustees of the University had been to look upon Negro state-supported colleges as institutions that were providing adequate and equal educational facilities in their undergraduate departments and, for that reason, applications of Negroes to the undergraduate departments of the three branches of the University of North Carolina had not been accepted.

Desegregation in institutions of higher learning in North Carolina has been limited primarily to the three branches of the University of North Carolina. The total Negro enrollment in the three branches of the university during the 1960-1961 session was approximately 70. However, it may be noted that Asheville-Biltmore Junior College and Charlotte Junior College, public supported institutions, opened their facilities to Negroes as of the first semester of the academic year 1961-1962.

Southeastern Theological Seminary at Wake Forest opened its facilities to Negroes in the fall of 1958, and has had one or more Negroes enrolled each year thereafter. Duke University at Durham and Wake Forest College at Winston-Salem, outstanding private institutions, have recently desegregated their graduate and professional schools, and Negroes have begun matriculating at these institutions as of the summer of 1961. Mars Hill College, a previously all-white private institution, admitted a Negro for the first time in September 1961, and it was announced on October 18 by the president that Guilford College, a Quaker college located in the Greensboro area, would admit several Negroes during the fall of the academic year 1962-1963.

The enrollment of white students in Negro colleges has been almost nil. Bennett College at Greensboro, Barber Scotia College at Concord, and Shaw University at Raleigh, private colleges, have had white students in their enrollments. There were no white students enrolled in a predominantly tax-supported Negro institution during the 1960-1961 academic year.

VIRGINIA

The University of Virginia was the first white institution in the state to desegregate. A Negro was admitted to its law school in the fall of 1950 by court order. The University has followed the policy of admitting Negroes to such graduate and professional programs as the schools of law, medicine, education, engineering, and the arts and sciences. Virginia State College, a Negro institution, is expected to meet the undergraduate and some of the graduate needs of Negroes since this institution offers the master's degree in a number of fields.

In the fall of 1960-1961 Negroes were enrolled in four of the thirteen previously all-white state-supported institutions of higher learning: Medical College of Virginia, Richmond Professional Institute, University of Virginia, and Virginia Polytechnic Institute. The Negro enrollment in the fall of 1960-1961 in these four states institutions was 57. A fifth school, William and Mary, has admitted Negroes to its graduate and professional schools, beginning in 1951, and has awarded degrees to two. In the past, Negroes have attended such previously all-white private colleges as Union Theological Seminary (Presbyterian), and General Assembly Training School of the Presbyterian Church of the United States, Bridgewater College, and Mennonite College. However, there were no Negroes enrolled at William and Mary during the academic year 1960-1961. Virginia Union University and Hampton Institute, Negro private colleges, have always been open to all students regardless of race.

No white students are enrolled at Virginia State College, the traditionally Negro college. The total enrollment in the two divisions of this college was more than 4,000 during the fall of 1960-1961.

FLORIDA

Three Negroes were admitted to the graduate school of the University of Florida, by court order, during the summer of 1959, and in the fall of 1959-1960 term, a Negro woman was enrolled in its medical school. These four persons were the first of their race to be admitted to the University of Florida or to any other previously all-white institutions of higher learning in the state. At the beginning of the 1960-1961 session a Negro was accepted in the University law school, and it is reported that he was the only Negro enrolled during the 1960-1961 academic year.

St. Petersburg Junior College, a public supported institution, joined the University of Florida when it opened its facilities to Negroes during the first semester of the school year 1961-1962. In addition, it may be noted that the University of South Florida at Tampa, a state-supported institution, announced that several Negroes had applied and that their applications were being processed.

Florida A. and M. University at Tallahassee is an all-Negro state-supported institution. This university maintains a college of liberal arts and sciences, a college of education, a college of agriculture and home economics, school of nursing, a college of pharmacy, vocational technical institute, a law school, and a graduate school which offers the master's degree in elementary education, curriculum, secondary education, administration and supervision, and guidance.

Negroes were admitted to the University of Miami, a private institution, during the summer of 1961.

GEORGIA

Two Negroes entered the University of Georgia in January, 1961, under U.S. District Court order. Georgia maintains one desegregated, three all-Negro, and fourteen all white public colleges and universities.

Georgia Tech, located in Atlanta, became the second previously all white Georgia public institution to desegregate when in September 1961, it admitted three Negroes. These students were very well received, and there were no reports of violence or disturbances of any kind.[1]

One formerly all-white private college in Georgia, Columbia Seminary (Presbyterian), accepts both Negro and white students, and several predominantly Negro colleges in the Atlanta area have small numbers of white students in their enrollments.

Thus far, Negroes have not been admitted to tax-supported institutions of higher learning in Alabama, Mississippi, and South Carolina. In fact, there has been no desegregation in any type of public or state-supported school in these states.

ALABAMA

Miss Autherine Lucy, a Negro, attended the University of Alabama, by federal court order, for several days in 1956, but was expelled for accusing university officials of conspiracy in the disorders that accompanied the desegregation. The court upheld the expulsion, but the school is still under court order to admit Negroes. Several Negroes applied at University Center in Montgomery in 1960, but were not accepted.

[1] *Southern School News (October, 1961)*. Vol. 8, No. 4.

Two private colleges in Alabama have enrolled both Negro and white students. In the fall of 1960-61, Negroes were enrolled at Spring Hill College, a Catholic institution, and white students were enrolled at Talledega College, a predominantly Negro institution. One Catholic college in Mississippi for the training of priests has been desegregated.

V. Conclusions and Implications

1. Desegregation in tax-supported institutions of higher learning was almost invariably initiated by court order with the U. S. Supreme Court decisions giving impetus and momentum to the movement. However, in recent years desegregation in many sections of the Southern region has been advancing at a steady rate under more desirable motivations with many high level officials, heads of colleges and universities, church groups, editors of newspapers, college professors, students, and other public spirited individuals and groups endorsing it because they felt it both legally and morally right.

2. Practically all of the Southern states admitting Negroes to formerly all-white schools began in the graduate and professional schools of their universities, and are gradually desegregating their undergraduate programs. The prevailing point of view was that Negroes should first exhaust all available offerings in the traditional Negro college before entering the all-white colleges and universities. Unfortunately, this point of view is still apparent in some states today, and if continued, will necessarily tend both to restrict the Negro enrollment in formerly all-white institutions and the number of schools involved in desegregated programs. It has been primarily by court order that many of these states have opened all phases of their institutional offerings to Negroes.

3. The increased enrollment of Negroes in the various departments and schools of these formerly all-white institutions of higher learning will conserve a vast reserve of human resources that could play a major role in the economic, social, and educational development of the Southern region.

4. It may be noted that the pace at which formerly all-Negro institutions of higher learning are desegregating is comparatively

slow. This may be partly attributed to the large number of good colleges available to white students, the inertia of local customs and traditions, and to a feeling of pressure that may come from those who control and determine the destinies of these colleges.

5. The change from complete segregation to varying degrees of desegregation has been taking place in public-supported institutions of higher learning in fourteen Southern states, and in all colleges and universities of the District of Columbia area, in an atmosphere relatively free of serious tensions, frustrations, and unfavorable incidents.

6. One or more formerly all-white private institutions of higher learning in the following thirteen states have admitted Negroes: Missouri, Maryland, West Virginia, Kentucky, Oklahoma, Texas, Arkansas, Tennessee, North Carolina, Virginia, Alabama, Georgia, and Mississippi.

7. The number of states that have not begun programs of desegregation is dwindling with only Alabama, Mississippi, and South Carolina maintaining complete segregation in their tax-supported institutions of higher learning.

8. The general effect of desegregation on the predominantly Negro college is frequently discussed in academic circles. Its existence as an institution for all people will depend largely upon the quality of its facilities and programs. There is reason to believe that during these times when the demand for a college education is so acute, the resources of all standard colleges will be increasingly used by all the people. The implication is that desegregation may enhance the growth of the predominantly Negro college which maintains high academic standards and superior facilities. On the other hand, it is very probable that the below-average Negro colleges with low academic standards will face difficulty in surviving in a "speeded up" program of desegregation.

9. It is likely that some of the graduate and professional offerings and specialized curricula in many of the traditionally tax-supported Negro colleges will be absorbed by formerly all-white universities to reduce unnecessary duplication of efforts as desegregation gains increased momentum.

X

Problems of Desegregation and Integration Confronting the Administrator

Katharine Dresden
Professor of Education
Chico State College, California

I. THE NEED FOR ACTION RESEARCH

SUPREME Court decisions will not solve all of the problems of desegregation in our schools. Indeed, in this instance, problems have been created where they did not exist before. Deep resentments, old animosities, and scapegoating will go on, at the least, for a generation. The administrator of a mixed school has always had these problems in a greater or lesser degree. The longer the mixed situation continues, however, the degree lessens, a fact that may bring a measure of comfort to the administrator in the newly mixed school who is facing the problem for the first time. And, by way of adding a further complication within the present, for the first time there will be Negro principals in schools where white children are enrolled.

These administrators, Negro or white, will have a two-fold task: first, they will need to take care of the immediate situation, with all of its tensions and complications; and, second, they will need to create a school and community climate that will eventually erase the problem entirely. Under these circumstances they may find it useful to introduce action research, in an effort to gain control of differing facets of their problem. What they will need to recognize is that people, not only the structure of the school, must undergo reconstruction, and that those who are to handle the operation must solve the problems and set up the system. Action research, in the view of many, is the best stimulus to growth in ability and to the transformation of attitude.

As outlined by those who have used it extensively, action research incorporates the following four steps:

1. *Defining the problem.* A clear definition by the practitioner of the problem he wants to do something about is necessary to orient his attack, and to make possible an appraisal of the results. A good definition should point to (a) the nature of the current inadequacy, and (b) the results that are desired. Unless rigorous precautions are taken, this may be done superficially, with the problem defined turning out not to be the real problem at all.

2. *Hypothesizing.* The planning of procedures to achieve the desired results involves a prediction that certain desired outcomes will follow from given practices. A good hypothesis must fulfill three criteria: (a) it must incorporate the best of current practices, (b) it must be in accord with accepted scientific principles, and (c) it must be testable—that is, it must specify the observable results that will be evidence of success or failure.

3. *Testing the hypothesis.* The procedures for collecting the evidence required to test the hypothesis are essentially those we associate with the scientific method. The hypothesis serves as a guide.

4. *Generalizing.* Investigations using action research are concerned with improvement of a program in the immediate locale. They do not necessarily lead to inferences as to what results may be achieved in another place, or indeed, at another time in the same place.

It is important to note, with respect to definition of the problem in an action research program, that as the project develops, the problem may become more sharply defined as those engaged in the research acquire greater insight. Ordinarily, in a formal research project, once the problem is defined, it must stay that way to fit the research design. In action research, however, the definition is more likely to evolve. The problem, for instance, is usually defined initially as an intention to use a certain procedure. This was well-illustrated in the experience of the California Current Materials Project, where the definition of the problem underwent three states:

1. How can we utilize current materials in the classroom?
2. How can we teach subject matter more effectively with the use of current materials?
3. How can we develop pupil initiative and effectiveness in attacking and solving problems in everyday life?

Since it is the expectation, in action research, that the definition of the problem will undergo an evolution, the hypothesis, too, must undergo adjustment. The entire design of the project is continually readapted to test new hypotheses developed, as it were, in mid-stream. Thus, it is clear, in the above instance, that the hypothesis advanced to solve the problem of promoting subject-matter learning would differ from the one advanced to solve the problem of promoting the broader purposes that emerged in the third state of the project.

One of the contributions made by the development of action research projects, which is a major concern of this writing, has been to identify the function of the administrator in contributing to their effectiveness. It is now generally accepted that action research should advance on the part of those engaged in it, in addition to serving as an instrument for program development. The activity should result not only in a revised program but, equally, in a staff whose increased insights and understanding will enable it to put the program into effect. The administrator, as he engages a staff in action research, may well be considered a director of learning. As such, he is responsible for establishing optimum learning conditions. The more important conditions for which he is responsible are discussed below.

Readiness of the Staff to Improve Programs and Procedures

Without interest and motivation, little of importance is learned in the class room. Similarly, the likelihood of improvement as a consequence of an action research program is slight unless the teachers, supervisors, and administration recognize the need for improvement and are ready to talk about and analyze the problems that trouble them. There are several reasons why they may be reluctant to become involved in such a program.

1. Unless the leaders are willing to admit the possibility of improvement in their operations, the staff may see no need to admit any limitations. One quickly learns from experience that to admit nothing is the most likely way to escape blame.

2. In many circles, creative ideas are viewed with alarm, rather than with interest, by both teachers and administrators.

3. If the program of research (or the planning for it) does not result in some form of action, a staff will soon become cynical. All teachers are familiar with the expressions, "What's the use? We meet and talk and plan, and nothing ever happens," which result when initial administrative excitement is quietly shelved.

Concern with Evidence

The elements of action research are simple: first, there is the need to specify what evidence will be necessary to test the hypothesis bearing, for instance, on the Study of Current Materials, stimulation and profit result from interchange of procedures and results. Many of the most important educational outcomes, indeed, are group achievements; and, as experience is gained, the responsibility for studying problems is more and more a group responsibility, rather than an individual one. Within action research the opportunities to learn to work effectively with others are many; hence, within the program itself techniques for group work may be learned through practice and evaluation. Direction of this learning, is an administrative responsibility.

II. A Specific Instance of Integration

Let us see how action research operated in a program of integration. The old Galena Street School in Milwaukee experienced the usual deterioration of an urban school in an expanding community. Built in the last decade of the nineteenth century, it was attended by the sons and daughters of the wealthy bankers, shippers, and brewers, whose ornate mansions surrounded the school. When the automobile made it possible for the elite to move to the suburbs, the homes were made into flats and light housekeeping apartments for brewery workers. When they, too, were able to build their own homes in fringe areas, foreigners moved into the vacated quarters.

The school is a district school. Its attendance is determined, therefore, by the residents of the area, and by 1940 the school, being in the center of a miserable slum, had experienced marked change in its student body. Many of the surrounding "residences" were uninhabited and uninhabitable. When the influx of southern Negroes to man the defense plants started, they drifted into this area. Milwaukee's compulsory school law really works. Every police man, every social worker, every pastor stops every school-age child on the streets during school hours. Merchants hurry the children out of their stores, theater managers will not sell them tickets. Hence, children of newcomers are soon herded into the schools.

Day by day Galena Street School became more Negro, moving from 10 percent Negro and 90 percent white to 25 percent Negro and 75 percent white to an unstable, with the flood still coming, fifty-fifty basis. Fights on the playground which were weekly occurrences at first began to occur daily, often several simultaneously. The old-time teachers talked with nostalgia of the "good old days" —when children were good, when they wanted to learn, when they were white. The principal, however, was not one of those "good old days" dreamers. He was living in the present. He annoyed his teachers with such questions as: "What are we going to do about it?"; "Are they really 'dumb'?"; "Why do they fight?"; "What ought we to teach them?"

He called regular staff meetings to discuss these problems. He inspired his teachers to analyze their problems from the points of view of psychology and sociology. Some of the teachers started child study projects. He invited every expert he knew to make a contribution in terms of time and knowledge. The head of the Urban League came to discuss the Negro, his culture, his education, his needs. A school psychometrist spent a week gathering data on "Are these children 'dumb'?" And so on, and on.

With study came knowledge, sympathetic understanding, and intelligent proposals to try out. For example, if a child from Mississippi brought a record showing him to be eleven years of age and in the fifth grade, the school knew immediately that he had, at best, attended school 100 days a year for four years. Milwaukee children, in contrast, attended 180 days for four years. Obviously these educational backgrounds were not equal, and this quite apart from the facts that the teachers in the two states had met differing credential requirements and the per capita expenditures on education in these states were not the same. Since it is not wise to place an eleven year old in the second or third grade, separate sections were established in some classes. Grouping was used in others.

As soon as they were available, Negro teachers were hired. This was for morale effect in the first instance, to give both Negroes and whites the opportunity to experience the respect which professional people have for each other. But, in the second instance, there was the need to offset the difficulty the southern Negro parent confronted in talking freely to white teachers. Some Negro children, in addition, found it easier to unburden themselves to Negro teachers. The white principal, in his effort to understand the southern Negro and his minority status better, enrolled in a southern Negro college one summer. He shared dormitory life with the other students and studied Negro sociology.

Meanwhile, greater emphasis was given to the social situation among the children than to strict academic learning. The music department made extra supervisors available for group experiences in choral work, band, and orchestra. Folk dancing was emphasized because of the physical contact involved. The problem of fighting on the playground was solved by providing a socially acceptable outlet, readily available on account of the current popularity of Joe Louis. Supervised boxing was permitted on the school grounds during recess, before, and after school. What had been rowdyism was converted to sportsmanlike contests.

By the close of the war the school was 90 percent Negro, 10

percent white. The school, however, had regained its academic respectability. Its "graduates" stand up well with other incoming high school students. This is an example, first, of proposed procedures; and, second, while the procedures are being used, the collection, if possible, of the indicated evidence. It is the awareness of the significance of evidence which is the essential difference between practices more or less casually tried out and practices deliberately planned and tested. This concern for evidence has broader and concomitant values in the total educational program. For example:

1. By pointing to the desired changes, consideration of evidence clarifies the objectives and suggests further promising procedures to make the objects of research.
2. By directing attention to pupil growth, teaching practices are improved as they become less self-centered and are evaluated in terms of what changes occur for, and in, students.
3. A test is provided which will differentiate fads from promising improvements in practice. When proponents of planned new practices are required to present evidence of their effectiveness, the danger of outside (or public) criticism is reduced and the educational cultist is checkmated.

The elements of action research may be simply stated but this in no way implies that the conduct of the research is easy. Technical competence and a critical attitude are required. To develop these requires the application of rigorous thought in numerous specific situations. This is a demanding process, sometimes a confusing one. It is not likely to be carried through in a staff without the thoughtful and sensitive leadership of the administration; and, perhaps, without the stimulation and guidance that occasional consultant services may provide.

Developing Effective Procedures for Group Activity

Action research is commonly a cooperative activity. The reasons for this have been indicated above. But even where all of the projects are individual, the results may be pooled with the total impact felt on each project and on the entire area. Thus individual research in the California program of stunts, games, scouting, and similar activities resulted in a sharp decline in the incidence of disease and in juvenile delinquency.

III. Planning to Live by the Law

The principal of Galena Street School did not know what he was getting into in 1940. Today every principal knows what the situation is and can plan for it.[1] First, however, he must accept the fact of the law, of the decision.[2] It has to be lived with as part of the culture. Administrators must accept desegregation and, especially white administrators must accept it emotionally, as well as intellectually. This will not be easy for many, yet the problem can be solved if there exists a determination to solve it. Unless this determination is generated, solution, is of course, impossible.

Before moving into a program of action, however, there are certain dominant factors in the situation which administrators will do well to review.

1. As we have indicated above, he must recognize the inevitability of the situation. The Supreme Court has ruled, the decision is here; hence, action must be taken.

2. Jefferson said that "The most sacred of the duties of government is to do equal and impartial justice to all of its citizens." The administrator is responsible for creating the educational situation in which boys and girls receive an education based

---

[1] The classic instance at the moment of planning the move to integration is presented by Omer Carmichael and Weldon James in *The Louisville Story* (the story of a southern city transforming its entire school system, New York: Simon and Schuster, Inc., 1957). In contrast, of course, the city of Little Rock, Arkansas, which equally planned through its officials a start toward integration at the high school level, was thrown into turmoil by the overt action to thwart its planning which the Governor of the State initiated. Between these extremes we have the illustrations of progress "along the border," in Maryland, West Virginia, and Washington, D.C., as well as notably, in Clinton and Nashville, Tennessee, and movements scattered from North Carolina to Texas. See *What's Happening in School Integration*, by Harold C. Fleming and John Constable (New York: Public Affairs Pamphlet No. 244, 1956.)

[2] That the "hard core" states have neither accepted the law nor given up their effort to escape its reach by the enactment of over-riding state law is one of the disturbing (and from a world view, shocking) phenomena of present-day democracy.

on free and impartial justice. Most school administrators, white and Negro, are basically in sympathy with this statement, and hence with integration. Philosophically, psychologically, sociologically, they say with the court, "We must consider public education in the light of its full development and its present place in American life throughout the Nation. . . . (Public education) is perhaps the most important function of state and local governments. . . . In these days, it is doubtful that any child may be reasonably expected to succeed in life if he is denied the opportunity of an education. Such an opportunity, where the state has undertaken to provide it, is a right which must be made available to all on equal terms."

3. The school, through its official leadership, the board of education and the superintendent, must take the action. No community can wait until parents and local courts take action; nor should it depend upon "outside" agencies to implement the decision. And, of course, after the administration has exercised appropriate leadership, it is the school personnel which will make desegregation and integration actualities.

4. There will be opposing forces. They should be met on an intellectual basis in a planned program. Social science has contributed facts derived from scientific studies of pressure groups, their activities, and how to meet them. No administrator dare ignore these studies.

5. The school is the formal institution through which the society transmits its culture to youth and through which it provides experience in democracy. It has been guilty often in the past of transmitting a perversion of culture and of teaching undemocratic principles. Some teachers have taught the myth of white supremacy; some schools have not given equal opportunity to all children. Some schools and some teachers have favored children from the "right side of the tracks." At times the one or two brilliant Negroes permitted to attend schools that are basically segregated have been over-played to prove the school's innocence in anti-Negro discrimination. Each administrator must look hard at his school system to remove these failures to live up to its high trust.

6. Each school is unique. There may be factors common to several schools, but the syndrome rearranges itself, admitting some factors and omitting others. This does not mean that the administrator will not get help and release by discussing his situation with other administrators in local or national associations. It does mean, however, that each faces a special problem.

7. Finally, it may be well to warn that desegregation and integration are not isolated, unique problems. They are part of the total web of society. They are inextricably bound up with society's attitude toward the dignity of the individual. If the society considers the individual precious, and acts accordingly, then there can be no choice as between white and Negro pupils. This means that the entire school must be organized to give every boy and every girl the maximum opportunity to develop optimally so that he can make his maximum contribution to society.

Having accepted these assumptions (or alternatives) the administrator should plan an appropriate program. In doing this he should work closely with the governing board of the school. Some administrators consider the board as an employer and are inclined to expect leadership from it. They fail to recognize that leadership in education is a professional prerogative and obligation. It may sometimes be unwise or unnecessary for the board to go on record in regard to the issue of desegregation and integration. But it is necessary that there be understanding and interaction among board members and administrators. The latter must know the attitude of each member toward the issue, and, likewise, the board members must know the administrator's program of action and be given opportunity to participate in it.

In some school districts there will be many administrative problems—shifting children, staff changes, equipment needs, and the like. Legal problems may be involved also. Here the administrator must be prepared to work closely and tirelessly with the board and other authorities. Upon him will fall the responsibility of easing tense situations, of keeping developments moving smoothly and quickly, of arbitrating between dissident persons, of going more than half way. On him, also, will fall the responsibility, in the final analysis, of going to the city or district attorney with those who persist in holding out against the law.[3]

IV. THE INDIVIDUAL TEACHER OF CRUCIAL IMPORTANCE

The actual success or failure of integration rests with the teacher, classroom by classroom. It is the teachers who show acceptance or rejection and who, thus, set the pattern, often unconsciously, which the children follow. Ideally, the teachers should be prepared for integration within the classroom before it happens. Actually, this cannot be. We may deal with this problem at the intellectual level and believe we are well prepared to meet it; but, in fact, its full character is not apparent until we are in the midst of it.

The white teachers who face a class of Negro children, or a class with only two or three Negroes in it, are already in need of help. The first faculty meeting of the year, therefore, may well be devoted to: "What problems do we face as a result of desegregation?" This approach may provide an emotional catharsis. It may release the guilt feelings of those who are conscience smitten because the Negro child constitutes a problem to them. It gives evidence to individual teachers that their colleagues are equally concerned. They need no longer guess about the attitudes of others. It is an intellectual approach, one that will place factors in their proper perspective. As discussion leads to a categorization of the problems teachers face and share, an orderly attack upon them can be made.

Each faculty must seek solutions to its own problems. It may decide to turn to a committee procedure, with each committee constituting an interest group that will do the basic research in one area and with all sharing results as the study proceeds. The

---

[3] It may of course be taken out of his hands, and away from all local authorities, by intervention at the state level, with a resulting need for federal action, as happened in Little Rock, Arkansas, in September, 1957. More likely, however, the experience of Little Rock will lead more communities to act with responsibility and promptness as was done in Nashville, Tennessee, at the same moment of time. And of course, other governors may not wish to become a participant in the Faubus story.

administrator, of course, will play a leadership role throughout, especially as he sees to it that the "research" does not become mere busy-work and that the end of action that will remove the problems (or, at least, lessen their immediate effects upon the life of the school) is held steadily in view.

As soon as the teachers start such cooperative work on their problems, it is fair to anticipate that their attitudes will change, as will their conduct of the classroom. Thus, the situation analyzed in the fall will not exist, or will be modified, by spring. As the staff grows professionally, other phases of the problem will be met with less strain and an enhanced confidence.

Within the classroom of course, each teacher may be expected to handle the situation in ways unique to him. Yet we may expect the teachers to share a common concern—namely, never to be accused of favoritism, whether of girls over boys, rich over poor, bright over dull, or Negro over white. When classes are conducted on the basis of problem solving or the unit method, or activities, or life situations, or experiences, to use other roughly comparable designations, a minimum of difficulty with Negro-white relations will be experienced. In these classes sharing and cooperation, rather than competition, will be normal attributes of the work and will provide a ground for the development of mutual respect.

A teacher may find it possible (though others may want to shun this as they would the plague) to develop a unit that is directly concerned with desegregation, integration, or the development of mutual respect. Such a unit would arise normally in the social studies and lead to such questions as: How does desegregation fulfill the spirit of democracy? How can South Africa avoid the historic American pattern of race relations? What is the relationship between economics and the acceptance of the Negro? Teachers of literature, art, and music on the other hand, may want to develop units on Negro contributions to the arts. Perhaps this would be a good time to review Othello, Langston Hughes, James Weldon Johnson, W. E. B. DuBois, Paul Lawrence Dunbar. *Uncle Tom's Cabin* could be analyzed in terms of the present. Negro musicians, athletes, and scientists could be given special consideration in music, physical education, or science classes—not because they are Negroes but because of their competence within these fields. Great care must be taken, quite obviously, to make such study genuine.

Thus will the teacher, who is deeply convinced of his responsibility to the youth of a democratic nation, approach the problem of developing good citizens. He will express immediate objectives in terms of desired pupil behavior. Through action research he will involve himself, Negro pupils, and white pupils in living and working together, thus changing attitudes which are the base on which the desired pupil behavior must rest. This will be difficult for some teachers, as it always has been difficult for some teachers for whom the problem is not new. But the administrator, by planning group discussions in faculty meetings and turning a sympathetic ear to these teachers may help them overcome their difficulties progressively. As he develops ways of bringing pupils together —committee work, group projects, sharing of responsibility, dramatic presentations, etc.—the teacher will, in turn, find the situation easier and less strained.

A teacher problem the administrator must handle with utmost care arises in adding a Negro teacher to an all-white faculty, or a white teacher to an all-Negro one. The choice should be made only when there is a teacher available who is up to the standard of the other staff members. He should be accepted professionally and socially, with dignity, and not with acclaim, fanfare, or maudlin sentimentality. Teachers, pupils, and parents should be prepared for the move so that his acceptance will not be questioned.

Further, as has been demonstrated since the 1954 Court decision, a part of the responsibility for making integration a reality will rest with the pupils. This is especially the case in the secondary schools. Careful preparation is required if the students are to handle the situation intelligently. Much will depend, of course, on how much leadership they have been accustomed to exercise. Where they have had little opportunity to exercise leadership, a start may be made by inviting potential leaders to take part in the deliberations of a faculty committee. Sociometric techniques must be used to select the leaders in order to do more than select those whom teachers *think* are leaders because they admire them for one reason or another. Negro and white pupils should be chosen, but there should be no attempt to provide an equal number or proportional representation. This is a false base on which to choose leaders, and the students must be made aware of this.

Student leaders may wish to tackle the problem independently. If there is a Student Council it may plan ways to deal with it. Otherwise, a special group, composed of the captains of the teams, editors of the periodicals, class presidents, and other comparable leaders may serve as a council substitute. However the group is composed, a faculty counselor, whose sole responsibility will be to advise the students as they identify and handle problems, conduct research, and evaluate content and process, should be made available to it.

Faculty and student leaders should work first to achieve basic understanding of the differing aspects of the problem of integration. It will then be necessary to devise means for making this understanding available to the entire student body. In some places, it may be necessary to keep emphasizing, "this is the law, this is the decision." But the important approach, of course, is functional. Some of the more obvious functional approaches are singing together in the choir, playing together in the orchestra, marching together in the band, performing together in drama, being on the same athletic team. In these activities the entire concern is to produce through the sharing of talent, a performance of which the individuals and the school may be proud.

In certain activities, such as a Student Council election, in which both Negroes and whites will be eligible, extreme care will need to be exercised. The principal (along with the teachers, of course) must be very close to his student body so that he may detect any developing whispering campaigns before they become rampant. A healthy, open campaign with parties, platforms, and real issues and slogans will do more than anything else to keep the election clean.

V. The Community Must Be Reached

When the administrator has his staff working on the problem in faculty meetings and in individual classrooms, when he has his student body cooperating in creating a democratic school, he has not finished his task. Simultaneously, he will need to create a program of community education. The details of this will vary community by community: how far integration has already taken place, how receptive the people are to it, what is being done by other agencies.

This last point is exceedingly important. Integration is not a school problem alone. The school is merely one facet of a total community. The principal may take the leadership role for a given school in getting his immediate community together as the superintendent will need to be a leader in the community as a whole. Genuine leadership in the community must be tapped. Presidents of men's service clubs, of the Ladies Aid, of workers organizations may be called upon; but only if they seem to be appropriate. How are the administrators to know upon whom to draw in building a School-Community Council? The National Citizen's Commission for the Public Schools can provide suggestions, as can the Extension Departments or the Adult Education Division of many state universities.

When the leaders have been identified the administrator may want to proceed with them as he did with the teachers, using the meeting to list problems, categorize them, and set up study committees. The task of working with and directing lay committees in a community that is inexperienced in working together is, of course, enormous. But heavy, intensive work for a short period will prevent the sorrow and irreparable harm that is almost certain to result if the task is not done. These committees share their studies with the entire group periodically, perhaps in the form of a film, a report by a social worker or minister, a lecture by an expert, or a panel discussion. Finally, a program of action must also be chalked out, action addressed to such questions as: How are we going to get this information to the organizations we represent? and What are we going to do when we have the information? All decisions must emerge from the group; the administrator, however, must serve as a guide as they are reached.

Press, TV, radio, and the pulpit should be represented on the School-Community Council. Whether or not separate committees are created to deal with segregation and integration through mass communicative media will depend upon local conditions. It is important to note, however, that the choice between a calm or hysteria approach lies rather largely in the hands of these who work in these media, depending upon the relative emphasis given constructive action and unfortunate incidents. The Student Council may find it helpful to have press, TV, and radio committees to handle releases to the public, as well as to initiate programs over the school inter-communication system.

Representatives of the police and the courts can form another subdivision of the School-Community Council. They will be especially concerned to foster preventive practices. The FBI and the police systems of many cities have already done yeoman work in this field and their experience is available to all law-enforcement officers.

Business and labor leaders should be involved in this community undertaking, also. They are influential in the economic situation, and economics is the base of much interracial conflict. Their attitudes, as expressed before students, at their own dinner tables, or through press and radio are as critical as when they are expressed through hiring standards and conditions of labor. The latter is of especial importance to the parents of the school children immediately and, in the very near future, will be important to the children as they seek employment.

The mother frequently sets the moral and spiritual tone of the home and particular programs should be created to give her an opportunity to clarify her thinking on the problem, especially in regard to race myths. Some of the more persistent myths, harmful to the development of good relations among school children, are: (1) The Negro is strong physically, but weak intellectually. If he shows intellectual achievement, this is because of an admixture of white blood. (2) Mixing, however, brings out the worst in both races. (3) Negroes are inferior people, primitive, closer to our common ancestor, the ape. (4) Negro women are fat, easy going, and slovenly. (5) Negro men are "end men," singing, dancing, cracking jokes, idling in the sun. (6) Negro men are eager to marry white girls.

The first five myths are easily disproven by evidence that parents may willingly accept. The sixth is a source of worry to many white mothers, however, who believe that socialization between the races will result in intermarriage; hence, a warning may not be amiss here. Socialization between classes, races, and religions is a touchy issue. One may well question, on the ground that a family responsibility is involved, the "right" of school officials to decree for or against such socialization in the school. Each family has its own standards in the matter of having its children avoid, or seek, friendships with certain other children. Parents develop attitudes in their children toward the ne'er-do-well, the renegade, the unmoral child. The school builds positively, however, to make self-respecting, moral citizens, by providing opportunities for their good qualities to develop. This involves cooperation and sharing not only within the classroom but within the total life of the school. This action does not involve dating, dancing, and other out-of-school activities, whatever the make-up of the school population. Administrators and teachers, having come to terms with the meaning of American democracy, will help parents realize that when their children (white or Negro) are educated together it does not follow that they will socialize, and perhaps marry, outside of set family standards. Merely to tell this to a mother, however, is frequently useless. She needs the chance, along with other mothers, to discuss the problem with experts in the field of race, as she also needs encouragement to build her own conclusions on a base of evidence.

An aspect of community-school relations which presents a problem not easily solved is the handling of undemocratic pressure groups. Such groups carry on campaigns of hate in every community where there is a possibility of the formation of anti-Negro groups. Where these groups operate in the open and above ground, they can be met by counter-action and education.[4] But all too frequently, they are clandestine or pose behind patriotic fronts. The administrator must be aware of each one. The police and press may know who and where they are. Once the groups are identified, the Community-School Council may develop plans to deal with them.

[4] This has been demonstrated in such communities as Baltimore, Maryland, and Washington, D.C., and, more recently, dramatically in Nashville, Tennessee.

Publicity which directs attention to the true nature of these organizations is frequently effective and police identification of the leaders is essential. The point is that this is not a matter for the administrator to deal with alone.

Many have wondered why administrators are so silent on the issue of desegregation and integration. A search of the literature, both professional and popular, and of the files of radio and television programs, shows that very few administrators have come forward "to be counted" on this issue. The advances made, as is proper enough, have been made by citizens—politicians, church leaders, influential editors and scholars (Negro and white), lawyers, and dedicated organizations such as the National Association for the Advancement of Colored People. But these people are not professional educators. Their achievements, however, have brought the problem to the door-step of the school administrator. What, then, shall he do and say? He should tell his community what his schools are doing. His voice should be heard on the air as he tells his fellow citizens how the democratic value of respecting the individual is pursued in his schools. He should be heard telling his school patron that his school is a microcosm of the macrocosm of society, that his school is populated by boys and girls, the future citizens of democracy—not by Negroes, whites, Jews, gentiles, or peons. He should accept responsibility for helping to mold public opinion concerning integration in education and he should be the author of accounts of implementation of the ruling. In sum, the school administrator should be guided, as he provides leadership to students, teachers, parents, and citizens generally, by convictions and principles of the following character:

1. He must accept the decision of the court in his heart as well as in his mind and move at once into a program of constructive action.
2. He has the responsibility of obtaining and directing the close and active cooperation of the school board in the total program of desegregation and integration in education.
3. He must direct his staff in the identification of the special problems it faces and help them in solving them.
4. He must encourage teachers to base their relationships to students on such democratic principles as respect for the individual, for

appropriate cooperative effort, and for rational thought—all, in this instance, designed to reduce the problems integration has brought to the fore.

5. Student Councils must be given sympathetic direction in approaching an analysis and solution of the problem in each school.

6. He must tackle the community aspects of the problem by providing for the active participation of the concerned and sensitive individuals and organizations.

7. He must learn to use the mass communication media to advance the understanding of the problems involved in desegregation and integration in education throughout the community, being especially concerned with those aspects of insight that will prevent the emergence of problems.

8. He must learn to identify the undemocratic pressure groups that work against integration and how to meet them with programs of education or, if necessary, with legal action.

9. Negroes and whites must be jointly involved in action, and often in study and research, on how to live together.

Thus will education help America fulfill her great destiny.

PART IV

THE FUTURE TASK

XI

Beyond Legislation and Litigation—What?

Dan W. Dodson
Professor of Education
New York University

THE strategies needed to provide further opportunity for the education of American Negroes will depend upon what local groups conceive to be the fundamental issue in present-day race relations, particularly as it relates to the power structure. Certain alternative positions are currently advocated.

One of these is that posed by Oliver C. Cox to the effect that the low status position of the Negro in America today is caused by economic forces. From this position, any attempt to work within the present power structure is collaboration. He says:

Collaboration proposes to achieve civil rights through indirect, ingratiatory, suppliant tactics. Its program is essentially that designed for Negroes by the white ruling class; hence it expects civil rights to be granted beneficently as a reward for development of good behavior and trustworthiness among Negroes. It places responsibility for civic discrimination against Negroes upon their own imputed lack of merit and economic stability It maintains, therefore, that Negroes should never struggle directly for civil rights, but should rather concentrate upon their education and material development. Civil rights will then follow as a sort of social luxury.[1]

This position despairs that the power structure can be changed within the framework of present economic organization. It would contend that the status of Negroes can be improved appreciably only by making common cause with other disprivileged economic elements of the society to wrest power from the ruling economic interests.

A good case could be made that the gains achieved over the past decade have resulted from the majority group's relinquishing some of its power because of the fear aroused by the threat to the present system during the war era. Many would contend that the reversal of the *Plessy* v. *Ferguson* doctrine stemmed from the threat to the western socio-economic system posed by the rising tide of pressure on the part of colored peoples in the world as a whole.

The alternative position is that American Negroes belong to the body politic in the same way as all other citizens; that a statusless society does not exist; that arbitrary power is continuously in process of being brought under social control, i.e., regulation by the people themselves in whose collective hands is the ultimate source of power; that regulation is increasingly vested in those responsible to its source, the people, and decreasingly in the hands of those who are privileged to use it for arbitrary and capricious ends.

The Negro community of America has good reason to feel despair over the rate of progress in race relations down to the present, and a person who is white runs grave danger of being misunderstood in attempting to outline strategy on so fundamental an issue. This chapter is predicated on the hypothesis that there are other sources of power than economic, that there is a relationship between economic and educational disprivilege, and that gains made on one front automatically strengthen the position on the other. It is the position of this writer that the destruction of the present economic power structure would not free those who are disadvantaged because of educational or social backwardness. A

[1] Oliver C. Cox, "The Programs of Negro Civil Rights Organizations," *The Journal of Negro Education*, XX (Summer, 1951).

reciprocal relationship exists between gains made on the legal and political fronts and the educational and social development of capacity to hold these gains. The one without the other means little.

This is not to disparage the great advances in civil rights accomplished through legislation and litigation during the past decade. The May 17, 1954 Supreme Court ruling and those of the subsequent Monday climaxed this great advance. These gains are documented in other chapters. They leave much still to be done in the definition of social policy through legal and political means. The gains accomplished in this way are themselves educational. The advances of the future, however, will perhaps be decreasingly legal and increasingly volunteer, positive, social actions in local communities. The strategies which will move us forward on the legal front should in no wise be diminished, however.

The broad non-litigation tactics involved in implementing the Supreme Court decision seem to fall in three categories. The first includes those strategies designed to bring private power and privilege, whether held by groups or persons, ever under social regulation. In many local communities, this means a continued operation utilizing pressure, the weight of public opinion, etc., to change policies of agencies, organizations, and businesses so that all the people of the community participate in services, employment opportunities, and other advantages on a common basis of privilege.

The second aspect of strategy involves perhaps the psychological integration of the people of local communities into a common sense of identification and belonging. Undoubtedly the greatest barrier to participation in the American dream that a person will be rewarded according to his abilities and energies, is the psychological sense on the part of minority group members of being shut off; the never being quite certain that one is accepted; the continuous question mark as to whether even special opportunities are offered because of justly earned merit or because of racial status. This is illustrated, for instance, in many northern communities where Negro children still constitute a small proportion of school classes but are elected to offices out of all proportion to their numbers. The Negro student is never quite sure whether he is elected because he merits it or because he is a Negro. The strategy for dealing with this problem is complex but exceedingly important.

The third aspect of strategy is much more positive. It involves "taking up the slack" that has been caused by the patterns of the past. Equality of opportunity is not enough if it is conceived as simply giving an equal chance to every person as he is presently constituted. There is no equality of opportunity for the person who has been shut out of the main stream of American life, whose ancestors before him were shut out, if he must compete with persons who have had superior advantages. This is as true within groups as between groups. This is treacherous, dangerous ground ideologically, but it is a problem that must be faced realistically.

TACTICS RELATED TO THE SHIFT OF POWER IN COMMUNITY LIFE

Much work needs to be done in almost all communities at the present time to provide a better basis for integrating minority groups into the common life of the community. There are many agencies, including those of local government, which are still "Jim Crow." By and large, private agencies have been exempted from the law in most civil rights legislation. Most of the private agencies working in the average community still practice rank discrimination. In addition, patterns of residential living, despite the Supreme Court decision outlawing restrictive covenants, continue to make the average American city a rigidly segregated community. New York City's Harlem is as famous as a ghetto as were any of the Jewish ghettos of central Europe a few generations ago. It is interesting that the Puerto Rican population, which has migrated to the New York City community principally within the past ten years, is far less segregated than the Negro community. The techniques of social action required to break these barriers are quite varied. Outstanding among them would be the following:

Protest

The outstanding approach to social reform in race relations has been social protest. Protest literature has appeared in significant volume and quality. The capacity of Negro leadership to interpret the position of Negroes in the local community has been varied but protest, especially as it has involved pressure group tactics, has accomplished outstanding results in numerous instances. The protest group more nearly represents the conscience of the minority in the average community than any other phenomenon.

Protest carried too far, however, tends to have a deleterious effect upon the growth and development of youth. The phenomenon of scapegoating in which the minority youth blames his failures upon the inequities of the social system is well known in educational circles. In other words, if too much reliance is placed on protest the tendency of people to resign themselves to the fate depicted by the protestations stifles effort.

Confrontation

A second tactic that should be tremendously effective in the immediate years ahead is that of confrontation. There are many agencies and organizations which have heretofore excused their segregated practices because of the separate but equal doctrine. They are at present confronted with a completely changed set of relationships. Many of these agencies have the responsibility of inculcating the basic American ideals and values in the youth of the society. They are today confronted with a responsibility for re-aligning their own practices. Illustrative of these types of situations are:

(1) *The Churches:* The institutions of religion are today confronted with a great challenge. A fundamental tenet of their beliefs, other than the faith in God, is the brotherhood of man. Kramer, in a study of 13,597 churches of three denominations, discovered some ten per cent which are mixed congregations.[2] Most of these, however, include only one or two persons of the minority group and the three denominations (Congregational, United Lutheran, Presbyterian) are heavily concentrated in the non-southern sections of the United States.

It is true that there is a great resource for community betterment

[2] Alfred S. Kramer, "Racial Integration in the Protestant Denominations," *The Journal of Educational Sociology* (October, 1954).

of race relations in many of these institutions. The Roman Catholic Church, for instance, has taken the lead in many communities in the integration of their school systems. On the other hand, this particular faith is not heavily represented in the South except in a few communities like New Orleans. It is a rare thing that a minister can take an opposition position such as the Reverend Bill Carter of Hobbs, New Mexico, who from his pulpit opposed the integration of Negroes and whites in the school system. In spite of the fact that in the average community the church is one of the most segregated voluntary institutions, religious leadership is setting its sails "four square" on the issue. A "round up" of church group reactions to the Court decision from the *Interracial News Service*[3] is typical:

Georgia: "Four church groups and the League of Women Voters urged Attorney General Eugene Cook to reverse his position (take no official part in hearings before the U. S. Supreme Court this fall) on how the Court should implement its decision outlawing segregation in Public Schools."

Methodist: "Methodist annual conferences meeting since the United States Supreme Court ruling . . . have gone on record as indicating that the churches will make every effort to urge their members to conform to the adjustments which must be made to comply with the law." Conferences of Baltimore, Southwest Texas, and Minnesota were cited for resolutions calling for support of the Court ruling and integration within their local fellowships.

Council of Churches of New Orleans passed a resolution approving the Supreme Court decision. They said, "We call upon the members of our State Legislature to find just ways of implementing in our State the decision of the U. S. Supreme Court. We ask that in every circumstance they exercise clear and calm judgment and Christian good will in all their attitudes and actions in accordance with the ideals of our Christian faith."

[3] *Interracial News Service,* XXV (July-August, 1954).

Atlanta: Seven Atlanta ministers told members of the Christian Council of Atlanta ". . . that the churches have an obligation to help carry out the Supreme Court ruling against segregation and that the churches must lead in the matter of integration of the races."

These instances are cited to indicate that, while organized religion has a long way to go to achieve integration, the repository of idealism and spiritual strength to be found in the church is an asset which undoubtedly can make a contribution to a more wholesome climate of race relations.

(2) *Other Character-building Agencies:* In every community of consequence there are other character-building agencies which are confronted with a comparable dilemma. Boy Scouts, Girl Scouts, YMCA, and similar agencies can no longer rationalize a position that since education is segregated without violation of civil rights, their programs must "follow suit." The boards of these organizations are usually composed of status persons in the community. They are now in the position of having to violate the basic ideals of American society or change their segregated practices. The Recreation Section of the National Social Welfare Assembly took the initiative, together with New York University, to hold a consultation with their membership in the Spring of 1954 on this issue. It is already evident that local groups are bringing a great amount of pressure to bear on the national offices of these organizations to supply guidance regarding problems connected with integration.

(3) *Employment:* Increasingly, employers are being confronted with the responsibility for bringing all groups into participation in the common economic life of the community. Organizations like the International Harvester Company have shown outstanding initiative in demonstrating that integration of employment can be achieved in southern localities such as Memphis, Tennessee.

(4) *Labor:* Labor unions likewise today face the necessity to re-align practices in many communities. Some labor groups have taken the lead in integration due to the realization that status of labor is always precarious if there is a vast reservoir of labor which employers can tap to foil union activity. The migration of

industry to the southern region of America within the past decade has been pronounced. Labor unions are rapidly realizing that Negroes and other disprivileged groups are a potential labor supply if a factory management decides to pull up stakes and go south.

(5) *Other Social Agencies:* Another group highly vulnerable to this approach is that of the social agencies. These run the gamut from child placement institutions to homes for the aged. The impact of the Supreme Court decision has produced a need for them to realign policies and re-evaluate programs.

Interpretation

The third approach is that of interpretation. In many communities there are many people of good will who desire to do the right thing but who blunder because of lack of understanding or ignorance. If dealt with intelligently, such persons frequently present enormous potentials for growth in understanding. Here the tactic of interpretation of the position or point of view of the minority persons cannot be minimized for its effectiveness.

Practically all persons possess "blind spots" in their social orientation coupled with stereotypes from a cultural heritage. To deal with these social limitations requires patience, tact, and understanding. Much harm has been done to intergroup relations by the assumption on the part of some minority persons and their friends that these stereotypes and blind spots, when they were exposed, represented bigotry and ill will. I recall an initial contact with a person who has since become outstanding in intergroup relations who started his conversation with the oft-heard statement that he had nothing against Negroes. In fact, he had an "old Negro Mammy" he loved as much as he loved his "own folks." If documentation of this point of view were needed, one has only to cite the scholarly conclusion of Professor Howard Odum, who wrote in his doctoral dissertation at Columbia University in 1910 to the effect that Negroes did not possess the capacity to learn beyond the early years. With the outstanding leadership he has given to the cause of intergroup relations, in the subsequent years, one dares say that had minority groups made him defensive about such a statement, his services to the cause would have been lost.

Not the least responsibility in strategy is the interpretation to those who are in power positions of what is involved in race relations. Evidence of what can happen without such interpretation, and in the absence of clear understanding of what is social policy, was represented at the time this was being written in Milford, Delaware, where parents were on strike because the schools attempted racial integration.[4] Local officials were impotent when attacked by organized fighting.

Another aspect of the interpretation approach involves the role of the press and other mass media. The climate of community opinion through which social gains are made is of enormous importance. It is interesting to note that the Southern Education Reporting Service has seven editors of outstanding southern newspapers on its Board of Directors. This means that an intelligent press in key communities has become increasingly sensitive to its role in interpreting race relations.

As this chapter was being completed, the function of mass media was highlighted by their treatment of the picketing of schools in Baltimore and Washington, D. C. Unfortunately, that which makes news is most often in the nature of conflict. Once the spotlight of public attention is focused on a conflict pattern, people who are involved begin to play roles for the public rather than operate as persons simply trying conscientiously to work out a situation. In a so-called "riot" incident involving racial groups in a high school in New York City a few years ago, the press distorted the picture tremendously, and what was worse, on the succeeding morning, it was testified, five carloads of reporters with cameras were lined up in front of the school waiting for "something to happen." It was alleged that one reporter offered a boy a quarter to start a fight so he could make a picture. Blow-by-blow accounts of interracial incidents are not conducive to amicable settlements based on good will.

TACTICS OF PSYCHOLOGICAL INTEGRATION

The psychological sense of not belonging is in many respects more damaging to the morale of minority persons than is depriva-

[4] See Chapter VIII, "Organized Resistance," pp. 205-207.

tion of the fruits of opportunity. Any activity or programming at community levels, which involves all groups helps give this sense of belonging. Educational work, for instance, such as appreciation courses and units on contributions of different groups, if done intelligently, provides a certain sense of "being included." Within this country, during the past decade, there have been many approaches to psychological integration through education. There are at present some six or seven centers in colleges and universities devoted to the human relations emphasis. These have been by and large interdisciplinary ventures in which the art and science of groups relating to each other are being combined.

In addition, in the summer of 1954 some 26 workshops in human relations were offered for teachers and community workers by different colleges and universities. The literature in the field of human relations has grown rapidly within the past few years. Interestingly enough, industrial organizations have become increasingly aware of the fact that production is influenced by whether people feel they belong in the plant and are considered an integral part of the team.

Another dimension through which the feeling of belonging has been developed is in the appointment to boards and public committees of persons of minority background. This has been accelerated tremendously in southern communities in the past few years as Negroes have acquired suffrage and had access to the ballot.

There is still a long way to go. For example, an unpublished study by a professor in charge of student-teacher placement in one of the leading northern states recently sent a questionnaire around to school superintendents of the state asking whether they would accept qualified Negro candidates if referred to them. In numerous instances the answer was, "No, we have no Negroes in our community." This sense of being shut out, of Negroes being employed only where services to Negroes are concerned, of not being in on community councils concerned with total community welfare, leaves a sense of isolation.

Another aspect of isolation is presented in the social relationships of the young people as they come through high school. A Negro graduate student recently described the experience thus:

"Through the elementary grades and the junior high school we were all together. Seemingly there were no differences. Each accepted the other for what he was as a person. Gradually, as we moved into high school the pattern changed. Negroes went their way and whites went theirs. Increasingly we were not invited. Soon the social worlds were parted completely."

Because of these aspects of isolation and because of lack of appreciation of their own cultural heritage on the part of minority children, there has frequently arisen what Kurt Lewin termed "group self-hate." The impact that it has on personality was spelled out by Dr. Kenneth Clark in the studies he made for the National Association for the Advancement of Colored People, the evidence of which was submitted in the Supreme Court brief. The studies tended to show that Negro children at an early age attributed those things which represented the dominant values of society to the whites and those things which represented the less good to Negroes. When black dolls and white dolls were presented, the white doll was the "good" doll, the Negro doll the "bad." The white was the clean and the black the dirty, etc.

These manifestations of distorted perspective, lowered aspirations, and psychological isolation seem to be almost inevitable concomitants of being set off and apart. They will persist until such time as we are able to produce a sense of belonging for all members of the community.

TACTICS RELATED TO ERADICATING PAST HARMS

The past decade has seen the greatest advance in the use of legislation and litigation for the advancement of minority peoples' rights since the Civil War era. Much yet remains to be done on this front, but as has been pointed out earlier, the advances of the future probably will be decreasingly legal and increasingly of a volunteer nature. Law produces broad policies and forced procedures but of itself is impersonal. It is that necessary but forced first mile in race relations.

The second mile is the permissive one. That task goes beyond segregation to the integration of all the people into the common life of the community on the basis of equality of opportunity for all. This mile cannot be traveled until people relate to each other in ways different from those that are possible by means of formal procedures. After the barriers have been broken, laws passed, or statutes reinterpreted, there still remains the ultimate question of how you change the lives of people.[5]

The great questions are: How do you provide positive creative educational leadership? How do you make up for the years of inequality of opportunity? How do you raise aspiration levels of those whose hopes for generations have been dimmed? How do you heal the traumas of past degrading experiences? How does education raise the cultural levels that are implied in social class, since second-class citizenship has for the Negro group relegated so many to lower social class status? These are the hard core questions for which education must find answers. They represent more than simply "equality of opportunity," because equal facilities, equal training of teachers, equal opportunity to share, do not mean, at least in the short run, equal participation.[6]

The experience in obliterating past inequalities in northern communities is not too heartening. Richard Plaut says that "in the past five years the National Scholarship Service and Fund for Negro students has alone found places for more than 2,300 Negro students in over 280 different interracial colleges in 27 states. It might have found places for five times that number, had the qualified candidates been available."[7] He cites a study conducted by his organization which examined the college qualifications of Negroes in 50 urban high schools stretching from New England to Illinois. The study

[5] It is not presumed here that these instrumentalities of law are any the less important because of the foregoing statements. It should also be pointed out that the proposal and passage of laws are of themselves an educational experience. In New York State, for instance, the Quinn-Ives hearings on the proposed State F.E.P.C. was one of the greatest educational experiences in race relations which the states citizens had ever undergone.

[6] This is no plea for racial favoritism. It is to say, simply, that the court has ruled, we believe, rightly, that separate education has produced inequality of opportunity. If this is so, education has the responsibility to go out of its way, if necessary, to make up for past harms.

[7] Richard Plaut, "Racial Integration in Higher Education in the North," *Journal of Negro Education*, XXIII (Summer 1954), pp. 310-311.

revealed that "in these schools Negroes constituted about one-third of the enrollment, but only .2 per cent of the seniors had fulfilled the minimum college qualifications, as measured by rank in class and subject requirements."

Kenneth B. Clark reports: "Children who have recently migrated to New York from the South or West Indian Islands tend to be superior in academic achievement to the native born Negro children in the fourth through sixth grades in the New York City public schools, that in a standard achievement test administered in some of the Harlem schools the average reading and arithmetic level was about two years behind their grade . . . There were some classes in which there was no measurable improvement in these school subjects from beginning to end of the school year.[8]

Dr. Clark goes on to say, "Not all this discrepancy can be blamed on the schools alone. Students from families with no tradition of higher education, with economic and social disadvantages are usually not stimulated to aspire to higher education. When, in addition to these factors, there is also insufficient, inadequate or stereotyped counseling in the schools; overcrowded classes and disproportionate pupil-teacher ratio; shunting to vocational courses without a sound teaching and counseling basis; then the obstacles to college qualification and aspiration for the bulk of Negro students become virtually unsurmountable."

In a youth opportunity project in New York City, the Urban League attempted through two years of group guidance to see what could be done experimentally toward raising social situations and aspiration levels of Negro and Puerto Rican youth. The counselor found that behind the low aspiration problem lay the ignorance of counselors and guidance people concerning resources for guidance and opportunities for Negro youth. Back of that was the structure of education which practically forced vocational choices at the time the children finished junior high school, for at that point either the academic or the vocational secondary school was chosen. Back of that were the stereotypes and anxieties parents harbored about their children getting hurt if they aspired too

[8] Kenneth B. Clark, Speech delivered at the conference "Children Apart," entitled "Segregated Schools in New York City," April 24, 1954.

high. One parent remarked to his son, "Boy, there is no use you trying to go to college. They're not going to give you a chance. I came to New York with a good voice but was not accepted because I was Negro. You better get ready to be an apartment house superintendent."

Behind these obstacles is a still more basic one of family and community resources. In many instances, youths were recognized for their abilities but the family and the community did not have the resources with which to assist. In addition, the larger community presents hurdles for all youths, but particularly for minority youths. The World War II veterans came home determined to get an education from their G.I. benefits and move into the mainstream of vocational and professional life. The number who took advantage of these benefits was phenomenal. The Korean G.I's who had grown up in the lush era after World War II have not been as anxious to go to college. They see little of the need when other occupations for which college training is not required are so lucrative. This is especially appealing to those young people from backgrounds where money has never been plentiful. This responsibility rests squarely at the door of the larger community of which the minority group is only a part.

The strategies for the improvement of minority groups in the future will be increasingly less those which "plead the cause." Undoubtedly they will be those which make "common cause." The great challenge to America today is how to go beyond mere "equal chance for everybody" and to bring all disprivileged peoples through the sociocultural gate into full participation in the common community life. In this responsibility, intelligent community action, education that gives direction to the social process, religion that reinterprets basic spiritual values, an economic system that assumes an obligation for the well being of all, a dynamic jurisprudence —all must lend a hand in the creation of new designs of community life if democracy is to prove that people have basic concerns for each other that transcend a raw power struggle for economic status.

XII

Appropriate Goals and Plans for the Future

Virgil A. Clift
Head, Department of Education
Morgan State College

THE story of the education of the Negro has contributed a fascinating chapter to the continuing history of education and democracy in the United States. The evolution of education for this group had its roots in the pre-Civil War period. Elementary schools for freedmen began in the southern states during the war. About a dozen so-called colleges and universities were founded for Negroes before the ratification of the Fourteenth Amendment in 1868. For the next seventy years southern states gave only scant aid to schools attended by Negroes. Northern philanthropy and church organizations continued their much needed support, without which the plight of the Negro would have been more dismal. In 1938, the United States Supreme Court ordered the states to provide "substantially equal facilities" within the states. This set into motion a feverish expansion of state-supported schools designed especially to deny Negroes admission to white state-supported colleges and universities. Private institutions for Negroes, which had contributed so much to their development, found it difficult to compete with state-supported colleges or even to remain in existence. Had it not been for the United Negro College Fund, many of them probably would now be extinct.

Desegregation was progressing slowly, even in the South, before the historic and far-reaching decisions of the United States Supreme Court of May 17, 1954 and May 31, 1955. These decisions shattered the foundations on which segregated education had rested by making invalid the doctrine of "separate but equal." In compliance with the first decision, school desegregation began in the fall of 1954 in a few large cities, notably Wilmington, Baltimore, and Washington, and in some scattered counties in Missouri, Arkansas and West Virginia. By the fourth anniversary of the Supreme Court's original decision, the desegregation process was at work in ten out of the seventeen states that previously had compulsory school segregation. In keeping with the court-ordained "deliberate speed" clause, desegregation moved faster in Kentucky, Oklahoma, and Texas than in Tennessee and North Carolina. But it did spread. Out of 2,889 southern school districts with both white and colored pupils, desegregation had begun in 764 by the end of four years.

Then, in the fall of 1958, desegregation appeared to have been brought almost to a standstill by deep southern hostility. New desegregation moves were limited to thirteen school districts in the entire South, and in contrast to this modicum of progress toward compliance, schools were closed in Little Rock, Arkansas and in sections of Virginia to avoid integration. Desegregation seemed to have been stopped short by seven states willing to dispense with public schools rather than to yield to racial mixing.

By the middle of the 1958-1959 school year, the situation had taken a different turn. Negro pupils had entered white schools in Alexandria, Virginia without incident, bringing a third new community into the desegregation column and not in a border state but in Virginia, the former center of massive resistance. Desegregation was thus on the move again, having met the ultimate test of school closing and proved, at least in Virginia, that parents placed sufficiently high value on public education for their children to endure a limited amount of integration. Georgia, Alabama, and Mississippi seemed not to be ready to back away from massive resistance. But the solid front had been broken, and desegregation was making some marked advances in its fifth year; it began again to be slowly but inevitably approaching.

The problem of providing for all American youth an adequate and equal educational opportunity which is truly democratic in all its aspects is a difficult one. This problem sometimes is made more difficult because of emotionalism, the lack of understanding of issues, and hot-headedness. In the pages and pages of discussion about desegregation and integration, most of it has emphasized the "right or wrong" of the issue, reasons some feel it will not work at this time, ways of circumventing the high court's decision, ways of dealing with massive resistance, what is or is not happening in desegregation, and what is likely to happen. Strange as it may seem, the persons and organizations having the most to say and receiving the most publicity have not usually been school people who must deal with this problem or the parents whose children will be affected by it. Also, almost completely ignored, devalued, or discounted are the opinions of students, be they mature graduate students working on the Ph.D. or professional degrees, or those on the lower level of education. When one looks at the list of persons who have had most to say and have tried hardest to exert influence, one finds that the vast majority of them do not have a reputation in the areas of school affairs, human relations, or in an understanding of democracy. Some influential politicians have capitalized on the issue for personal gain and votes. Consequently, the issues are confused; the waters are muddy.

If we are really seeking for appropriate goals and plans for the future in trying to deal with this domestic problem, it is first necessary for the people in this country to understand fully all of the facets of it as well as its far-reaching significance. They must understand that it is not just because of pride and the desire to be recognized that has caused Negroes to press for complete desegregation of the schools. These are factors to be sure, but they are far from being the most significant. Negroes realize that it is impossible within a segregated pattern to receive an education that is truly equal and does not discriminate against them. They recognize that available tax resources and the prevailing attitude of some southern whites are mitigating factors making it impossible to have equal educational facilities and opportunities when measured by national norms. They feel strongly and keenly that compulsory segregation in education inflicts injuries upon the personalities of children, and that this is true regardless of how equal the facilities and teaching staff may be. Their belief that forced segregation results in lowering of motivation, impairing of ability to learn, and distorting of personality is abundantly supported by social psychologists and other social scientists.

The desire for integration in the schools is related also to a much larger pattern which is overlooked by some, but which nevertheless is ever present in the thinking of Negroes. Throughout much of the nation Negroes find themselves in a position of disadvantage in employment, family income, housing, use of public facilities, recreation, justice or equality before law, hospitalization and health facilities, and politics and government. With reference to economic conditions, Ira De A. Reid wrote the following:

It is painfully evident that despite the great changes in the occupational characteristics of the Negro population during the last fifteen years, and despite the several national and local efforts to effect more and better employment for Negroes, the status of the Negro's economic adjustment remains substantially below that of the white population.

. . . we are given evidence to support the contention that after almost three generations as members of the industrial work force, more than half of the Negro male workers and nearly two-thirds of the Negro female workers (as compared with one-sixteenth of the white male and female workers) are employed in occupations below the semi-skilled level. Furthermore, virtually no progress has been made in reducing the differentials in the rates of unemployment experienced by the white and Negro groups, and there seems little prospect for doing so unless the country maintains a "full employment economy." This is the relative status of the Negro working population after a decade of unusually favorable employment conditions.

The money income gap between the white and Negro population is closing for the urban populations but shows the usual differentials in the rural populations. "Half as much" continues to represent the relative family income of the Negro group when compared with the white. Statistically and socially significant are the broad estimates that of every

1000 white families reporting incomes in 1950 there were 268 with annual incomes under $2000, 519 with incomes between $2000 and $4999, and 213 with annual incomes of $5000 or more. Among every 1000 nonwhite families (predominantly Negro families) there were 650 in the lowest bracket, 312 in the middle group, and 38 with annual family incomes of $5000 or more.[1]

As is well known, housing is related to income. With the Negro, housing is both a social as well as an economic problem. He finds himself most seriously handicapped in both the ownership and rental markets. Housing facilities for the group are improving, but he still must pay artificially inflated prices of occupancy and ownership. The "opening up" of new neighborhoods to Negroes and the creation of racially mixed neighborhoods have done little to eliminate the ghetto quality of the modern residential areas for them.

The pattern which has been pointed out in employment, income, and housing prevails in all other aspects of the Negro's life. Therefore he sees little hope of improving any of these conditions as long as segregated schools exist. *He is firmly convinced that the segregated tax-supported school is an institution which, more than any other, is teaching the youth of the nation to follow and to continue discriminatory practices in all areas of life and human endeavor.* Therefore this problem must not be considered as one based only upon pride, the desire for recognition, and the desire to have the races mixed in schools. It is much deeper, much more far-reaching, and one which relates to the entire physical, social, cultural, and economic well-being of the Negro.

Furthermore, Negroes see the segregated school as a factor contributing to the delinquency of their children, as a factor contributing to many forms of social maladjustment and unacceptable social behavior. They feel that forced segregation distorts the personality of their youth and results in a lowering of motivation to the extent that it is impossible for their youth ever to compete in the wider society and to make the contribution they should to it.

Another aspect of this problem that the American people need to understand more clearly and vividly than they now seem to is

[1] Ira De A. Reid, "The Relative Status of the Negro in the United States," *The Journal of Negro Education,* Vol. XXII, No. 3 (1953), p. 446.

that this is a serious domestic problem that is doing great damage to our basic democratic ideals and the "American Dream." But, it is not only a domestic problem. During this critical time when the United States of America is exercising a role of leadership on the international scene, this problem is causing people all over the world to lose respect for us and to discount the true value of our democratic institutions. How can we expect to be the leaders of the free world and to influence people to have faith and confidence in our ideals and values unless we find a better solution to this domestic problem?

With this brief introduction on the nature of the problem and a statement as to why it is imperative that we begin dealing constructively with it, let us now explore appropriate goals and plans for future action. In this discussion it is assumed that we should and will operate within the framework of the Supreme Court Decisions on segregated education. It is assumed further that since there is a trend toward desegregation in many areas of community life involving various social institutions, some lessons can be learned from these. Some of the principles and practices which have been found to be successful in other areas of community life can probably be applied to the situation in the schools. Presented in the remainder of this chapter are suggestions for individuals, community groups, school personnel, and citizens in general, who will in some way, either directly or indirectly, have to make some contribution to the solution of problems in desegregating education.

I. THE PUBLIC AS A WHOLE MUST BECOME BETTER INFORMED ON THE MANY FAR-REACHING FACETS OF DESEGREGATION

The first step in dealing with this problem is to develop a widespread understanding among the citizenry as to the nature of the problem and the reasons why it must be solved. We need to understand what it is doing to people, what it is doing to our nation, and what it is doing to the basic things for which we aspire. This understanding is not going to "just happen" any more than it "just happens" that funds are raised for the Red Cross, the Community Chest, or for the United Negro College Fund. It has not "just happened" that the free public school system has emerged into the great institution that it now is. Things are achieved in this society by a concerted and planned effort. It is now time for the radio, the press, civic organizations, social agencies, churches, and even the schools themselves to make a much greater contribution in helping all people gain a better understanding of all aspects and issues in this problem. There now exist enough agencies and organizations concerned with the general walfare of the nation to exert tremendous impact, not in propagandizing for one side or the other, but in an open forum of information related to desegregation in education. We need sober discussions and information-seeking exchanges rather than rambunctious rabble-rousing appeals to emotionalism. When given facts and information, the American public can be counted on to support plans and actions which are good for the nation and the general welfare. Neither Negroes nor the South, both of which are in a sense minorities on these issues, need be fearful of the future.

To cite one example of how this might be accomplished, reference is made to the Great Decisions Discussions organized throughout the nation by United Nations associations to explore and help people become better informed on our role in international affairs. Each week for nine weeks these informal discussion groups study the issues involved in one of the great decisions or conflict areas of international affairs. They then meet and discuss the pros and cons of the issues and, on the basis of all they have read and talked about, they try to draw conclusions on an individual and group basis as to appropriate action our nation should take in important policy matters. In many significant ways this procedure is related to the old New England Town Meeting which laid many of the cornerstones in our democratic way of doing things.

There are many groups and organizations which are willing to devote time, discussion, and energy to the important domestic problem of school desegregation. Both camps, the desegregationists and the segregationists, could well afford to appeal to these groups and organizations to organize discussion groups on the issues involved. The history of this nation, as it has moved progressively toward the democratic ideal, supports the contention that this is a good approach to solving problems, resolving conflicts, and extending the general welfare. This approach or one related to it has never permitted a minority group to ride roughshod over the majority, nor has it permitted the majority to keep the minority at a disadvantaged position out of relationship to the extension of the common good.

II. ALL COMMUNITIES WILL NOT BE ABLE TO USE THE SAME APPROACHES, METHODS AND TECHNIQUES IN DEALING SUCCESSFULLY WITH DESEGREGATION

The second step is one of establishing the realization that communities are not the same, their problems are not identical, and therefore the approaches used to deal with the problem of desegregation should not be the same in all communities. When one considers seriously the total trend toward desegregation, including the progress that has been made in the states of the "hard core" South, one begins to realize that specific factors responsible for desegregation vary from situation to situation, institution to institution, and from region to region. Kenneth B. Clark[2] lists twelve such factors which include: population changes, voluntary public opinion pressure, referendum electorate, threat of publicity, moral arguments, activity of community action agencies, personal decision of responsible authority, non-judicial governmental action, legislative action, threat of court action, pending court decision, and court action. This list can now be expanded to include many others.

During the past fifteen years there have been many areas of American life in which change has taken place from racially segregated to nonsegregated patterns. This has been true not in the North alone, but throughout the nation. There has been an increasing rate and extent of desegregation in such areas as the church, the Armed Forces, housing, interstate transportation, public accommodations, recreational facilities, organized sports, labor unions and industrial employment, and politics and government. This point need not be labored with examples, but to list a

[2] Kenneth B. Clark, "Desegregation: An Appraisal of the Evidence," *The Journal of Social Issues*, Vol. IX, No. 4 (1953), p. 20.

few, Negroes are being accepted in politics and government when we consider that they have been elected to school boards and to other similar responsible positions in the South. Mitchell[3] has reported that 700,000 Negroes were in unions in the South. Many Catholic and Protestant churches have membership of both races, not to mention the fact that several outstanding churches now have Negro ministers. In organized sports, Negroes have been accepted if they can make a contribution, even in the World Series.

As we look at these and many other examples, it must be recognized that the same forces which were operating in baseball were not necessarily operating in other areas where desegregation has been achieved. The evidence points to the fact that careful and detailed studies are needed in each community confronted with problems involving school desegregation. Information is needed on resources available in persons and organizations which can contribute to the successful solution of many facets of the problem. Careful thought must be given to plans of action. Techniques for providing understanding and open discussion of issues must be devised. Techniques must be devised for dealing with the rumor monger and the troublemaker.

III. Resource People Must Be Available to Give Technical Advice and Problem-Solving Techniques in Communities where These Are Needed

If these things are to be done successfully, resource people with special training and information must be available in communities to give assistance when it is needed. These resource people are available in both the private and public colleges and universities in this nation. In every state in the union, and this includes the "hard core" states of the South, there are located private and public colleges and universities where are to be found professors who are willing to give their knowledge, time, and energy to help interested citizen groups deal with problems in this area. This is not to say that they are ready and willing to carry on a campaign for any

[3] George S. Mitchell, "The South Charts Its Course," *Interracial Review*, Vol. XXVI, No. 5 (May, 1953), pp. 78-81.

special group in any community on any issue. It is intended to emphasize the willingness of many persons in our institutions of higher learning to come to people when they are called to give their studied and intellectually considered opinions and advice on any issue, regardless of how controversial, if it relates to an extension of democracy and the general welfare.

In the deep South, at the present time, there are many graduate students enrolled in institutions of higher learning, white and Negro, public and private, who are working on research studies which relate directly to desegregation. Citizens in almost any community, regardless of how remote, could profit much from the knowledge and information of this human resource if they chose to do so. In this connection, the Negro college professor in the social sciences and in the field of education has a fertile field within which to operate. If these scholars truly believe in the principles which produce a system that enabled them to rise to their present stature in spite of impending forces, it follows that it is their responsibility and obligation to make a contribution to solving this problem at the grass-roots level.

IV. The Moral and Ethical Aspects of the Problem of Desegregation Have Not Been Emphasized Sufficiently

An appeal to the ethical and moral nature of the problem has not been emphasized sufficiently, as was pointed out recently by Thompson.[4] A great majority of the people in America, in fact all but a very small minority, are deeply committed to democratic and Christian ideals. They believe fundamentally in the principles of fair play. The whole history of America has been highlighted by events which have demonstrated their devotion to these things. Their unselfish contributions to the underdeveloped nations of the world, their personal assistance and sacrifice to help others in times of stress and disaster, and their continuous willingness to share their abundance and to extend rights to all have caused the people of the world to look upon them and their ideals as being

[4] Charles H. Thompson, "The Moral Issue in Desegregation," *Journal of Negro Education*, Vol. XXVIII (Winter, 1959), pp. 1, 2.

the greatest and the most noble expression of man in his relationship to man. Here is to be found a great potential in solving this problem.

Existing public opinion and public support for these principles and ideals have not been given a chance to function effectively in the school desegregation situation. The efforts to desegregate schools is not one supported alone by a few Negroes, the NAACP, and the Supreme Court. Without the help of the white people in the South who are devoted to the "American Dream" there would have never been a Negro lawyer in the South who could move freely and unmolested in that area and present his case at the bar of justice. Without the assistance of white people, there would probably never have been organized and prepared an *Appendix to Appellants' Brief*[5] entitled "The Effects of Segregation and the Consequences of Desegregation: A Social Science Statement." This appendix was submitted to and accepted by the United States Supreme Court during the October term, 1952, and represents something very important as the social scientists see it. Eminent American social scientists who are deeply concerned about desegregation as it relates to the future well-being of our nation helped to prepare this statement. It is not a statement by Negroes of what Negroes want, but rather a statement by Americans trained in the field of social science who do not want to see this problem do violence to our concept of democracy.

Masses of people in the United States, concerned with principles which make this nation strong, represent a potential which has not been organized or used effectively in this controversy. It is not the social scientists and the social psychologists alone in this country who have a concern in this issue. Negroes have been encouraged to take the stand they have because almost daily they find white counterparts encouraging and advising them to keep up the fight and not weaken. Many people of this nation would have a deeper appreciation of what the school has taught in democratic concepts

[5] The data which was a part of this appendix was considered in connection with the legal briefs submitted in South Carolina (*Briggs* vs. *Elliott*); Kansas (*Brown* vs. *Board of Education of Topeka*); and Virginia (*Davis* vs. *County School Board*), before any of these went to the U. S. Supreme Court.

if they knew the degree to which the laundryman, the milkman, the insurance man, the farmer, the small businessman, and others take the Negro customer off to the side and in deep confidence encourage him to press for school desegregation. These kinds of expressions are not organized and made as impressive through the press and other similar agencies as expressions coming from other sources. To the outside observer, the laundryman, the small businessman, and others seem to be whispering in a wee small voice to encourage the Negro as compared with the voice of a Faubus or Almond. Somehow the Negro must learn to pool this resource that gives him encouragement. This human resource is in nearly every community.

Nevertheless, these people of good will who believe in principles of fair play cannot be expected to carry on a crusade for desegregation, especially when on the other side of this issue they see some men who are supposed to be statesmen and leaders conducting themselves in such a peculiar way as related to morals, ethics, and democracy. They cannot as individuals afford reprisals, rebuff or disapproval. Yet if they understood more clearly the issues involved and if they could see more clearly through all factors, and if they had better ways of expressing themselves positively as a group, much of what seems to be resistance to desegregation would cease to exist. Scholars in the behavioral sciences could make a great contribution to providing techniques and "know how" which would enable these citizens to express themselves in a more positive manner.

V. DURING AND AFTER DESEGREGATION, NEGRO LEADERSHIP MUST PLAY A NEW ROLE AND DISCHARGE NEW RESPONSIBILITIES

This brings into focus a fifth approach to solving some of the difficulties involved. Negro leadership is faced with a new role in trying to help culturally deprived people face up to and assume their full responsibilities in the wider community. Integration, which is taking place in many aspects of American life, places an obligation and responsibility upon people of minority status which did not exist before. When the Negro child is admitted to school without regard to race, the parent will find that his responsibility does not end there. Previously, the typical Negro parent accepted the school that was built in his community, he played little or no part in the policy of the school, he was restricted from participation in the broader activities of the community-wide Parent-Teacher Association, and his active participation in civic organizations to support and improve schools was not expected. With integration, his responsibilities in these and in many other similar areas have become heavier.

In many communities parents will be reluctant to discharge their duties in these things because of past habits of conduct, a feeling of not being wanted, timidity, and the lack of understanding as to how they can make their greatest contribution. A very great and significant service must be rendered by the Negro leaders who can give advice and guidance to parent groups who so urgently need it. In some instances adults will need a type of education which will equip them for these new duties and responsibilities.

VI. BEFORE DESEGREGATION AND INTEGRATION CAN OPERATE SMOOTHLY, MORE ADEQUATE WAYS MUST BE DEVISED FOR DEALING WITH ATTITUDES AND EMOTIONAL STATES WHICH CHARACTERIZE MANY NEGROES

Minority consciousness and feelings of inferiority on the part of the Negro are factors which tend to operate against complete and smooth intergration in the schools. Studies of large urban areas reveal that there is strong group consciousness among Negroes which is expressed in militancy, racial pride, and efforts to compensate for their status either through competition with the majority group or by withdrawal into self-sufficiency. Their experience has frequently been that after their best efforts to improve conditions as individuals, there was still ineradicable identification with their group. Thus, it is natural that they have become inhibited in thoughts, aspirations, and activities by their own conceptions of themselves and their group. This kind of minority consciousness is usually not revealed through verbalized conduct, but can be observed in the apathy and indifference which often defies the best intentions of groups and organizations offering them many opportunities and being most willing to accept them on merit. In many communities notable for programs of integrating all segments of the population, there seems to be an unwillingness on the part of Negro citizens to participate in many activities open to them. This kind of conduct is misunderstood by whites and Negroes. The clubs, churches, and social groups are predominantly, if not completely, of one racial group or the other. Restrictions are imposed upon neighborhoods and employment. People of both groups, regardless of age and place of birth, have been exposed to many situations which make them aware of certain things which affect attitudes, even though they as individuals may not be conscious of them. Thus the Negro becomes aware of his race, that his position in society is altered more or less by his race, and that the differential is usually not favorable to his fullest participation in the society in which he lives. Yet, in conversation there is usually no feeling of resentment or inferiority. But on the other hand, when opportunities for full participation are open and encouraged, he behaves with apathy and withdrawal.

There are many implications in this whole situation for Negro parents and children. Some approach must be designed to deal effectively with attitudes and emotional states. Our community groups and community leaders must become cognizant of this problem and find ways of dealing with it if all citizens are to contribute as fully as they should to the general welfare. Very little planned and organized effort has been given to this phenomenon in our communities even though it affects most ethnic groups in our urban areas.

VII. Institutions Preparing Teachers Must Provide for Effective Experiences which Will Enable Teachers to Deal with the Factors of Desegregation and Integration

In general, institutions preparing teachers for the public school have done little, and in most instances nothing, to help prospective teachers to understand the social and psychological aspects of desegregation. This is an important area which must be given more attention in our plans for the future. This involves much more than preparing for the integration of a racial group in schools. It involves also migrant groups who must adjust in urban areas; it involves many related problems implicit in the social and physical change which is characteristic of much of the United States. Changes, noticeable in all our cities, which have to do with urban renewal, migration of southern mountain folk, migrant labor groups, changing patterns of housing, and the like, create problems. The increasing mobility of population in the nation tends to throw together in institutions, such as the school, a large number of people with a variety of cultural backgrounds. An effort to integrate all these divergent cultural elements into a pattern consistent and harmonious with the ideals of American democracy is a difficult problem in many American communities. If teachers in public schools are to function well in such situations and make the contribution they should, much more stress will have to be laid upon aspects of these problems in the teacher education programs.

Implicit in this is the need for educating our prospective teachers, both white and Negro, for self-understanding that can lead to a real and fundamental concern for both the specific needs and the readiness level of every child. In many cases, there has been so much deprivation and retardation among children of minority groups that many teachers give their time to the able and responsive few and simply let the rest go.

The teacher needs instruction in the problems of human relations. She needs to know the value systems, purposes, and motivation of children of backgrounds different from her own in order to be able to understand the children she will teach. For example, the low income of teachers may cause some of them to reject children of well-to-do families. On the other hand, children of deprived families may seemingly have no interest in reading or education. The teacher must understand the values of this group and must not become personally disturbed about the seeming lack of interest, yet must provide sufficient motivation for the children to do something about these deficiencies. In another area, some teachers fear the child with a high intellectual capacity and reject him. Somewhere in their training, teachers should be alerted to these prejudicial tendencies in themselves toward students of differing racial, socio-economic, and social status. Teacher education institutions can do much by providing for a human relations emphasis in existing courses, including wherever possible workshop opportunities with participants who come from different backgrounds and disciplines.

VIII. More Knowledge and Information Is Needed about Social Groups in Our Society and the Forces Operating in Them

Educated people in general, and teachers especially, should understand more about society, the structure of social groups, and forces operating in them. Superintendent Hansen[6] in Washington, D. C., tells a story which illustrates this. Immediately after the May, 1954 decision of the Supreme Court, 73 percent of the students and 25 percent of the faculty members were in desegregated schools in Washington. In October, there were a series of racial demonstrations by white students which seemed to be, in part at least, a result of the warm weather that made it pleasant to be outdoors. In one instance, white boys were clustered in a hallway talking about joining their friends who were picketing a particular school. A young Negro student who had been in class with this same group of white boys, was standing close by. As they were leaving, they turned to the Negro boy and asked, "Aren't you coming with us?" Startled, he asked, "Who? Me?" was the reply, "You're one of us, aren't you?"

This little story suggests that though we cannot discount the racial factor in the students' demonstrations, what may appear to be racial hostility can have other causes. At least we have to consider the mixed motives involved in such a situation. The definition of "one of us" can sometimes transcend racial identification, even in a "racial incident"! This same principle applies not only to children in the school, but to the wider community.

This story helps to point up the need for a better understanding of the social structure and the forces operating in it. American children are often victims of social forces that they do not under-

[6] Carl F. Hansen, "Proceedings of the Pennsylvania State Teachers College Conference on Intergroup Relations and Teacher Education," Lock Haven State Teachers College, November 1958, p. 6.

stand. We must admit that our teachers do not know how to operate effectively in situations where class-caste phenomena affect the value systems of the children they teach.

IX. Leaders and Groups with Authority and Prestige Should be Encouraged to Make Their Positions Known on Desegregation

A ninth factor in the accomplishment of efficient desegregation with a minimum of social disturbance depends upon the position taken by leaders with prestige and other authorities.[7] Tumin states:

However one evaluates the Little Rock events, there can be little doubt that Faubus played a highly influential role. And the situation would have been drastically different had Faubus not taken his stand and implemented it as he did.

Other governors and mayors, other officials who have been able to persuade their constituents one way or the other, have also shown us, over the years since the Supreme Court edict, that the roles played by leaders, official and otherwise, can be critical. This is always the case when we are in the midst of a situation where the issues at stake are of deep concern to everyone, and where the competing leaderships are vying for the adherence of a relatively volatile and varied constituency.[8]

When desegregation is approached and planned for on the local level, it has been found that problems were solved and issues resolved in direct proportion to the support given by persons of high status in leadership roles. It has been noted that when persons in authority and organizations which are higly respected express a positive unequivocal position for desegregation, incidents were few, if any.

It is interesting to note that four important religious groups voiced support of school desegregation during 1958. In October, the

---

[7] For further study of the roles of power, leadership, and public opinion, see Chapters 2 and 3, in *Desegregation, Some Propositions and Research Suggestions* by E. A. Suchman, J. P. Dean, R. M. Williams, Jr., *et al.*, New York: Anti-Defamation League, 1958.

[8] Melvin M. Tumin, *Desegregation: Resistance and Readiness*, Princeton: Princeton University Press, 1958, p. 151.

Protestant Episcopal Church's House of Bishops issued a statement calling for equality of opportunity in education, housing, employment, and public accommodations "without discrimination and without separation." The following month, both the Roman Catholic Bishops of the United States and the Methodist Council of Bishops issued strong statements in support of the Court's anti-bias rulings. In November, 309 white Protestant and Jewish clergymen in Atlanta called upon "community leaders and state leaders to give creative thought to maintaining a sound public school plan. Such a plan must be consistent with the law of the land, respect and preserve the rights of all citizens and assure the preservation of our system of public education."

These are excellent examples of forthright and positive statements from highly respected groups. These statements are certain to influence thinking and action. Such statements have been late and many of our highly respected leaders in other walks of life have not made their positions known. When they do, their influence will be significant. It is important therefore to pool and use this resource in working out more harmonious relationships in school desegregation.

The pressure for Congressional action to promote compliance with the Supreme Court's school desegregation decisions has been growing steadily recently. The factors contributing most to this have been the positive position taken by groups similar to those indicated above and to a more positive stand on the part of respected leaders.

X. FEDERAL LEGISLATION IS NEEDED TO ALIGN THE CONGRESS AND
THE EXECUTIVE ALONGSIDE THE SUPREME COURT IN ACCEPTING
LEGAL AND MORAL RESPONSIBILITY FOR DESEGREGATION

The history of race relations in the South supports the thesis that citizenship rights for the Negro are possible only when the three branches of the Federal government support these rights. In the school desegregation cases, the Supreme Court has interpreted the Fourteenth Amendment of the Constitution as being the law of the land. Hearings before Congressional committees on a variety of civil rights bills have disclosed that southern governors, attorneys general, and other state officials have refused to acknowledge this. They have come before the committees of Congress not to plead for time to effectuate an orderly transition to integration, but to defy the law and to insist that they would never comply. The testimony of Governor John Patterson of Alabama is typical. He said, "The citizens of Alabama will not tolerate or support an integrated school system. They will scrap their public school system rather than submit to integration of the races."

Some southern state officials have sought to popularize the belief that the decisions of the Supreme Court are not the law of the land and that they can be disobeyed with impunity. There is no doubt that the success they have achieved in this is because the other branches of government have failed to support the judiciary. The executive branch has been committed to a policy of inaction with the result that little has been done to enforce the law. The legislative branch has had hearings on civil rights bills, and finally at this late date, three sets of bills which deal directly with desegregation in education have been introduced in this session of Congress.

There are those who insist that federal power from the three branches of government should not be used to desegregate schools. They feel that the National Association for Colored People has aroused strong emotions among those anxious "to do the decent thing." They hold that society cannot be changed by law.

Yet, never in its history has the South as a region, without outside pressure, taken a step to grant the Negro his citizenship rights. It is true that paternalistic good feeling has existed and there has been widespread individual toleration and respect, but on a purely individual basis. The NAACP, which was founded half a century ago, appeared in the United States Supreme Court in 1915 on a voting registration case. After many many law suits, and nearly thirty years later (1944), the major legal battle for the franchise was finally won. For more than thirty years Negroes have sought to improve their educational opportunities within the framework of the Consitution by litigation through the courts in order to get equal salaries for equal training, equal facilities and equipment, equal expenditures per pupil enrolled, equal opportunities for graduate and professional training, etc. This has been a long, patient, and peaceful struggle within the letter and spirit of the supreme law of the land. In spite of the fact that great discrepancies and gross inequalities still exist in the education for this group as compared with that for other citizens, tremendous progress has been made in "closing the gap." This progress can be attributed primarily to legal action which caused state and local governments to operate more consistently with the Constitution of the United States.

Therefore, the Negro feels that a resort to law and governmental sanction is an all important force in improving his citizenship status. There are those who say that we cannot change society by law. The Negro understands that it was the Thirteenth Amendment as a law that removed the chains of chattel slavery. He understands also that it has been government enforcement of law that has improved his educational opportunities and given him a larger measure of citizenship rights in education. The Negro has supreme faith in the idea expressed by Thomas Jefferson, the great architect of democracy and freedom, who said, "The most sacred of duties of government is to do equal and impartial justice to all its citizens."

To this writer, it appears that the next appropriate step is to provide for federal legislation which will align Congress and the Executive alongside the Supreme Court in accepting the legal and moral responsibility for upholding constitutional rights enunciated in the Fourteenth Amendment. This legislation should provide the branches of government with the tools of technical, financial, and legal assistance necessary to carry out the obligation government has to its citizens.

The principal provisions of such federal legislation should include the following:

1. There must be a declaration that the federal government accepts the legal and moral responsibility for implementing the constitutional requirements for desegregating the schools.
2. Provision must be made for urgently needed federal technical and financial assistance in states and local communities where schools are still segregated. Data must be gathered and distributed, surveys must be made, conferences must be held, human relations services must be established, and advisory councils

must be available. Federal authorized appropriations should be available for several years to support such activities.

3. Federal legal assistance must be available in securing equal protection under law, especially where private parties are unable to vindicate the constitutional rights of school children. The Attorney General of the United States should be authorized to file civil suits to prevent denials in equal protection cases because of race, color, religion, or national origin. Senator Paul H. Douglas of Illinois and sixteen of his colleagues have introduced Senate Bill 810 which contains this provision. This provision is urgently needed, as Senator Douglas has pointed out:

. . . because without it the weakest, the poorest, and those most subject to intimidation and coercion are required to fight their case with their own resources against the legal talent, power, legislation, and economic resources which a state opposed to desegregation can throw into the breach. Because of the anti-barratry laws (which make it a penal offense in some Southern states for anyone to offer financial or legal assistance for court actions to interested parties suing to protect their constitutional rights), the anti-NAACP laws, school placement laws and the multitude of other barriers thrown up to resist the law of the land, the scales of justice can only be evenly balanced if these legal and economic burdens of enforcement are borne in part by the federal government, whose duty it is to enforce the law.

To require, as is now the case, that this burden be placed solely on the backs of the fathers and mothers of Negro children in areas which are overwhelmingly hostile to them is to apply that concept of justice made famous by Anatole France's remark that the "law in its majestic equality forbids the rich as well as the poor to sleep under bridges, to beg in the streets, and to steal bread."

The idea of injunctive relief is highly controversial, but it is not novel. The injunction has long been used to secure compliance with the law. Unfair labor practices, national emergency strikes, anti-trust law violations, wage and hour law infractions, defense production act violation, and scores of other affecting both personal and public rights are reached by similar actions under existing laws. The writer has attempted in this chapter to present some suggestions and ingredients for a hopeful approach to the solution to the most compelling problem facing our country. Due cognizance and recognization has been given to the deep roots of resistance in the South, the social customs and practices. For that reason special emphasis has been given to a transitory approach to compliance with the law in a reasonable, conciliatory, and affirmative manner, with special stress being placed on a maximum of cooperation and agreement between federal and local governments.

Index